Instruction for All Students
Table of Contents

P9-DJA-783

Instruction for All Students
Table of Contents

Instruction for All Students
Table of Contents

Table of Contents

Introduction

The purposes of these introductory pages are to introduce new readers to the text and to inform those familiar with the text that this second edition is "an old friend in a new dress."

The content changes in the second edition of **_Instruction for All Students_** are based on new research, new learning, and new experiences. The use of the first edition of this text in workshops all over the world for the past thirteen years provided clear data about what organizational changes needed to be made in the text. Furthermore, the availability of technology resources led to the inclusion of templates and exemplars on a CD-ROM.

What is the Same?
- Holds student learning as the central goal of our work
- Is based on the premise that the best management program is a strong instructional program
- Includes practical applications of research-based practices
- Is presented in a teacher-friendly format
- Printed in easy-on-the-eyes font sizes
- Features K-12 practitioner examples
- Is based on the same philosophical underpinnings as the first edition. To that end the following is reprinted from the Introduction to the first edition:

> A wise educator said: We will conduct all of our interactions with students based on the most current data, research, and current thinking in our field. When this information changes, we will change our practice.
>
> I do not believe that this statement in any way implies that we should continue to hop from bandwagon to bandwagon looking for materials and programs that will ensure quick fixes or successes. Quite the contrary. It means that we must constantly reach out to analyze, reflect on, and react to the massive body of research on teaching and learning that comes, not only from those doing formal research, but also from those of us working directly with students.
>
> There are three additional ideas that we must come to terms with before we can accomplish all we might. The first is that we and our students have the capacity to achieve far more than we have so far. Ron Edmonds called us to action when he said that whether or not we and our students achieve more depends, to a large extent, on how we feel about the fact that what we've been doing has not brought all the results we seek.

The second important idea is that we cannot accomplish all we might until we see ourselves as part of a greater whole and expand our efforts for working collaboratively. The third major component is that we must agree on, and become much more clearly focused on, what students should know and be able to do; then we must focus our time and energy on moving all students toward those goals. It is no longer good enough for the lesson to be a "good lesson", it must also be the "right lesson."

This book is based on an analysis of the research base on teaching and learning, and on the work of educators in schools around the world. The ideas presented here have been productive for educators in many situations, but there is absolutely no guarantee that all of the material and ideas will work for you. There is, however, a strong likelihood that we will all accomplish far more if we engage in our practice with:

- A sense of self-efficacy
- A focus on clearly articulated standards
- An ever growing repertoire of skills for teaching and assessing diverse learners
- A passion for engaging all students in the learning process
- The use of data to make and assess instructional decisions
- A mission to promote high standards and expectations for both students and educators
- A commitment to collaborate with colleagues and parents

What is New?

- An up-to-the-minute review of initiatives that are in the news and influencing our thinking
- Clearly articulated purposes for each of the strategies for actively engaging students
- A greater focus on the range of diversity in our classrooms and strategies for working with all students
- Strategies for vocabulary development and supporting struggling readers
- Multiple approaches to lesson and unit design with a focus on using the standards-based planning process
- Cutting-edge information on technology integration

- Thought-provoking information on formative assessment
- An expanded focus on 21st century thinking skills that promote rigor and relevance
- An array of formats for creating learning communities and opportunities for job-embedded learning and collegial collaboration

What New Tools are Included?

- A CD-ROM of templates including multiple templates for lesson and unit design, learning buddies, and organizational tools
- Exemplars of standards-based units of study on the CD-ROM
- Multiple self-assessments both embedded in the text and on the CD-ROM
- An updated list of resources and references
- A mini-index of the uses and purposes of the active learning strategies (pages 88-89)
- An extensive index of the book
- The use of the Top Ten Questions to provide focus for chapters II through IX (The questions explored in each chapter are highlighted on the second page of each chapter.)

What Support Materials Are Available?

- A set of **Visual Tools** on CD-ROM is available separately. You can use these tools to create full color handouts, charts, overhead transparencies or embed them in PowerPoint and KeyNote presentations.
- A free **Study Guide** is available on the Just ASK website. The **Study Guide** can be used to focus individual work or to facilitate a book club on the text.
- The text, *Leading the Learning: A Field Guide for Supervision and Evaluation*, is cross-referenced to *Instruction for All Students*. This helps administrators provide explicit suggestions during coaching and supervisory conferences.
- The text, *Why Didn't I Learn This in College?*, provides new teachers and their mentors an abbreviated look at instruction aligned with the information in *Instruction for All Students*. It also adds essential information about creating a positive and productive learning-centered environment so that new teachers can implement a strong instructional program.
- The text, *The 21st Century Mentor's Handbook*, is cross-referenced to both *Instruction for All Students* and *Why Didn't I Learn This in College?*

ASK Framework for The Study of Teaching & Learning

The components of the **ASK Framework for the Study of Teaching and Learning** addressed in this text are marked below. One * means some information is included and two ** means extensive information is included.

(Diagram labels: Planning Instruction, Professionalism & Collegial Collaboration, Implementing Instruction, Organizing a Productive Environment, Assessing Learning & the Instructional Program, Orchestrating a Positive Environment)

Planning Instruction
** Standards-Based Teaching, Learning and Assessment
** Lesson, Unit and Course Design
   Content Specific Pedagogy
** Learning Styles, Multiple Intelligences and Brain Research
** Diversity of Students
** Active Learning
** Connections to the World Beyond The Classroom
 * Integration of the Curriculum

Implementing Instruction
** Framing the Learning
** Dealing with Naive Understandings and Misconceptions
** Communicating Purposes, Expectations, and Directions
** Using a Repertoire of Strategies, Materials and Resources
** Designing Rigorous Questions and Assignments
** Promoting Connections and Meaning Making
** Incorporating Literacy Instruction
** Differentiating Instruction
 * Accommodating and Adapting for Special Needs Students

Assessing Learning & the Instructional Program
** The Assessment Continuum
** Checking for Understanding
** Designing, Selecting, and Assessing Paper and Pencil Assessments
** Designing, Selecting, Implementing, and Assessing Performance Tasks
** Designing and Using Rubrics and Performance Assessment Task Lists
** Using Assessment Results to Inform Teaching Decisions

ASK Framework

Orchestrating a Positive Learning Environment

* Building a Community of Learners
* Having and Communicating High Expectations to All Students
* Using Attribution Theory to Re-Frame Belief Systems
* Building Capacity Through Learning How to Learn Strategies
** Using Errors and/or Lack of Background Knowledge and Skills as Learning Opportunities
** Building in Reflection and Metacognition
** Developing Thinking Skills for the 21st Century
* Building Appropriate and Positive Personal Relationships with Students

Organizing & Leading a Productive Learning-Centered Environment

Creating and Using Organizational Systems for Professional and Instructional Materials
* Developing and Implementing Organizational Systems for Learners and the Classroom
* Planning Proactively to Work with Reluctant and Resistant Learners

Professionalism & Collegial Collaboration

The Ways We Collaborate: Consultant, Collaborator, and Coach
** Formats for Collaboration and Job-Embedded Learning
** Peer Observation
* Mentoring
* Co-Teaching
Professional Responsibilities
Parents as Partners

The components of the **ASK Framework for the Study of Teaching and Learning** addressed in this text are marked above. One * means some information is included and two ** means extensive information is included.

Acknowledgements

The first people to come to mind when I think about who has significantly influenced my thinking about teaching, learning, and leading are my two sons, Doug and Mike, and my grandchildren, Will, Carter, Kelly, and Quinn. When it is personal, educational theory quickly becomes grounded in reality.

In addition to those acknowledged in the first edition: Clint Van Nagel and Paul Eggen of the University of North Florida; Jon Saphier, Executive Director of Research for Better Teaching (RBT), as well as all my colleagues in that organization; and incredible educational leaders, Katherine Ruh, Mary Alice Price, Janie Smith, and Mary Herrmann, the contributions of the three ASK Group Senior Consultants, Brenda Kaylor, Bruce Oliver, and Louise Thompson to this work must be noted. In addition to constantly teaching me what they know, these three continuously challenge me by asking hard questions that cause me to think deeply and re-examine old understandings.

This book also represents what I have learned from the thousands of educators and students I have had the good fortune to work with in schools and workshops throughout the past thirty plus years. Educators of special significance are those who have so willingly shared their expertise and thinking by providing specific examples of strategies that have worked well in their instructional programs. They are cited by name and school district; their contributions are presented on pages with the sub-title: Through the Voice of... These colleagues have taught me much about teaching and learning and truly exemplify the concept of collegial collaboration.

A special thanks goes to the women who worked with me as graphic designers and administrative assistants as I wrote the first edition. They are: Karen Grady, Anna Daley, Margie Spendiker, Valerie Fairchild, Kris Saum, Jennifer Wiley, Connie Phares, and Mary Crohn.

The second edition could not have made it to print without Donovan Goode and Mike Rutherford's patient reformatting, Caitlin Cooper and Bruce Oliver's amazing proofing and editing skills, Shilpa Shah's incredible cover design, and Laura Pavlock-Albright's organizational skills.

The biggest thanks goes to the person who is still president of my fan club and believes in me beyond all reason, my husband, David.

In The News
& Influencing Our Thinking

1

VOL. 11, NO. 25 • Second Edition • $3

 # The N4ALL News
That's Shaping Our Thinking

Vocabulary Development

Read through this list of words related to the integration of technology.

- teacher and student-made videos
- class blogs
- Google Books
- Flex cams
- Inspiration
- classroom web sites
- WebQuests
- PDF
- Photo Story 3
- podcasts
- CyberGuides
- Skype
- streaming video
- KeyNote
- TeacherTube
- webcast
- Wikis
- key pals
- Fly Pens
- Google Scholar
- Classroom response systems...Clickers

If you have any questions do a Google search or ask a digital native, that is, according to Marc Prensky, anyone under 40.

Some Things Never Change!
Ralph Tyler's Questions in *Basic Principles of Curriculum and Instruction*, 1949

- What educational purposes should the school seek to attain?
- How can learning experiences be selected which are likely to be useful in attaining these objectives?
- How can learning experiences be organized for effective instruction?
- How can the effectiveness of learning experiences be evaluated?

We are All on the Same Team

What do Judith Warren Little, Susan Rosenholtz, Ann Lieberman, Jon Saphier, Shirley Hord, Rick and Becky DuFour, Bob Eaker, Kent Peterson, Terry Deal, Linda Lambert, Michael Fullan, and Roland Barth have in common?

They all have written extensively on creating a culture for learning. They describe a culture where all the adults in a school use data, common vocabulary and concept systems, and work collaboratively around a shared mission and vision to promote student learning.

The challenge is clear. Now it is up to us to make it happen.

N4ALL Recommended Books

- *A Whole New Mind* by Daniel Pink
- *Classroom Instruction That Works* by Marzano, Pickering, and Pollack
- *Concept-Based Curriculum and Instruction* by Lynn Erickson
- *Content Area Reading and Learning* by Lapp, Flood, and Farnan
- *Instruction for All Students* by Paula Rutherford
- *Results Now* by Mike Schmoker
- *The World is Flat* by Thomas Friedman

VOL. 11, NO. 25 • Second Edition • $3

The N4ALL News

That's Shaping Our Thinking

Questions on Our Minds

- What do schools look like when they organize around a commitment to the achievement of high standards by all students?
- How do we use data to inform our practices?
- How can we provide multiple pathways to learning?
- How do we make assessment a learning experience?
- What learning experiences will connect with the digital natives in our classrooms?
- How do we work together to maximize student learning?

What should students know and be able to do?	How will the students and I know when they are successful?

 The 21ˢᵗ Century Standards-Based Planning Process

Given my task analysis, what learning experiences will facilitate student success?	Based on data, how do I refine the learning experiences?

When we constantly examine our practices and instructional decisions in terms of desired outcomes and student learning we are more likely to ensure that all students achieve at high levels.

Do You Hear What We Hear?

standards-based planning process
English language learners
learning-centered
formative assessment
mentoring and induction
differentiation
inclusive education
technology integration
repertoire building
smaller learning communities
data-driven decisions
rubrics
homework
graphic organizers
rigor, relevance, and relationships
common assessments
high stakes testing
response to intervention
literacy across the curriculum
co-teaching
concept-based instruction
creating a culture for learning

Marzano's High Yield Strategies

1. Identify similarities and differences
2. Summarizing and note taking
3. Reinforcing effort and providing recognition
4. Homework and practice
5. Nonlinguistic representation
6. Cooperative learning
7. Setting objectives and providing feedback
8. Generating and testing hypotheses
9. Questions, cues, and advance organizers

Curriculum, Instruction, & Assessment

Curriculum: What is Taught and Learned

The curriculum is the structured set of learning outcomes for a prescribed course of study. Most districts have aligned, or are working to align, their curricula with state and national standards. The curriculum is often expressed in terms of broad standards, time or grade specific benchmarks, and indicators that identify specific knowledge, processes, and skills students need in order to reach mastery of the standards. This set of learning outcomes provides the criteria and framework around which instruction as well as both standardized and classroom assessments are designed.

Instruction: How We Teach

An instructional repertoire is the array of teaching and learning strategies we use to design experiences which promote student learning of the curriculum. Thoughtful professional educators work throughout their careers to build extensive repertoires so that they can provide varied learning experiences and make purposeful selections to best meet the needs of their learners. An instructional focus on concepts and big ideas provides students with rich and rigorous learning experiences.

Assessment: How We Know What Students Have Learned

An assessment repertoire allows us to have students demonstrate what they know and what they can do in a wide variety of ways. Daily activities, assignments, and homework provide formative assessment data that allow both teachers and learners to make instructional and learning decisions. Both formative and summative assessment are most effective when the tasks are engaging, authentic, and rigorous. Assessment tasks and measures must be aligned with curriculum and standards.

> All students, including special and remedial students, need to learn what is in the curriculum; it is the instructional and assessment methods that may be different. The curriculum is designed to prepare ALL students for successful living in society.

4

Yesterday & Today...
Where We've Been & Where We Are Going
Curriculum

What is taught	What is learned
Chapters covered and workbooks completed	Identification of what student should know and be able to do
Academic context	Life context
Textbook as resource	Multiple resources
Individual subjects	Integrated subjects
Basics emphasized for all; thinking skills emphasized for gifted	Basics and thinking skills emphasized for all

Instruction

Teacher centered	Learner centered
Organized around time	Organized for results
Single teaching strategy	Multiple teaching strategies
Teach once	Reteaching and enrichment
Fixed groups	Flexible groups
Whole group instruction	Differentiated instruction
Passive learning	Active learning

Assessment

Bell curve	Public and precise criteria
One opportunity	Multiple opportunities
After instruction	Integrated with instruction
Paper and pencil based	Performance based
Grades averaged	Standard met or not met
Proving and accountability	Diagnose and prescribe
Focus on product	Focus on product and process

The Learning-Centered Classroom

Words of Wisdom

Lev Vyostky's **zone of proximal development** posits that students in the future can do independently what teachers support them in doing today. In today's classroom that translates into **scaffolding**. When we provide support through scaffolding tools such as graphic organizers, note taking aids, time management tips, manipulatives, and vocabulary instruction, students develop the background knowledge and skills they need to achieve success independently in the future.

William Glasser's **Control Theory** is based on the construct that survival, love/sense of belonging, power, and freedom are driving forces in the decisions we make about whether or not to learn or otherwise engage in an activity. In today's classrooms, teachers who use Glasser's Control Theory in their instructional decision making engage students in active meaningful learning experiences that are relevant to them in that they provide opportunities for social interaction and help students make real world connections.

Structuring Schools for Student Success, a 1991 report from the Massachusetts Board of Education, provided recommendations for creating a learning-centered environment that decreases discipline issues and increases student attendance. The following recommendations are based on that report.

- Employ active learning strategies so students are interacting with the information, the materials, and each other. Decrease time spent in whole group instruction and individual seat work.
- Provide non-evaluative feedback that gives students a clear sense of their progress. Consider some class work to be works-in-progress for which you provide clear but non-evaluative feedback.
- Have students evaluate their learning, the effectiveness of their effort, the classroom learning environment, and instructional program on a regular basis. Have them support opinions with data.
- Use a range of consequences matched to the frequency, intensity and cause of any misbehavior. Be purposeful in using consequences that are designed to move students back into a learning mode rather than remove them from the learning environment.
- Teach students within the context of their academic learning the interpersonal and communication skills they need to work and learn collaboratively. This includes skills such as speaking clearly, listening, clarifying, asking for help, and disagreeing agreeably.
- Ensure that students are not only consumers of information, but also producers of information.

The Learning-Centered Classroom

Establishing a Brain-Compatible Classroom

The body of research on how the brain works expands daily! The implications for educators are huge as we work to have **more students learning more** of what we have identified as important to know. We've moved from Binet, past the Bell Curve and, thanks to the technological revolution, on to the powerful brain research of the 21st century. When we study and use the work of Howard Gardner, Daniel Goleman, Renate and Geoffrey Caine, Robert Sylwester, Pat Wolfe, and others, we and our students benefit from that new knowledge and its application in the classroom. Not one of these extraordinary researchers claims to have "the" answer, but each offers valuable insights. One thing we know for sure is that there is a great deal more for us to know in order to "be smart about intelligence!"

When we use what we know so far about how students learn and how the brain works we can be explicit about establishing a **brain-compatible, learning-centered environment**. In 1998 the Association for Supervision and Curriculum Development (ASCD) published several videotape series that featured four components summarizing how we can use research to create such learning environments. When we include these four components in our planning we increase the likelihood of student engagement and learning. They are:

- **varied sources of input**
- **meaningful active learning**
- **timely appropriate feedback**
- **a safe, nonthreatening environment**

Such an approach to teaching and learning does not mean that teachers abdicate responsibility for what students learn or for holding and using expert knowledge. In fact, this constructivist approach requires that teachers be knowledgeable and skillful about not only the content to be learned but also about the students who are to learn it. It means that the teacher role changes from **sage on the stage to guide from the side** and that the learner role changes from reproducer of facts and theories to an active, reflective, analytical participant and producer in the learning process.

Tell me,
I forget.

Show me,
I remember.

Involve me,
I understand.
- Ancient Chinese Proverb

The Quest Continues
High School Reform

Breaking Ranks

Breaking Ranks: Changing an American Institution, published in 1996 by the National Association of Secondary School Principals (NASSP), declared that high schools must:

- be learning communities
- prepare students for the next stage of their lives, whether it is further formal education or the work force
- prepare all students for a life of learning
- give students the tools to be good citizens and active participants in a democracy
- include experiences that meet the social needs of students
- prepare students to live and work in a highly technological world
- build student capacity to thrive in a diverse country and world where acceptance and collaboration with those different from them is a basic skill

Breaking Ranks II: Strategies for Leading High School Reform, published by NASSP in 2004, presents seven "cornerstone strategies" to improve student performance:

- core knowledge
- connections with students
- personalized planning
- adapting to differences
- flexible use of time
- distributed leadership
- continuous professional development

To obtain more information about *Breaking Ranks* go to www.nassp.org.

High Schools for the New Millennium
Smaller Learning Communities (SLCs)

The Bill and Melinda Gates Foundation and the U.S. Department of Education have provided millions of dollars to help districts create smaller learning communities (SLCs).

One of the goals of the Gates Foundation's grants is to prepare students for college, work, and citizenship by offering ... "the new 3Rs—rigorous instruction, a relevant curriculum, and meaningful, supportive relationships." The Gates Foundation report, *High Schools for the New Millennium*, explains the possibilities for SLCs and describes several successful schools. Read the entire report at

The Quest Continues
High School Reform

www.gatesfoundation.org/UnitedStates/Education/TransformingHighSchools/

The **Smaller Learning Communities (SLCs) Program of the U.S. Department of Education** has provided grants to districts to "support the implementation of SLCs and activities to improve student academic achievement in large public high schools with enrollments of 1,000 or more students." The SLC formats supported include "freshman academies, multi-grade academies organized around career interests or other themes, "houses" in which small groups of students remain together throughout high school, and autonomous schools-within-a-school."

Visit the website of the **Coalition of Essential Schools** to learn about the coalition's small school project: www.essentialschools.org and **The Education Alliance** website: www.lab.brown.edu/db/ea_catalog.php to access multiple downloadable publications on SLCs and other high school reform initiatives.

Results that Matter: 21ˢᵗ Century Skills and High School Reform

The Partnership for 21ˢᵗ Century Skills, established in 2002, has over twenty-five member organizations including Microsoft, Apple, Adobe, AFT, NEA, Dell, PBS, and Time Warner. The Partnership's 2006 report *Results that Matter: 21ˢᵗ Century Skills and High School Reform* recommends redefining rigor to include mastery of:

- the core subjects identified by the 2001 reauthorization of the Elementary and Secondary Education Act of 1965 known as No Child Left Behind
- 21ˢᵗ century content including global awareness, financial, economic, and business and entrepreneurial literacy, civic literacy, and health and wellness awareness
- learning and thinking skills comprised of critical-thinking and problem-solving skills, communication skills, creativity and innovation skills, collaboration skills, contextual learning skills, and information and media literacy skills
- information and communications technology literacy
- life skills including leadership, ethics, accountability, adaptability, personal productivity and responsibility, people skills, self-direction, and social responsibility

The report further states that student learning must be measured with a balance of assessments including both high-quality standardized testing and classroom assessments using modern technology.

The entire twenty-six page report can be accessed at www.21stcenturyskills.org.

Data-Driven Discussions & Decisions
Job-Embedded Learning

In the 1980s Bruce Joyce, Beverly Showers, Judith Warren Little, and Susan Rosenholtz wrote about the power of collegial collaboration, training sessions followed by job-site practice with feedback, peer observations, and teachers asking for and providing one another assistance. Art Costa and Robert Garmstron extended our thinking with their cognitive coaching model and Jon Saphier and Matt King wrote about creating cultures for learning that emphasized collaboration and reaching out to the knowledge base on teaching and learning. In the 1990s Rick DuFour and Robert Eaker along with Shirley Hord began writing extensively about professional learning communities and Linda Lambert wrote about building teacher leadership capacity.

At last, in the 21st century, teachers across the country are engaged in multiple job-embedded learning formats. Professional Learning Communities (PLCs), as described by DuFour and Eaker, are the Rolls Royce model to which we all aspire. There are, however, formats any group of educators can initiate. Listed below is an array of those formats, many of which are described in **Chapter XI: Collegial Collaboration**.

- Action Research by Individuals, Teams, Entire Staff
- Data Analysis
- Journals: Planning and/or Reflective
- Looking At Student Work
- Lesson Study
- Peer Review of Plans and Products
- Book Clubs
- Demonstration Teaching
- Co-Teaching
- Mentoring Relationships for All
- Presentations by Internal Experts
- Observations for "Peer Coaching and Peer Poaching"
- Learning Walks (Rutherford)
- Analysis of Videotaped Teaching/Learning Episodes
- 3-D Teams (Rutherford)
- Study Groups
- Case Studies
- Learning Clubs
- Cognitive Coaching
- Group Problem Solving
- School Improvement Teams Focused on Teaching and Learning
- Role Playing of Difficult Situations: What Do You Do When...?

Through the Voice of...
Job-Embedded Learning

Team Leaders at Pine Crest Elementary School in Montgomery County Public Schools, Maryland, conduct three, 60-minute grade level team meetings per month. As a part of their collaborative planning time together they lead their teams by:

- Identifying common values and norms
- Developing a team mission statement
- Facilitating meetings that are focused and a productive use of time
- Modeling effective meeting strategies
- Addressing/seeking answers for team member concerns in a timely manner
- Eliciting input from the team to represent the views of the team at a team leaders meeting
- Ensuring all stakeholders' views and needs are taken into consideration when decisions need to be made by a team leader or at the team level
- Providing timely communication from the team leaders meeting to the group

80% of team meeting time is used to

- Develop quarterly content maps in reading, math, science and social studies to increase communication with all stakeholders
- Engage in lesson study
- Target strategies, activities, and lessons aligned with lesson plan development
- Conduct on-going data analysis activities to answer:
  - How will we respond when students experience initial difficulty with learning?
  - How will we deepen their understanding for students who have already mastered essential knowledge and skill?
- Write/score/discuss common grade level assessments using a protocol
- Analyze the expectations of statewide assessments
- Create grade level action plans based on identified areas of need through building walk-throughs
- Conduct action research projects
- Identify needs related to the acquisition and use of instructional technologies
- Engage in collaborative problem solving to ensure all students are successful at a high level
- Lead or participate in a book study based on identified student/school needs
- Collaborate to create a presentation for staff development (i.e., another grade level team, faculty meeting, etc.)

In summary, teams meet regularly to identify essential student learning, develop common formative assessments, analyze current levels of achievement, set achievement goals, share strategies, and create lessons to improve learning.

Meredith Casper, Principal, Pine Crest Elementary School, Montgomery County Public Schools, MD

21st Century Thinking Skills

Voices Beyond the Halls of Academia

Jennifer James, Daniel Pink, and Thomas Friedman are among those leading the charge in calling, directly or indirectly, for PreK-12 education to focus more on 2026 than on 1996. James is an urban cultural anthropologist and author of **Thinking in the Future Tense**, Pink is author of **A Whole New Mind**, and Friedman the foreign correspondent for the New York Times and author of **The World is Flat**. All three books are on our recommended books list.

On **Jennifer James**' website (www.jenniferjames.com) she lists eight thinking skills that she sees as important for the 21st Century. They are:
- perspective (seeing with new eyes)
- awareness of patterns (recognizing the future)
- critical thinking (understanding the social context)
- response time (the ability to change and help others change)
- context (understanding the past to know the future)
- effectiveness (doing more with less)
- diversity I.Q. (profiting from diversity)

Daniel Pink (www.danpink.com) writes and talks about the need for our students to:
- be able to do big-picture thinking
- be creative
- empathize with others
- tell stories and listen to others' stories
- recognize patterns
- be intrinsically motivated

Pulitzer Prize winner **Thomas Friedman** (www.thomaslfriedman.com) names the following skill sets as important for our students in the global workplace because this work is not likely to be outsourced in the near future:
- collaborators
- orchestrators
- synthesizers
- explainers
- leveragers
- adapters
- personalizers
- math lovers
- localizers

Given this information, what are the implications for our instructional decisions?

Rigor, Relevance, & Relationships

Much of the literature about rigor, relevance, and relationships, the new 3 Rs to be added to but not replace the original 3 Rs, is focused on high school reform. Respect, responsibility, resiliency, and results are often added to the mix when we extend the alliteration of the Rs. Another important R is the **reality** that we need a focus on rigor, relevance, and relationships not just in high schools but in all classrooms PreK-12.

To achieve rigor we need to
- design courses that explicitly address standards and essential understandings
- task analyze so that we can scaffold instruction appropriately
- align all learning experiences, class assignments/projects, homework, and assessments with the learning standards
- develop consensus about what student work does and does not meet standards
- teach students to self-assess and self-adust as a result of that self-assessment

To obtain relevance we need to
- help students build on what they already know
- explicitly make real-world connections
- integrate the technology they are using outside the classroom

To build relationships we need to
- get to know our students well
- provide opportunities for them to know each other and other adults
- work with parents as partners
- recognize and applaud effort rather than speed
- focus on equity rather than equality

Rigor/Relevance Framework
Willard Daggett and his colleagues at the International Center for Leadership in Education, Inc. have developed a very practical framework called the **Rigor/Relevance Framework™**. The framework builds on Bloom's Taxonomy. This model adds an application component that focuses planning on the context in which the knowledge will be used. The contexts are: knowledge in one discipline, application in one discipline, application across multiple disciplines, application to predictable real-world situations, and at the most complex level, application of knowledge to unpredictable real-world situations.

See page 235 and visit the website at www.leadered.com to explore the framework in depth.

Literacy Across the Curriculum

Mike Schmoker and Katie Haycock have both written about the "crayola curriculum." They contend that in many classrooms students spend more time coloring than they do reading and writing. On the other hand, as Marzano has written, visuals, graphic organizers, and other non-linguistic representations are important to the learning process. Clearly we must carefully craft the assignments we give our students and provide both variety and balance.

Journals and interactive notebooks support the emphasis on integrating literacy across the curriculum and can provide opportunities for rigor and relevance. Interactive notebooks provide students the opportunity to create relevance and use non-lingusitic representations to extend their learning.

Journals may be kept in hard copy or on computers. Blogs are a great way to engage our students, provide a motivating and engaging writing opportunity, and create opportunities for language and communication skills development.

Uses of Journals and Interactive Notebooks

- To record daily thinking and learning...aha's and questions, implications, general musings
- To prepare for discussions...questions, key ideas, etc.
- To summarize lessons and ideas...such as 3-2-1 or "As a result of today, I..."
- As an alternative to homework assignments when unclear as how to proceed
- To make predictions about next steps, rationales, effects of actions
- To identify and solve problems
- To promote vocabulary development
- To make connections to prior learning and/or life beyond the classroom
- To respond to discussions, printed text, videos, demonstrations or lectures
- To generate possible topics for research
- To let off steam
- To set priorities and schedules
- To record and evaluate study habits, efforts, and academic progress
- To create graphic organizers, pictures, poems, charts, etc.

The use of journals and interactive notebooks appeals to the verbal/linguistic and intrapersonal learners. Journaling may open learning avenues for these students in content areas that are usually presented in a more logical/sequential manner.

See page 228 for more information on interactive notebooks.

Literacy Across the Curriculum

Willard Daggett, President of the International Center for Leadership in Education, says "Once a student leaves high school, 90% of his reading will be information reading. Only 10% of his reading will be for pleasure." This statement from Daggett reinforces the responsibility we have to explicitly teach students how to read informational material in all our classroom settings.

Profile of Proficient Readers

Based on their review of the literature, secondary educators in Fairfax County Public Schools, Fairfax, Virginia, identified the following as behaviors by proficient readers across the curriculum. Proficient readers:

- Set a purpose for reading
- Access prior knowledge and relate it to new information
- Construct meaning
- Reread, skim, summarize a chapter
- Paraphrase and predict based on chapter headings
- Frame and re-frame focus questions prior to, during, and following reading
- Look for important ideas in charts, tables, and graphs
- Test their understanding of technical information
- Identify patterns in the text that serve as examples of the main idea
- Use graphic organizers to organize ideas
- Sequence events, e.g., in an explanation of historical facts
- Look for relationships, e.g., between math concepts
- Read ahead for clarification, e.g., of scientific terms and concepts
- Mentally execute directions in a manual
- Have a repertoire of strategies and know when to use which
- Think about reading strategies before, during, and after reading
- Monitor their understanding of difficult explanations

Secondary content-area teachers can use the components of a balanced literacy program, such as guided reading, modeled reading, and discussion groups, to help their students develop and use these skills. Other essential tasks of the secondary teacher include the teaching about, and providing practice with, content specific vocabulary through the study of commonly used prefixes and suffixes, as well as Latin and Greek roots, and the structure and parts of the textbooks used in the study of the discipline. Information, patterns, connections, and processes that are clear to teachers who are experts in their field may well escape the learner who is encountering this material for the first time.

Vocabulary Development

Looking words up in a dictionary or a glossary and writing down the definition even when followed by using the word in a sentence does not always do the trick! Students need to work with the vocabulary words in context and in connection with other words they already know and use. They need to do so in a way that promotes **mastery** (the capacity to use the word in both their receptive and expressive language), **retention** (the capacity to use the word over time), and **transfer** (the capacity to use the word appropriately in other contexts). Many educators are calling this **word study**.

Graves and Slater, in *Content Area Reading and Learning*, identify six levels of vocabulary development. While looking up a word in a dictionary or glossary may be appropriate for some of them, it is not the best approach most of the time. When you identify vocabulary words to preteach or to emphasize during teaching, consider the relationship the students already have with the word when selecting the instructional strategy. The levels are:
- Learning to read words already in oral vocabulary
- Learning new meanings (content specific) for known words
- Learning new words for known concepts
- Learning new words representing new concepts
- Clarifying and enriching meanings of known words
- Using words currently in the students' receptive vocabulary (listening and reading) and in their expressive or productive vocabulary (speaking and writing)

Instructional Strategies to Use in Vocabulary Development

Word Splash - Dorsey Hammond "invented" the idea of a word splash. Early readers can use a "picture splash." The idea is to have students look at words that are known to them, and decide how they might be related to one another and to the focus of their study. This is not a strategy to use with new words, but rather with words being used in a different context or with a different meaning. See page 18 for an example of a **Word Splash**.

Word Walls - Selected concept/vocabulary words from the current area of study are placed on the wall in the classroom. They may be arranged in a randomly angled way to encourage students to make guesses about what they mean, why they are important, and how they are related to the topic under study and to each other.

Vocabulary Development

Alternatively, they may be grouped by category and even printed on different color paper to explicitly identify the group to which each term belongs. The important point is to have the words on display for students to refer to in their discussions and while they are writing. This approach is appropriate for all levels of vocabulary development. It is especially useful for English Language Learners and for promoting use of the terms and concepts in written and spoken language of all learners.

Frayer Model - This visual organizer is useful in helping learners separate critical attributes from interesting information about a concept. This is a recommended approach for new words for new concepts. See the following page for a visual representation.

Word Sorts - The name **List-Group-Label** is used in the reading literature for the word sort strategy and is useful for helping students clarify and enrich meanings of known words. As the name implies, students list all the words they can think of related to a given topic. They then group the words and label the groupings. These three steps are the first stage in Hilda Taba's inductive thinking model, which was originally presented as an elementary social studies strategy.

Three Column Charts - This strategy is a good one for helping students identify their own level of use and expertise with words. Use the headings **I Know and Use It in My Speech and in My Writing, I Recognize It and Understand It When I Hear and Read it, I Am Not Sure of the Meaning**. See page 113 for more information about **Three Column Charts**.

Graphic Organizers - Descriptive graphic organizers, or **mind maps**, are particularly useful in helping students refine their understanding and use of terms, as well as to integrate the terms within a context. Students could create their own mind maps, work with a partner to refine their mind maps, and then create a class mind map on the board. This is an excellent way to review an important and complex concept that has vocabulary that is challenging and/or vocabulary that is being used in a new way.

Inside-Outside Circles (Kagan, 1994) - When it is necessary to have students look up words up in a dictionary, and they do not need to work on glossary or dictionary skills, have each student look up one word. Have them write the word on one side of an index card and the definition on the other. See page 93 for more information on **Inside-Outside Circles**.

The Frayer Method

Students list as many attributes of the word as they can think of, then cross out those that are not essential. The remaining essential attributes will help define the new word. This model helps students build skills at crafting rich definitions of concepts and vocabulary words.

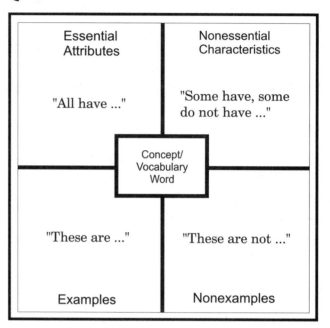

Word Splash

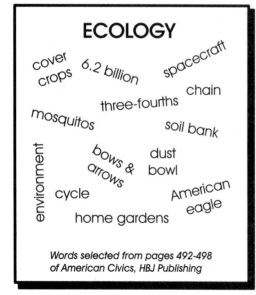

A word splash is a collection of key terms or concepts from a reading. The terms should be familiar to the students. The purpose is to relate the terms to each other and to the new topic of study. It is a particularly powerful strategy when different meanings of some of the words are being introduced. Prior to reading, viewing, or visiting a site, students brainstorm and generate complete sentences to predict the relationships. After the learning experience, they review their predictions and make corrections.

Vocabulary Development

Robert Marzano has identified a six-step process for teaching vocabulary. The six steps are presented below with suggestions as to how to implement them.

Explain - In this step, the teacher gives a student-friendly, relevant, and perhaps humorous, description, explanation, or example of a new term. The explanation can be enhanced by pictures, computer images, mental images, and stories.

Restate - Next, students generate their own definition and consider how the term relates to their own life experiences. They should share their definition with a learning buddy or with their table group and discuss the similarities and differences. Students often keep a vocabulary notebook, a collection of vocabulary cards, or include their vocabulary work in their interactive notebooks.

Show - Students generate a visual to capture the essence of their current understanding of the term. This visual might be a picture, a symbol, or a graphic organizer. Depending on time and resources computer graphics could be accessed and/or created. If the term represents an abstract concept, provide multiple exemplars or other scaffolding.

Have students complete the first three steps when a term is first introduced. They will have multiple opportunities to revise both their explanations and their visuals in the next three steps which are spaced over time.

Discuss - This step uses the principle of learning, cumulative review, in that students revisit terms they have previously studied. Too often we have students study vocabulary or spelling words for a week, do multiple exercises with the terms, and take a test on Friday. We all know that two weeks later we have often forgotten the word. This step spirals the study of the terms throughout the year and asks students to find the words in context both inside and outside of school. Because 75% of our learners are talk processors, the opportunity to use and discuss the terms over time promotes their learning.

Refine and Reflect - If students are expected to repeatedly use the terms in complete sentences and use them to frame questions about their learning, their ownership of the terms increases significantly.

Engage in Learning Games - This final step is designed to have students "play" with vocabulary. The commercial and student-made learning game possibilities are limitless. Be sure to collect some of the student-generated games for use in future years. These games make excellent learning centers.

Meeting the Needs of Diverse Learners

Who Are Our Students?

Some of our students have traveled abroad, some have lived abroad, and others were born abroad. Some have not yet traveled beyond state borders or city limits. Some were born into affluent families and others into families with far less financial means. Some speak English with everyone they know and others speak two or more languages on a daily basis and English may or may not be their first language. In both groups there are some who cannot read or write proficiently in any language while others read well beyond grade level not only in English but other languages as well. Some of our students are born with special needs and all are born with interesting and possibly challenging quirks. Certainly all process information and learn in different ways. What's a teacher to do?

What's a Teacher to Do with Second Language Learners?

The answer is straight forward: recognize, appreciate, honor, and respond to the differences in an inclusive and culturally responsive way. NCREL's **Strategic Teaching and Reading Project Guidebook** describes culturally responsive practice as
- Inclusive, meaning the curriculum reflects the cultural, ethnic, and gender diversity of society
- Building on the students' prior knowledge, culture, and language
- Stimulating students to construct knowledge, make meaning, and examine cultural biases and assumptions

What's a Teacher to Do with Struggling or Special Needs Learners?

- Focus on individuals first and exceptionality or speciality second
- Ensure that inclusive education includes inclusive language and professional practice
- Make data-driven decisions about instructional strategies or interventions to use with students

See **Chapter VIII: Differentiation of Instruction** for more information.

This Means

We need to be sure that we connect with all students in ways that cause them to see us as trustworthy and invested in their success. We need to, in word and deed, send the messages that:
- We do not equate not being able to read with not being able to think and learn
- We do not equate not speaking English with not being able to think and learn
- For us, all means all, even if some students do not look or dress like us
- We believe that we have not taught if they have not learned

Inclusive Education
Meeting the Needs of Diverse Learners

Public Law 94-142 (Education of All Handicapped Children Act) passed in 1975 required that students with disabilities be taught in the "least restrictive environment." At that time we brought most of our students back to their home schools from outside placements. That first step at mainstreaming led to the establishment of self-contained classrooms where core subjects were taught by special education teachers and resource rooms where special educators worked the students in either a remedial or compensatory approach. What went on in these classrooms was usually driven by IEP goals with little consideration of the curriculum or program followed by the rest of the students in the school.

PL 94-142, now known as Individuals with Disabilities Education Act (IDEA), as amended in 1997, requires that all students have access to the same rich curriculum as all other students and that they be held to the same level of accountability as all other students. With those requirements, there can no longer be different curricula and standards and all students must have instruction from teachers who are not only well versed in pedagogy, learning theory, and working with disabilities or language challenges (the special educators and second language specialists), but with teachers who are also knowledgeable and skillful with the content to be taught and learned (the general educators). This clearly requires that teachers collaborate in ways that have not previously been the norm.

The 2004 reauthorization of IDEA included the statement: [Schools will] "not be required to take into consideration whether a child has a severe discrepancy between achievement and intellectual ability ..." [Section 1414(b)] Instead schools can now use an approach called **Response to Intervention (RtI)** which permits the use of data about the students' response to scientific, research-based intervention to determine the type and level of support the child should have, and requires that the learner's general education teacher be a part of the team that determines whether or not the child has a specific learning disability. The important point of this change is that interventions can occur earlier and may take place in the regular classroom. That is, the student does not have to fail in school before receiving additional support; that support is to be provided in a three-tier model and may or may not include special education services. It is also important to note that students cannot be found eligible for special education services because of lack of scientifically-based reading instruction, lack of instruction in math, or limited English proficiency.

Go to wvde.state.wv.us/ose/RtiImpGuide91906.DOC to access the West Virginia Department of Education's **Response to Intervention (RtI) Implementation Guide**. Appendix A has an extensive list of recommended readings and websites.

Through the Voice of... Rethinking Assessment Practices
Assessment as a Learning Experience

We often assess the way we were assessed when we were in school without stopping to think about why we do what we do, or whether it is the best way to determine if students are truly learning. Following a review of the literature, I outlined the following **Top Ten Suggestions for Rethinking Assessment Practices** to capture my learning about how we can make assessment a learning experience.

Emphasize learning, not grading

Some educators lose sight of student learning as the ultimate goal. Some become so wrapped up in grading practices that the focus on our primary responsibility, student learning, is lost. Recently I encountered a student who received a "D" on his report card when he had earned a "B" on the summative unit assessment. In the teacher's list of "grades," he had missed two homeworks, one journal entry and received an "F" on a pop quiz. The teacher's grading practice allotted a certain percentage to each category in the grade book. In short, she followed the practice of averaging grades instead of focusing on what the student ultimately learned.

Give students multiple opportunities to show what they have learned

Assessments should not be a one-shot, do-or-die undertaking for students. We should apply the same common sense to assessing student learning as we do to teaching a loved one or colleague something new. When we teach a teenager to drive, we don't just continue to tell him he's failing or give him a "bad grade." We give continuous feedback and allow him to try and try again until he learns. If we teach a colleague a new technology application, we sit with her and answer her questions until we see that she can use the skill independently. As learners ourselves, nothing is more frustrating than having a knowledgeable individual present us with information and then leave us floundering as we struggle to figure out new learning on our own. We should use the teaching practices with our students that we want for ourselves when we are tackling new learning. One principal established the practice in her school that she called "A, B, C or Do It Over." Students were expected to work until they had earned a minimum of a grade of "C." The emphasis was on teaching students to persevere until they had achieved a goal.

Eliminate zeros

There is no practice in education that discourages students more than the practice of giving a zero for an incomplete assignment or an assignment that is not turned in. When a teacher gives a zero, it is the expectation that the grade will be a wake up call for the student who will then be motivated to improve his or her performance. The practice often has the exact opposite effect.

Assessment as a Learning Experience

Typically a student will shut down and stop working because he or she knows that it is impossible to rebound from that zero. I have also heard of situations where teachers follow the unfortunate practice of assigning zeros as a punishment to students which is a misuse of a teacher's authority. I am not sure where the idea of zeros came from but it is a practice that is counter to our goal of motivating students to learn.

Be up front with students about how learning will be assessed

It is critical that assessments be aligned with the standards that are taught. The guideline for teachers should be to **take the mystery out of mastery**. As Paula Rutherford writes, educators should follow **The Three Ps** in relation to assessment: **Prior** to giving an assessment to students, the teacher should be **public** about how students will be assessed as well as telling the students **precisely** how learning will be measured. All of us are better able to work toward achieving a goal when we know what the goal is.

Build student confidence

When teachers use assessments accurately and appropriately, student success follows. When students experience success on a regular basis, they develop confidence and build optimism. They develop a strong desire to succeed, learn to analyze their mistakes, put forth a high level of effort and take risks as they stretch themselves as learners. On the other hand, repeated failure results in pessimism, a sense of hopelessness, decreasing effort, and expectations that assessment results will be negative. Teachers have the power to build student confidence through the way that they plan lessons, and that is the kind of power a teacher should always exert. By task-analyzing assignments and assessments, teachers can differentiate instruction and provide scaffolding to ensure that all students can accomplish the work that is being assigned.

Offer choice

When students have some ownership in their learning, they become more engaged and interested in participating in the learning experience. By allowing students some choice in how they learn (research topics, books for reading, projects, outlining, free writing, webbing, etc.), they become more intrinsically motivated. When a teacher allows students, on occasion, to choose how to demonstrate their learning, the essential understandings become more personal and long-lasting. See pages 183-188 for an extensive list of products students can create.

Assessment as a Learning Experience

Use formative assessment data properly

Formative data can be misused by teachers. The results of formative assessments (pre-assessments, checks for understanding, student self-assessments, journal writing, quizzes) are often used to determine a student's final grade for a marking period. Formative assessments provide information to both the teacher and the student as learning is taking place. Once students have had the chance to use teacher feedback and formative assessment data, a teacher can administer a summative assessment which allows students to show what they have ultimately learned.

Expand assessment repertoires

My belief is that we should do whatever it takes to promote and measure student learning. Educators should be lifelong learners who are constantly adding to their instructional approaches as well as ways to assess student learning. Teachers need opportunities to routinely collaborate with their peers and exchange assessment ideas and must continuously seek out new strategies and approaches. In short, we should be searching for the keys to student success.

Think long range

Our ultimate goal as educators is to have our students learn to self-assess by reflecting on their own efforts and learning and then self-adjust. We want our students to think of assessment and adjustment of behaviors and practices as not only steps in the learning process but also as essential life skills. We can promote this mind set by carefully structuring the learning environment for students.

Remember the person behind the numbers

We must remember that a student cannot be reduced to a number or a grade. The more personal interest we take in each of our students, the greater the likelihood that the student will become more involved in the learning. As human beings, we all want to experience success. We have feelings and aspirations. Our students are no different. When frustrated, they often resort to acting defensively or seemingly uninterested.

Bruce Oliver, ASK Group Senior Consultant
Adapted from "Rethinking Assessment Practices," *Just for the ASKing!* April 2006. All rights reserved.

Through the Voice of...
Growth-Producing Feedback

Feedback is an incredibly powerful teaching tool; Grant Wiggins writes that when growth-producing feedback is provided, most students can achieve at the same level as the top 20% of students. He also asserts that feedback has a positive impact on student engagement. Put quite simply, students who are given specific information about the accuracy and quality of their work will spend more time working on their academic assignments.

It is important to have a clear definition of growth-producing feedback. Wiggins says that feedback is not about praise or blame, approval or disapproval. Good feedback describes what a student did or did not do for the purpose of changing or maintaining a behavior or performance. Robert Marzano and associates concur that effective feedback should provide students with an explanation of what they are doing correctly and what steps they must take to continue to make progress. Typical feedback includes such comments as "Nice work," "Unclear," "You need to improve your study habits," "C+," or "75%." These types of statements or grades show either an approval or disapproval of what a student has done, and are evaluative in nature. This type of feedback has very little effect on student learning and can have a negative impact on student motivation to learn. Students tend to ignore comments when they are accompanied by grades or numerical scores. Students pay much closer attention to written comments when they are not accompanied by a grade. Stephen Chappuis and Richard Stiggins found that "replacing judgmental feedback with specific, descriptive, and immediate feedback benefits students." Productive feedback tells students where they are on the continuum of mastery of given standards or benchmarks, what they are doing right and next steps to take toward mastery.

Providing students growth-producing feedback is not enough. Students must have the opportunity to respond to the feedback, make adjustments in their work, and resubmit their assignments for further comments.

When teachers provide specific growth-producing feedback, students begin to develop the skills of self-assessment and self-adjustment. We do not want students to be completely dependent on their teachers to let them know if they are learning. These life skills can result in our students having greater aspirations to succeed in the future, enjoying greater satisfaction from their learning, and setting future performance goals.

Bruce Oliver, ASK Group Senior Consultant

Adapted from "Growth Producing Feedback," *Just for the ASKing!* October 2006. All rights reserved.

Technology Integration

How Are We Doing?

Do we create learning experiences in which students are using technology to access, retrieve, select, collect, process, collate, display, analyze, evaluate, create, and communicate information?

Do learners produce written products in which they communicate in different formats using text, tables, pictures, graphics, and sound?

Do students use graphical, statistical, and presentation software to create and present multimedia presentations for varied audiences?

Do learners access news reports from multiple sources including international sources and analyze the causes and effects of the different perspectives?

Do students access databases and carry out research using technology?

Is the learning environment structured so that students systematically build and practice telecommunication skills for both using and troubleshooting technology?

Do students participate in online discussions such as e-mail to and from experts, Keypals, electronic bulletin boards, chat rooms, and blogs?

Our Technology Learning Tools: Do We Have Access To and Use...

- the Internet
- electronic U.S. and world atlas
- interactive dictionaries
- electronic encyclopedia
- simulations
- electronic thesaurus
- webcasts
- desktop publishing programs
- database programs
- e-mail
- integrated learning systems (ILS)
- SmartBoards
- webcams

- graphic organizer programs such as Inspiration
- word processing programs such as Word
- presentation programs such as PowerPoint and Keynote
- graphic programs such as Adobe Photoshop
- scanners
- spreadsheet programs such as Excel
- digital cameras
- streaming video
- Podcasts

Listen to the Natives!
Technology Integration

Jeff VanDrimmelen, UNC Chapel Hill, wrote in a posting on EduTechie.com his suggestions about what teachers can do to get our digital native students really engaged in the learning process. He suggests using technologies like blogs, wikis, podcasts, and online video. The general guidelines he provides are:
- Make final products shareable
- Give students projects not assignments
- Encourage students to use popular technologies that are a part of their lives
- Give students options

Stu Smith, Barker Road Middle School, Pittsford Central School District, New York, shared via a November 2007 email the following pointers about using the Internet and, in particular, using teacher web sites for technology integration.

Using the Internet
- Teachers no longer have to send their students home with a deck of flash cards to practice basic facts. There are a plethora of interactive and fun sites that promote learning.
- Teachers today can take advantage of the thousands of web sites on the Internet. New sites are created every day in all curricular areas. Students can access them in the classroom or at home. They can play instructional games, take practice quizzes, or watch interactive videos, which when selected by the teacher can help students build competency with the identified objectives.
- There are sites where students can take online quizzes, either created by the teacher or ready-made. The quizzes are scored automatically and the results are sent to the teacher complete with an item analysis.
- Everyday there are more and more teacher sites where lessons and ideas are shared. Teachers are finding out they no longer have to reinvent the wheel day after day. Lessons can be used "as is" or modified to meet specific needs.

Using Your Own Classroom Web Site
- Teachers can post class news, homework assignments, upcoming tests, and projects.
- Assignments can be uploaded so students who are absent have access to them from home.
- Parents and students can download supplemental assignments for remedial or enrichment work.
- Teachers can create links to web sites that they want their students to use.
- Exemplars can be posted so both students and parents know what is expected.

Teaching & Learning in the
21ˢᵗ Century Standards-Based Classroom

The headings in this section come from the *Facilitator's Manual for Developing a Common Ground* developed by a team of educators from Centennial BOCES, Longmont, Colorado; they were early scouts in the standards movement.

Standards guide all classroom decisions.

This statement represents where we want and need to be. Across the USA educators have access to standards developed at the state, and often at the local level, that should guide instructional decision making. The reality is that few educators can say that they are **standards-based**. What they can say so far is that they are **standards-referenced**. That is, many of us refer to the standards to see if we can justify what we had planned to teach based on teachers' manuals or on programs purchased by the district or by what they have "always" done. Teachers who are new to the profession seem to more readily engage in practices that are **standards-based** because they have no "old habits," units, lessons, or activities to give up.

Moving from Standards-Referenced to Standards-Based

- Knowing that the standards exist.
- Knowing where to find a copy.
- Reading the standards: It is possible to read part of a standards document without understanding the depth and breadth of the standards for a course of study. There is also a danger that we might march through indicators in much the same way that we, in the past, marched through pages in texts or workbooks. These issues mean that we need to read the entire standards document so that we can begin with the end in mind.
- Posting the standards: Posting standards in "educationaleze" in primary classrooms or posting and announcing the standard, benchmark, or indicator by number in any classroom does not meet this criteria. The information should be presented in accessible "student-friendly" language.
- Occasionally referring to the standards during planning.
- Checking to see if what is being taught can be found in the standards: It is at this point in the journey that many of us get stuck.
- Beginning to understand the power and focus the standards provide and working to identify the essential understandings that are embedded in and that transcend the standards as they are written in the documents.
- Being able to say "I am **standards-based** because I used the standards to design assessments and instruction, and I used student work to judge whether or not the instruction was well-designed for this content with these learners."

Teaching & Learning in the 21ˢᵗ Century Standards-Based Classroom

The first six bullets are more representative of **standards-referenced** than they are of **standards-based**. Teachers have to include the last two before they can say that they are **standards-based**. The next five headings further clarify variables that must be in place before teachers can accurately say, "**I am standards-based**."

The focus is always on student learning.

"**I have so much to cover**" continues to be the cry of many teachers. It is true that the amount of information and the number of skills they are asked to ensure that the learners master is mind-boggling. Given that, we teachers have to be thoughtful and focused about **how we spend the currency of education: time**. We need to make sure that every single learning experience students engage in is not only an interesting activity, but also the right exercise for moving their learning forward. Just because an exercise is next in the textbook, or because our teammates have been using it for years, is not sufficient reason for having our students do it. We have to ask the following questions:

- **Is this the right lesson for these students right now?**
- **Given the school-year time frame, is this learning experience worthy of the time it will cost?**
- **Is there another way to approach this learning that might work better for these learners or be more efficient in moving them along?**

In the first years of teaching it is difficult to know the answers to these questions, so it is essential that as we move through those first years we keep good reflective/analytical records of what worked and what did not work, and about the cost in terms of time. That way we can be even more purposeful in the years to come.

Expectations for learning are the same for all students, even those who have traditionally performed at low levels.

At the same time the standards movement was sweeping across the land, IDEA made legally imperative what was already our moral responsibility. It required that all students have access to the same rich curriculum and be held to the same level of understanding as all other students. The implications are huge. The percentage of students who have been labeled as "special needs" and the percentage of English Language Learners (ELLs) is staggering.

Teaching & Learning in the
21st Century Standards-Based Classroom

This mandate and these students are the reason we hear so much about **differentiation of instruction**. Differentiation must start with a strongly focused curriculum based on the standards. We need strong knowledge and skillfulness with our content, a thorough understanding of how our students learn, and a deep and wide repertoire of instructional strategies for connecting the students and the content. Only then can we provide scaffolding and multiple pathways to learning. The current move away from a deficit model in identifying students who need special education services increases the need for us to have that knowledge and these skills. Response to Intervention (RtI) provides us with an incredible opportunity to be more collaborative in our work, more purposeful in our selection of strategies, and more data-driven in analyzing the effectiveness of those decisions.

The final determination of the effectiveness of instructional practices is whether or not they result in higher levels of achievement for students.

Are we making progress? We need to first gather and analyze **pre-assessment** or baseline data about what our students know and can do as they enter the learning experience. The analysis of that data leads to an instructional plan which includes the ongoing gathering and use of **formative data. Summative assessment data** informs us and the learners about whether or not the students are moving toward mastery of the identified standards. The question is not did they complete all the assignments and do their homework, but rather, did they learn what they were supposed to learn, did they retain it over time, and can they use it in ways that demonstrate that transfer has occurred.

Assessment results are used to inform the teacher about the effectiveness of curricular and instructional decisions.

This fifth category is different from the previous one in that it forces the issue of using not only **classroom data** but **external data** to inform our practice. The data we glean or that we are given may reveal that the pacing of instruction needs to be adjusted, that the curriculum needs to be re-examined, or that instructional practices need to be revamped to promote retention and transfer. We can look at assessment results across schools, departments, and classes so that we can examine and redesign instruction to more closely align with what is working most effectively in similar settings. We can look at the data longitudinally across the year and over several years. When we reach the point where we do this work collaboratively, we should see astonishing results in student achievement.

Lesson & Unit Design

II

Planning Instruction for the Year

All decisions are based on district standards combined with your knowledge of the disciplines you teach and of the students who are to learn this curriculum.

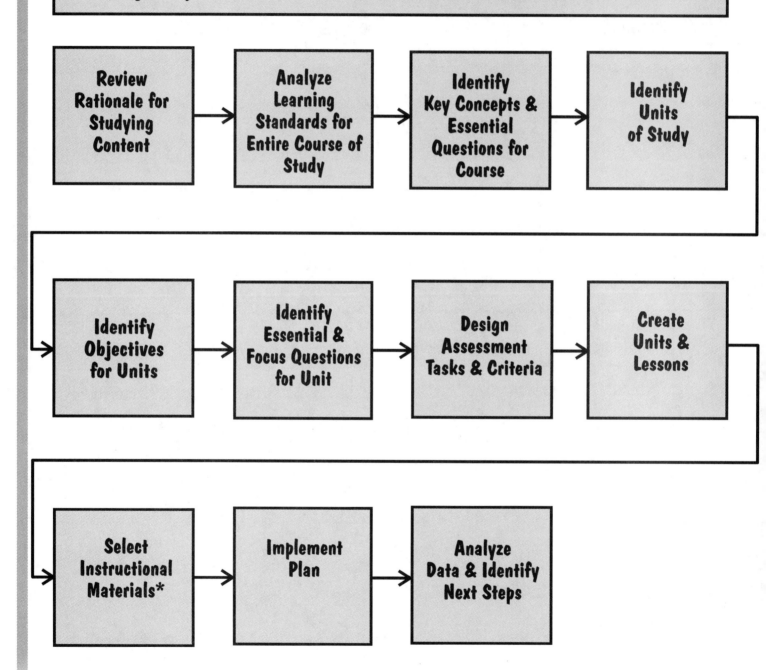

Review Rationale for Studying Content → Analyze Learning Standards for Entire Course of Study → Identify Key Concepts & Essential Questions for Course → Identify Units of Study

Identify Objectives for Units → Identify Essential & Focus Questions for Unit → Design Assessment Tasks & Criteria → Create Units & Lessons

Select Instructional Materials* → Implement Plan → Analyze Data & Identify Next Steps

* "Select Instructional Materials" is placed at this point in the sequence to ensure that the focus is on teaching to the learning standards in ways that match the students needs, interests, and backgrounds rather than how much time to spend on each chapter in the textbook. The textbook is a valuable tool but we must remember that we teach students not textbooks.

Self-Assessment
Course & Unit Planning

Assess your practice around each of these variables in the planning process.
Almost Always (A), Sometimes (S), Not Yet (N)

Do you...

_____ **Frequently review the learning standards for your state and district?**

Analyze the curriculum to

_____ examine the guidelines the department, school, district, or state provide?

_____ consider the conceptual themes or big ideas that form the framework for this course?

_____ design essential questions to guide students to an understanding of the key concepts and big ideas?

_____ ask what major thinking skills are used in this course?

Chunk concepts, themes, and skills into units by asking

_____ how concepts and thinking skills can be incorporated into units?

_____ what products and performances could students create/do to demonstrate mastery of these skills and concepts?

Design units around authentic assignments and assessments and

_____ ask yourself how the proposed activities explicitly move the students toward what they should know and be able to do by the completion of the unit?

_____ plan tasks that require the use and analysis of processes important beyond the classroom?

_____ ensure that the tasks are academically rigorous?

_____ plan assignments engaging and relevant enough to motivate students?

_____ orchestrate learning experiences that require the use of a wide variety of thinking skills?

_____ identify specific audiences other than the teacher?

_____ provide precise criteria for assessment of the work known to students prior to the beginning of the work?

_____ check to see that necessary skill building is integrated into meaningful activities rather than being presented as isolated drills?

_____ provide learning experiences that call for in-depth inquiry into concepts cited in the standards and on topics of interest to the students?

The Planning Process
in a Standards-Based Environment

Planning in a standards-based environment is often called "backwards" because we "begin with the end" in mind. In fact, we almost always begin with the end in mind when we plan vacations or weddings or purchase new automobiles. It is the way our colleagues in business and industry do project management/action planning. In school, teachers have always planned with "the end in mind." Often though, the end we had in mind was to work our way through the book, chapter by chapter, or through the year, project by project.

In a standards-based environment, we must be clear about "the end" we have in mind and be certain that we are working together from pre-kindergarten through twelfth grade to lead students to the achievement of commencement level standards. It is within this context that we focus on the standards, benchmarks, and indicators that have been identified as the ones students are to master during the grade or courses we teach. The end in mind cannot be a particular activity or project, chapters in a book, or completion of a packaged program. We have to be clear about how what students are doing in the classroom is tied to the outcomes we seek this year and throughout their K-12 educational experience.

Just like we have a clear picture of that perfect vacation, car, wedding, or ad campaign, we need to have a clear picture of what it looks like when our students are competent with what we want them to know and be able to do. Just as that vacation, wedding, or ad campaign will not happen without an action plan, we need an action plan for guiding our students to be able to demonstrate the learning we have in mind for them.

The first step in this planning process, both inside and outside the classroom, is identifying the outcome we want. The second step is creating our vision of what it looks like when we get there. Next we analyze the outcome and vision to figure out what we have to do in the third step in order to accomplish the first and second steps. It makes no sense to start the third step without **THE END** in mind.

SBE Planning Process*

1st What should students know and be able to do?

2nd How will the students and I know when they are successful?

Task Analysis

3rd What learning experiences will facilitate their success?

4th Based on data, how do I refine the learning experiences?

***Access SBE Ovals template on CD-ROM.**

What Elements Are You Using?
Standards-Based Education

Give yourself a boost of confidence by taking this quick assessment to identify the elements of Standards-Based Education (SBE) you are currently using.

Curricular materials are selected or developed because they address content standards.

Never	Seldom	Sometimes	Often	Always

Instructional strategies are selected or developed that give students opportunities to learn and practice the expectations outlined in the standards.

Never	Seldom	Sometimes	Often	Always

What students know and are able to do is clearly defined before a unit of instruction begins.

Never	Seldom	Sometimes	Often	Always

Documentation of student learning other than grades is provided to students and parents.

Never	Seldom	Sometimes	Often	Always

Students share the responsibility for monitoring their progress toward the standards.

Never	Seldom	Sometimes	Often	Always

Student performance on assessment is used to revise and refine the selection of curriculum, instruction, and assessment activities.

Never	Seldom	Sometimes	Often	Always

Instruction and assessment are adapted to accommodate students with special needs or alternative learning styles.

Never	Seldom	Sometimes	Often	Always

Lesson plans focus on what is to be learned rather than what is to be taught.

Never	Seldom	Sometimes	Often	Always

Developed by the SBE Design Team, Centennial Colorado BOCES, Longmont, CO

TOP TEN QUESTIONS
to ask myself as I design lessons

1. What should **students know and be able to do** as a result of this lesson? How are these objectives related to national, state, and/or district standards?

2. How will **students demonstrate what they know and what they can do**? What will be the **assessment criteria** and what form will it take?

3. How will I find out what students already know (**pre-assessment**), and how will I help them access what they know and have experienced both inside and outside the classroom? How will I help them **build on prior experiences, deal with misconceptions**, and re-frame their thinking when appropriate?

4. How will new knowledge, concepts, and skills be introduced? Given the **diversity of my students** and the **task analysis**, what are my **best options for sources and presentation modes**?

5. How will **I facilitate student processing** (**meaning making**) of new information or processes? What key questions, activities, and assignments (in class or homework) will promote understanding, retention, and transfer?

6. What shall I use as **formative assessments** or **checks for understanding** during the lesson? How can I use the **data** from those assessments to **inform my teaching decisions**?

7. What do I need to do to **scaffold instruction** so that the learning experiences are productive for all students? What are the multiple ways students can access information and then process and demonstrate their learning?

8. How will I **Frame the Learning** so that students know the objectives, the rationale for the objectives and activities, the directions and procedures, as well as the assessment criteria at the beginning of the learning process?

9. How will I build in opportunities for students to make **real-world connections** and to learn and use the **rigorous and complex thinking skills** they need to succeed in the classroom and the world beyond?

10. What adjustments need to be made in the **learning environment** so that we can work and learn efficiently during this study?

Using the Top Ten Questions

The ten questions on the opposite page provide the framework for Chapter III through Chapter X of this book. These questions can be found on the first page of each chapter. The questions addressed in each chapter are highlighted there.

Additionally, here and on the next page are the questions with page number references. If one of these questions is of particular interest, turn to the referenced pages for immediate study.

An expanded version of this worksheet is found on the CD-ROM in the back of the book. Print out that worksheet as many times as needed for use in planning lessons.

The questions are cross referenced to the first three ovals in the SBE Planning Process. See pages 36, 56, 84, 122, 150, 182, 196, and 218.

1st Oval

1. What should **students know and be able to do** as a result of this lesson? How are these objectives related to national, state, and/or district standards? How are these objectives related to the **big ideas/key concepts** of the course? Consult your state and district learning standards and your district curriculum for guidance with this question. See pages 43-45 for information on big/ideas and key concepts.

2nd Oval

2. How will **students demonstrate what they know and what they can do**? What will be the **assessment criteria** and what form will it take? See pages 149-180.

3rd Oval: Questions 3-10 address the 3rd Oval

3. How will I find out what students already know (**pre-assessment**), and how will I help them access what they know and have experienced both inside and outside the classroom? How will I help them **build on prior experiences**, **deal with misconceptions**, and re-frame their thinking when appropriate? See pages 57-61.

Using the Top Ten Questions*

4. How will new knowledge, concepts, and skills be introduced? Given the **diversity of my students** and the **task analysis**, what are my **best options for sources and presentation modes**? See pages 55-82.

5. How will **I facilitate student processing (meaning making)** of new information or processes? What key questions, activities, and assignments (in class or homework) will promote understanding, retention, and transfer? See pages 122-148.

6. What shall I use as **formative assessments** or **checks for understanding** during the lesson? How can I use the **data** from those assessments to **inform my teaching decisions**? See pages 154-156.

7. What do I need to do to **scaffold instruction** so that the learning experiences are productive for all students? What are the multiple ways students can access information and then process and demonstrate their learning? See pages 195-216.

8. How will I **Frame the Learning** so that students know the objectives, the rationale for the objectives and activities, the directions and procedures, as well as the assessment criteria at the beginning of the learning process? See pages 57-61 and 123.

9. How will I build in opportunities for students to make **real-world connections** and to learn and use the **rigorous and complex thinking skills** they need to succeed in the classroom and the world beyond? See pages 135-140, 181-194 and 217-248.

10. What adjustments need to be made in the **learning environment** so that we can work and learn efficiently during this study? See pages 249-266.

Guiding Questions for
Unit Design
in the **Standards-Based Classroom***

1st Oval: What should students know and be able to do?

1. On which content standard(s) will the students be working?

2. What are the key ideas, major themes, big concepts, or essential understandings embedded in, or which transcend, the standards listed above? See pages 43-45.

3. Given the essential to know key concepts and ideas identified in #2 how will this unit be different from what/how I taught and asked students to do in years past? If this is a new unit, skip this question.

4. When and where (inside and outside of school) have the students encountered information about and had experience with these key concepts/big ideas before? Think horizontally and vertically across the curriculum.

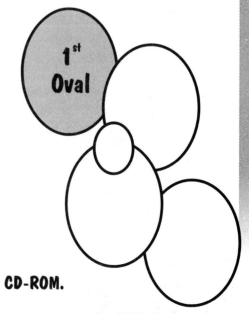

1st
Oval

***Access a template for the Guiding Questions
for Unit Design and other formats and tools for unit design on the CD-ROM.**

Guiding Questions for
Unit Design in the
Standards-Based Classroom*

2ⁿᵈ Oval: How will the students and I know when they are successful?

5. What would it look like when students can demonstrate that they understand the big ideas and have the essential skills? That is, what are some ways they might demonstrate their capacity to use the newly learned concepts/information appropriately in a new situation? See pages 124-140, 159-174, 176-180.

6. What task/products would best demonstrate student understanding? Should I use a rubric or a performance task list, and what criteria should I include?

7. What does a task analysis reveal about the skills, the knowledge, and the level of understanding required by the task? See pages 46-47.

8. Do I already have sufficient pre-assessment data or do I need to gather more? If so, what method shall I use? What does the pre-assessment data tell me about the skills and knowledge on which the entire group will need to focus? Are there individual students who will need additional support if they are to have a realistic opportunity to demonstrate mastery? In which areas will they need support? See page 153.

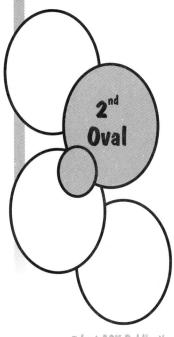

2ⁿᵈ Oval

*Access a template for the Guiding Questions for Unit Design and other formats and tools for unit on the CD-ROM.

Guiding Questions for Unit Design in the Standards-Based Classroom*

3rd Oval: What learning experiences will facilitate their success?

9. How will I "Frame the Learning" so that students know what they are going to be doing, what they will know and be able to do as a result of those activities, how they will be assessed, and how everything they are doing is aligned with the standards? See pages 57-61.

10. How will I help students access prior knowledge and use it productively, either building on it or reframing their thinking as appropriate? See pages 88-116.

11. What methods of presentation and what active learning experiences can I use to help students achieve the standard? Could I provide multiple sources of information and exercises that would help all students to make real-world connections and use sophisticated thinking skills? See pages 12-13, 14-19, 63-82, 157-158, 219-248.

12. What assignments, projects, and homework will help students see the relevance of the learning? How might I provide multiple pathways to learning? See pages 123-148, 201-216.

13. What classroom activities/observations, as well as formative quizzes and tests, would provide me and my students information on their progress toward the standard? See pages 22-25, 154-155.

14. What materials and resources do I need to locate and organize to provide multiple pathways to learning? How should I organize the classroom and the materials to provide easy student access? See pages 202-203, 251-266.

15. What else might I do to provide challenging and meaningful experiences for both struggling and advanced learners? Are there other human, print, or electronic resources I might consult to refine/review my plan? See pages 12-13, 26-27, 133-134, 197-216.

3rd Oval

*Access a template for the Guiding Questions for Unit Design and other formats and tools for unit design on the CD-ROM.

Guiding Questions for Unit Design in the Standards-Based Classroom*

4th Oval: Based on data, how do I refine the learning experiences and/or the assessment?

16. How did students do on the performance task? Were there some students who were not successful? What might account for that? What could I do differently next time?

17. What else do I need to consider in my advance planning the next time I am focusing on this standard?

18. Did all of the learning experiences guide students toward mastery of the standard? Are there learning experiences that need to be added, modified, or eliminated? Am I using these learning experiences because I have always used them or have I analyzed them to be sure that they are the most effective and efficient tools at my disposal?

19. Overall, was this unit effective for addressing the standard(s)? Are there other standards that I could incorporate into this unit or are there other units of study where I can have the students revisit these standards or essential understandings?

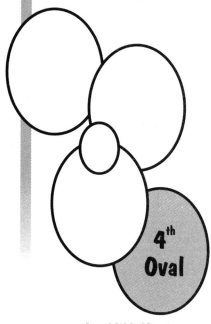

4th Oval

*Access a template for the Guiding Questions for Unit Design and other unit design tools and formats on the CD-ROM.

Facts are Important...But They Aren't Enough!
Concept-Based Instruction

The brain can hold only so many isolated facts. It continually seeks a connection or patterns on which to hook new information. The more we know, the more we learn.

We have obtained an increase in student achievement by aligning the curriculum to learning standards. Much remains to be done. To see further increases, it is essential that we adjust instructional practices so that students have a greater chance of retaining and transferring knowledge and skills to new situations.

High school teachers in Greece Central School District, New York, were not able to create interdisciplinary units until they moved beyond the standards and indicators in each of their courses. Through the use of Lynn Erickson's book, **Concept-Based Curriculum and Instruction**, they moved beyond thinking that they had little common ground in their courses to seeing that they could indeed design meaningful integrated units while preserving the integrity of each course. The key points that moved the work forward are explained below.

Essential Understandings
- are generalizations that show the relationship between two or more concepts
- may be written as statements or questions

Concepts
- are big ideas that are timeless, universal, broad, and abstract
- have a set of examples that share common attributes

Facts
- are pieces of information to know
- are embedded in concepts

Therefore
- Essential knowledge is fact-based.
- Essential understandings cannot be fact-based. They must be concept-based!

In addition to the fact that students learn at a higher level when we use concept-based instruction, it is important to note that this instruction also leads to higher standardized test scores as well. Even though many standardized test questions are written at the factual or recall level, when students learn at a conceptual level they are better able to sort through the possible answers in a multiple-choice item and eliminate the alternatives that do not fit the big idea of the question.

Concepts & Generalizations
Creating Essential Understandings

Read through this list of concepts and identify those that are embedded in a subject you teach. The combination of two or more of these concepts (plus the addition of content-specific concepts) results in a generalization or essential understanding that can serve as the driving force of units and even courses of study. If you teach more than one subject look for concepts that are embedded in more than one subject. If you teach only one subject, discuss the concepts you identify with a colleague who teaches a different subject and explore the concepts shared by the two subjects.

Stimulus	Individual	Revolution	Organization
Belief	Balance	Renaissance	Attitude
Probability	Communication	Object	Estimation
Values	Number	Community	Message
Change	Interaction	Curiosity	Honor
People	Variables	Challenge	Love
Celebration	Projection	Fairness	Loyalty
Production	Influence	Justice	Reaction
Time	Relationship	Equilibrium	Survival
Space	Knowledge	Economics	Wellness
Order	Limit	Geography	Stamina
Force	Motion	Solution	Fitness
Complexity	Consequence	Tradition	Group
Culture	Music	Reciprocity	Matter
Interdependence	Tension	Stability	Sequence
Perspective	Opinion	Cohesion	History
Scale	Habitat	Disparity	Rotation
Property	Needs	Factor	Success
Behavior	Diversity	Density	Intelligence
System	Wants	Faith	Style
Adaptation	Rhythm	Fantasy	Failure
Structure	Pace	Division	Speed
Role	Conflict	Unity	Truth
Freedom	Pattern	Family	Capacity
Competition	Control	Patriotism	Power
Symbol	Beauty	Parallel	Supply

Through the Voice of...
Concepts, Key Ideas, & Generalizations

Framing lessons and units around concepts, key ideas, and generalizations leads to improved teaching and learning. Generalizations, also known as essential understandings, can be presented as statements or questions. The question format promotes learner curiosity and facilitates inquiry. The following statements and questions were developed by participants in the workshop series **Instruction for All Students**.

- All living things need to adapt to their habitat to survive and thrive. (Grade 4 Science)
- All living things need each other to survive. (Grade 4 Science)
- How does the study of language help us understand and experience the world around us? (Languages Other Than English)
- What makes a book worth reading? (Middle School English)
- How do geographical, economic, technological, religious, and social variables affect the course of history? (Grade 5 History and Social Science)
- There are positive and negative consequences of revolutions. (Grade 5 History and Social Science)
- Math is a language. Effectively communicating mathematical ideas is a critical component in solving real-life problems. (Geometry)
- Numbers tell the story of a business. (Accounting)
- Is the world a fair and just place? (High School English)
- How does literature affect your life, and how does your life affect your interpretation of literature? (High School English)
- The three big ideas of Chemistry are structure and properties of matter, atomic structure, and chemical reactions. Everything we study will fit into those categories. (Chemistry)
- Observations lead to model building that helps explain past observations and predict future events. (Grade 2 Science)
- The study of mathematics is the study of how to organize information to solve problems. (Mathematics K-12)
- Why war? (Middle School Social Studies)
- All life on earth is interdependent. (Grade 4 Science)
- Data that occurs in real world situations can be examined for patterns and trends. These patterns may exhibit linear or non-linear relationships. (High School Math)

Task Analysis

Task analysis: (*noun*) The systematic breakdown of the tasks we ask students to complete. Task analysis allows us to identify the skills, both academic and process, that the students need in order to successfully complete the task, assignment, or project.

How To Analyze a Task

- Make sure the task is worth doing.
- Note and list all the **components** that go into accomplishing the task.
- Note and list all the **skills (procedural knowledge)** and bits of **declarative knowledge** students need to have in order to be successful with the task.
- Identify the levels of understanding they will need to complete the task.
- Use **cognitive empathy** to check through the task one more time. Better yet, if this is a high stakes assignment, have someone not in your class (student, teacher, or friend) read through the task and the directions to check for possible problem areas.
- Identify **which students have mastered which skills**. If unknown, decide how to find out or how to circumvent the need for the skill.
- **Design your instruction** by deciding what to do about the skills or knowledge the entire group needs and what to do about those students who lack the prerequisite skills to be successful even with the beginning components of the task. While there will no doubt be many skill sets and chunks of knowledge you will plan as learning experiences for the entire class, you may choose to organize **mini lessons** to teach focus groups needed skills, have **students teach each other** the problematic skills, or **provide the information** students will need to complete this part of the task. **Prevention of problems** or failure, rather than intervention later, will make you and your students **more successful**. In the end, it will save time and energy for all involved.

The ultimate goal is for our students to task analyze independently. This is not only a school skill, but a life skill as well.

Task Analysis

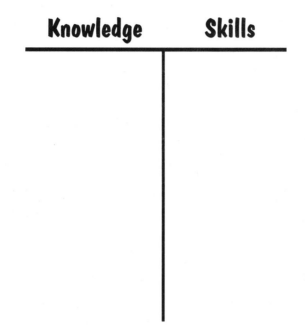

Knowledge	Skills

- Is there background knowledge or a level of understanding the entire group is lacking? How about individual students?
- Are there skills the entire group is lacking? How about the skill level of individuals?
- What shall I do in a proactive way to prevent frustrations and problems with learning?
- What shall I do with students who already know and can apply this information?

Students	Potential Problem	Possible Intervention

Approaches to
Integrating the Curriculum

Side by Side

In this model, two or more content area teachers examine their curriculums to identify broad concepts, as well as social skills and thinking skills, that could be taught simultaneously in both/all classes. Topics or units of study are rearranged and sequenced to coincide with one another. Similar ideas and skills are taught at the same time although the courses remain totally separate classes.

For example, an English teacher might have students read **The Diary of Anne Frank** while they are studying WWII in their history class. Additionally, the two teachers might agree to focus on inductive thinking or on conflict resolution skills during the first quarter of the semester.

That's What Friends Are For

Two or more teachers identify concepts and skills that are taught in both/all courses. Through collaborative planning teachers organize lessons that can be taught by one of the teachers, perhaps to quite large groups of students at one time.

For example, formatting of bibliographies, use of graphic organizers, problem solving, consensus building, and communication skills are taught and re-taught across the curriculum. With just a little communication, teacher energy and time, learning could be maximized; and groups of teachers could be freed up to collaborate in the design of future learning experiences or to examine student work.

We Are Family

Entire grade level teams, departments or entire schools identify a theme around which teaching and learning can be organized. Elementary teachers are masters of this approach because they each teach many curricula and naturally build bridges between what can sometimes seem like fragmented subject areas.

To organize instruction around a theme, a high school could decide to design a unit around a significant anniversary of the school, around an issue of current importance in the community or the world, around the arts, etc., while an elementary school might focus on habitats, space exploration, or conservation. Concepts such as justice, conflict, fitness, or diversity are also possible areas of focus. It is important to identify key concepts and skills of each curricular area included in the thematic unit so that those important components do not get lost in the energy and excitement generated by the integrated study.

Approaches to
Integrating the Curriculum

I Heard It Through the Grapevine

In this approach, the learner is bombarded with a selected big idea no matter where he or she turns. Teachers identify and weave thinking skills, social skills, multiple intelligences, technology, or study skills across all the course offerings and co-curricular events of this school.

For example, the staff might identify analytical thinking skills as the focus for a particular time period. Each department/teacher would identify ways to emphasize those skills in their instructional program. Once the areas of focus are identified, individual teachers need only look for opportunities to reinforce the identified skills and explicitly reference their usefulness in this setting, throughout the academic day and in life beyond school.

We Are The Champions

In this **Go for the Gold** model, courses, teachers, and students are integrated. This interdisciplinary approach matches subjects or overlaps in topics and concepts with team teaching in an authentic integrated model.

Courses titled Humanities that frequently feature a combination of English, social sciences, and fine arts are examples of a team-taught interdisciplinary course.

Many high schools are now organized into smaller learning communities that use this integration approach with a career academy focus. Even in this setting teachers learning to work in SLCs often pass through these phases of development as they create and implement their integrated curriculums.

*Access tools for integrating the curriculum on the CD-ROM.

Lesson & Unit Design using
Multiple Intelligences*

Use these questions to plan lessons and units:

1. How might I have the students process information by reading, writing, speaking, and listening? How might I ensure that students use a balance of these four communication skills?

2. How might I teach students to process information and demonstrate learning through the use of numbers, calculations, logic, classifications, and patterns?

3. How might I use color, art, and graphs to explain key concepts? How might I have students process information or demonstrate learning through visualization, graphs, color, art, manipulatives, or metaphors?

4. How might I have students process information through rhythms, patterns of sound, and mnemonics? How can I incorporate music or environmental sounds to create a mood or make a point?

5. How might I have students process information and demonstrate learning through movement and dramatics? What "hands-on" experiences might I include?

6. How might I help students learn to use effective collaboration and communication skills in learning and working situations? How might I have students demonstrate and assess their learning and the effectiveness of their efforts in collaborative situations?

7. How might I promote reflection and metacognition? How might I include multiple opportunities for goal setting and self-assessment?

8. How might I bring the outdoors and nature into the learning environment?

*See pages 127-132 and access template for using Multiple Intelligences Theory in lesson and unit design on CD-ROM.

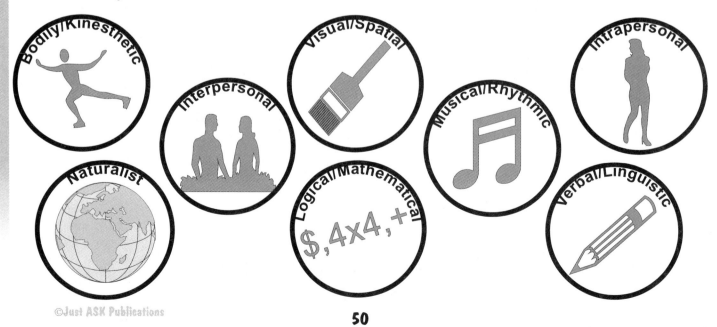

Lesson Design using
Direct Instruction

Rosenshine (1987) states that the explicit teaching or direct instruction format can be a useful approach when the objective is **skill-building or memorization of a body of knowledge**. He reports that research indicates students need to achieve an **80% success rate during initial practice**.

1. Previous work is **checked and reviewed**.

2. Teacher states **objectives** of the lesson and the **purposes** of the activities.

3. Teacher **explains** concepts or operations and gives **examples** and/or **demonstrates**. Information is presented in **small chunks**.

4. Teacher **checks student understanding** after **each** small chunk of information.

5. Students **practice with guidance** through direct monitoring, feedback, correction, help and hints from the teacher.

6. Students **practice alone** (seat work or homework).

7. Teacher **re-teaches as needed** to those students who need additional information and/or alternative instruction in order to build identified skills.

8. Teacher gives **frequent tests**.

9. Teacher **reviews** frequently.

Used in isolation, this method can yield misleading test results. Some students can regurgitate information or perform the skills in a contrived setting without having made any sense or meaning of their "learning." This often leads to forgetting, frustration (for both the teacher and the learners), and the need to "teach" the same information over and over again...year after year! It is essential that all skill building leads to meaningful and engaging work within the same unit of study.

Madeline Hunter's
Elements of Lesson Design

Madeline Hunter always described these components as **variables to be considered in lesson design**; she never indicated that all lessons should have all of these elements. Hunter's elements, as outlined below, are one **application of the direct instruction model**. The **three categories of decisions** she identified (1982) as components of a teacher's planning of any lesson are:

a.   **what content to teach next**

b.   **what the student will do in order to learn and to demonstrate that the desired learning has occurred**

c.   **what the teacher will do to facilitate that learning**

1.	**Anticipatory Set**	What might I do to focus the attention of the students on the concepts we are about to study?
2.	**Communicate Objectives**	How shall I let students know what it is that they are to know and be able to do? How will I let them know why it is worth knowing?
3.	**Input**	What new content, concepts, information, and skills are to be studied?
4.	**Modeling**	How shall I present/explain the new skill or content?
5.	**Checking for Understanding**	How will I know if and when the students are learning the new information?
6.	**Guided Practice**	How will I help the students practice the new skills with immediate feedback and corrections in class?
7.	**Independent Practice**	What assignments and homework shall I have the students complete to facilitate long-term retention?

Lesson Design using
Cooperative Learning

Big Picture Decisions
- What are the objectives for the lesson?
- What sources will be used to provide essential information about key concepts?
- What are the social skill/group process objectives?
- What cooperative learning model shall I use?
  - Learning Together and Alone (Johnson and Johnson)
  - Jigsaw (Aronson, Gonzales)
  - Students Teams Achievement Division-STAD (Slavin)
  - Jigsaw II (Slavin)
  - Team Games Tournament-TGT (Slavin)
  - Group Investigation (Thelen, Sharon)

Group Composition Decisions
- How many students will be in each group?
- How will I form the groups?
  - Random (number off, draw cards, etc.)
  - Heterogeneous by past performance (STAD and TGT, and perhaps other models)
  - Heterogeneous by learning/information processing style
  - Interest
  - Student choice

Group Interdependence Decisions
- Should roles be assigned to group members? If so, what roles?
- How should positive group interdependence be structured?
  - One product/performance/paper from each group
  - Randomly selected spokesperson from each group
  - Group points for individual members improvement over own previous scores/averages
  - One set of materials to share
  - Limit time for task (One person would not be able to do task within that time limit.)
  - Each member has only part of the information
  - Other
- How will I communicate the forms of interdependence and the rationale for my decisions to the students?

Cooperative Learning

Individual Accountability/Assessment Decisions

- What forms of individual accountability should be used?
  - All group members sign off
  - Individual quizzes
  - Individual tests
  - Random selection of one paper from group for grading
  - Random oral quiz
  - Individual homework or products as follow-up
  - Other
- How will I communicate to students, at the beginning of the work, how they are expected to work and to demonstrate learning?
- Should I use a rubric or a task performance list?

Social Skills/Group Process Decisions

- What social skills/group process skills do students need to complete this task?
- Do we need to review/reflect on past work?
- What social skills/group skills do I want students to develop?
- How will I communicate the social skills focus?
- Do I need to model, role play, or develop a see and hear chart?
- How will data be collected for assessment of social skills/group process growth?
- How will individuals and groups give, receive, and reflect on feedback?

Adapted from Mary Ann Haley-Speca

Presentation Modes
Updating Old Faithfuls

III

TOP TEN QUESTIONS
to ask myself as I design lessons

The focus questions for this chapter are highlighted below.

1. What should **students know and be able to do** as a result of this lesson? How are these objectives related to national, state, and/or district standards?

2. How will **students demonstrate what they know and what they can do**? What will be the **assessment criteria** and what form will it take?

3. How will I find out what students already know (**pre-assessment**), and how will I help them access what they know and have experienced both inside and outside the classroom? How will I help them **build on prior experiences, deal with misconceptions**, and re-frame their thinking when appropriate?

4. How will new knowledge, concepts, and skills be introduced? Given the **diversity of my students** and the **task analysis**, what are my **best options for sources and presentation modes**?

5. How will **I facilitate student processing (meaning making)** of new information or processes? What key questions, activities, and assignments (in class or homework) will promote understanding, retention, and transfer?

6. What shall I use as **formative assessments** or **checks for understanding** during the lesson? How can I use the **data** from those assessments to **inform my teaching decisions**?

7. What do I need to do to **scaffold instruction** so that the learning experiences are productive for all students? What are the multiple ways students can access information and then process and demonstrate their learning?

8. How will I **Frame the Learning** so that students know the objectives, the rationale for the objectives and activities, the directions and procedures, as well as the assessment criteria at the beginning of the learning process?

9. How will I build in opportunities for students to make **real-world connections** and to learn and use the **rigorous and complex thinking skills** they need to succeed in the classroom and the world beyond?

10. What adjustments need to be made in the **learning environment** so that we can work and learn efficiently during this study?

Self-Assessment
Framing the Learning

Assess your practice around each of these research-based strategies for structuring the learning environment in ways that help students process, retain, and transfer their learning

Almost Always (A), Sometimes (S), Not Yet (N)

At the Beginning of the Lesson: Making Connections

_____ I explicitly communicate the learning outcomes, the relationship of the learning experiences to the outcomes, the assessment, and the assessment criteria before we begin the lesson.

_____ I help students recall what they know about the topic to be studied and/or where they have used or learned related information.

_____ I have students make predictions about the content and give rationales for their predictions.

_____ I work with students to set purposes for study and to generate questions to be answered during the lesson.

During the Presentation of New Information

_____ I pause to have students process/summarize at meaningful points. (I practice **10:2 Theory**.)

_____ We assess old predictions, make new predictions, and/or identify significant information at the processing points.

_____ I help students relate new information to prior knowledge.

_____ I use visuals, manipulatives, props, and realia to provide nonlinguistic representations.

_____ We collaboratively generate more questions throughout the lesson.

At the Close of the Lesson: Locking In the Learning

_____ I facilitate student processing/summarizing of the whole lesson.

_____ We evaluate predictions and use new learning to re-frame thinking.

_____ I ask students to note similarities and differences between the new material and what they already know.

_____ We return to the purposes set for study to see if they were accomplished and identify additional information that would be interesting or helpful.

Framing the Learning

We seldom start out for an automobile trip without having in mind a destination and a plan for getting there. If only the driver knows the destination and the plan, the passengers are limited in their ability to make the trip alone or to explain it to someone else. The same is true for learners in the classroom. Information is power, so put students in the driver's seat by letting them know where the learning is headed.

Communicate Standards, the Learning Process, and Assessment by

- Explaining what students need to know and be able to do
- Clarifying why students need to know and be able to do what the standard targets
- Delineating the activities and assessments students will experience in order to process their learning
- Articulating how students will demonstrate learning and the criteria to be used for assessment
- Providing models for processes and products

We need to clearly articulate these variables at the beginning of the learning experience and provide opportunities for students to translate them into their own words.

Letting students know the desired outcomes in **age appropriate language** is an important part of **Framing the Learning**. Telling students that they will be working on "telling time" or on "solving problems with irrational numbers" is NOT telling them the topic. Instead, we want to say something to the effect of, "**By the time we finish this lesson (or unit) you will know and/or be able to**...". "We will know that you know that and/or are able to do that because you will be assessed by...". Many learners also need a rationale for "learning this stuff" and unfortunately, "Because I said so!" is not a sufficient reason. In fact, for some students the fact that it is "going to be on the test" is not the least bit motivational. We have to be clear in our own minds about the essential understandings we are asking students to learn. In order to "market and sell" the knowledge and skills we want them to acquire, we also need to be clear how what we are asking them to learn is used in the world beyond academics.

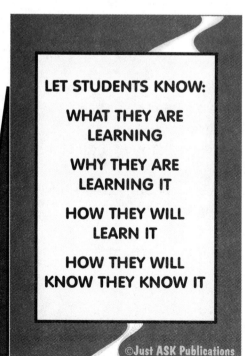

LET STUDENTS KNOW:

WHAT THEY ARE LEARNING

WHY THEY ARE LEARNING IT

HOW THEY WILL LEARN IT

HOW THEY WILL KNOW THEY KNOW IT

©Just ASK Publications

58

Framing the Learning

Provide the Agenda/Outline for the Day, Unit, and Year

Depending on the age of the students, the agenda may be written daily on the board or be included in a unit overview packet. An important consideration is explicitly linking whatever appears on the agenda to the learning outcomes as the students engage in the agenda items.

Identify Student Naive Understandings and Misconceptions

Our students are not the only ones with naive understandings and misconceptions about the world around us and how it works. We all have them. Ours may be about how the stock market and the Dow Jones Average are related, how a fax machine works, what a well-to-do neighborhood in New Delhi looks like, or whether it is better to lease or buy a car. When those discussions are going on around us, we often pretend that we know what people are talking about, or we may tune out. If we are reading about something for which we do not have the prior knowledge to fully understand (we may not even know we do not know enough) we may force connections or just skip that part. That is exactly what students do in classrooms. It is essential that we surface those naive understandings and misconceptions or students will hook new learning to inadequate or incorrect knowledge, perhaps without even knowing that they are doing it.

Help Students Access Prior Knowledge and Make Connections

- To past experiences both inside and outside of school
- Between concepts/activities at transitions
- To future areas of study and life beyond the classroom

Have Students Process, Summarize, and Use Learning

Students need to apply new learning in meaningful ways in order to promote retention and transfer.

See Chapter IV Active Learning for ways to help students make connections!

Framing the Learning

Whether you use demonstrations, discussions, field trips, guest speakers, lectures, multimedia presentations, printed text or any other mode...
This Is Not Multiple Choice!

In speech-making, the rules of the road are to tell the audience what you are going to say, say it, and then tell them what you said. The rules of the road for teaching are to **Frame the Learning** by asking them what they already know, presenting new information, and asking them to make connections as you go. At the end of the lesson, have students tell you what they have learned and the connections they have made or questions they are pondering.

Marzano, Pickering and Pollock, in their book *Classroom Instruction that Works*, identify nine categories of instructional strategies that have proven to promote student achievement. Several of those categories can be used in the context of **Framing the Learning** at the beginning, during, and at the end of lessons or units. For example, generating and testing hypotheses, questions, cues and advanced organizers, nonlinguistic representations, summarizing, and note taking are variables to consider when planning how to **Frame the Learning** for your students.

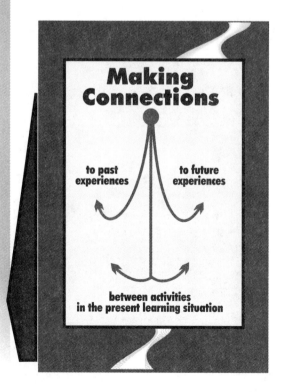

In the Beginning: Making Connections

- Help students recall what they know about the topic to be studied and/or where they have used or learned related information.
- Have students make predictions about the content and give rationales for their predictions.
- Through accessing prior knowledge and pre-assessments, identify misconceptions and naive understandings and use those as starting points for the learning.
- Work with students to set purposes for study and to generate questions to be answered during the lesson.
- "Beginnings" occur frequently. Each learning session is a new beginning for students even if the topic or area of study is a continuation from the day before.

Framing the Learning

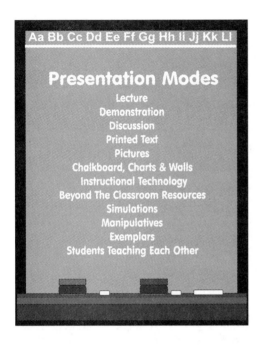

Presentation Modes

Lecture
Demonstration
Discussion
Printed Text
Pictures
Chalkboard, Charts & Walls
Instructional Technology
Beyond The Classroom Resources
Simulations
Manipulatives
Exemplars
Students Teaching Each Other

Presentation of New Information

- Process/summarize at meaningful points.
- Assess old predictions, make new predictions and/or identify significant information at the processing points.
- Relate new information to prior knowledge.
- Collaboratively generate more questions throughout the lesson.

Wrapping Up: Connection Making and Locking In Learning

- Process/summarize the whole lesson.
- Evaluate predictions.
- Return to the purposes set for study to see if they were accomplished.
- Identify additional information that would be interesting or helpful.

Implementation Tips

These **making connections** components are important at the beginning of new units of study, throughout units to build bridges between fragmented learning segments, and at the close of lessons and units. **Do not rush to cover material without having students pause for processing!**

PAUSE for PROCESSING:
PRACTICE 10:2 & WAIT TIME

Updating Old Faithfuls
Presentation Modes

Old Faithfuls for the presentation of information to students include: demonstrations, lectures, discussions, printed text, and audio visual sources. These modes of information are extremely useful when used in balance with other techniques, and when used in ways that promote student interaction with the information. Most of us have not had formal instruction in the design and implementation of these **Old Faithfuls** but have modeled our practice after that of our own teachers. Only recently have teachers widely studied such powerful strategies as the Socratic Seminar or Paideia Seminar. Much valuable guidance is provided in the reading literature about setting purpose for reading, using graphic organizers, and designing connection-making questions and examples. Unfortunately, most of us have had only one three-hour course, if any at all, in the teaching of reading. Our exposure to those important findings has been severely limited and we have not been explicitly asked to apply, or been guided in the application of, those strategies to presentation modes beyond the printed text. Given the strength of learning theory through the ages and the power of the current brain research, we need to combine the old and new methods to ensure that when we use demonstrations, lectures, discussions, printed text and audio visual sources, we do so in ways that promote the transfer and retention of the learning.

No matter what mode of presentation we select, we need to **Frame the Learning** to ensure that students recognize connections to past learning and experiences and make connections to the new learning. Framing the learning also helps students see the connections between the standards of learning, the activities in which they are engaged, and the assessments they are asked to complete.

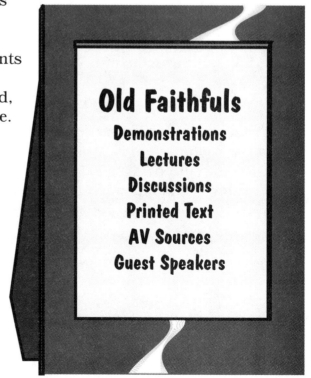

This chapter provides guidance on how to update the tried and true presentation modes and on how to **Frame the Learning** so that students focus on and retain essential to know concepts and build skills that enable them to not only score well on standardized tests, but to function well in society. See Chapters IV through IX for additional presentation modes that include students teaching each other, strategies to promote a wide range of thinking skills, and strategies for differentiation of instruction.

Old Faithfuls
Demonstrations
Lectures
Discussions
Printed Text
AV Sources
Guest Speakers

Demonstrations

Demonstration (*n*) 1. **visual presentation** that clarifies or explains a procedure, product, or process; often illustrates a clearly articulated sequence. 2. **procedure** that gives information, provides an introduction, or shows how to do something. May prove a point about safety, form, or outcome. 3. **sequence of actions** that makes noticeable the essential steps or elements in a procedure, and indicates which steps are optional.

Tips for Giving an Effective Demonstration

Classroom demonstrations occur on a regular basis, but there is little written about how to do an effective one. It appears that we are just supposed to know how to do demonstrations because we are teachers.

- Identify the most important points of the demonstration so that you can be sure to emphasize the critical. Demonstrations are more effective if you plan in advance the important points you want to demonstrate, and how you will emphasize them.

- Tell the students what to watch for, have them watch it, and have them **process what they saw**.

- Complex or lengthy demonstrations are best broken down into meaningful chunks. Allow students to process and practice between segments.

- The processing of significant information is essential, because we often watch and/or notice the wrong components. **Practice 10:2 Theory throughout any demonstration**.

Hints

- As learners, we usually believe we can do that which we see done. But in reality, we often miss important steps. Check with your students to see if they caught what you taught.

- If students have trouble duplicating the steps you lay out in a demonstration, try a **Think Aloud**, described on the next page. This strategy allows the teacher to point out potential pitfalls and common problems.

Demonstrations

- how to hold a musical instrument
- how to use a Bunsen burner
- how to construct a paragraph
- how to position fingers on a keyboard
- how to outline a chapter
- how to enter a kindergarten room
- how to throw a shot-put
- how to do a double back flip
- how to clean up a work area

An Alternative to Demonstrations
Think Alouds

Think Aloud *(n)* an alternative to a demonstration in which the teacher assumes the role of a student "thinking aloud" about how to work through complex or confusing tasks or problems. The purpose of this format is for the teacher to point out potential pitfalls and common misconceptions or behaviors of learners, and model strategies and ways of thinking for working through the problems.

Our students think that we were born knowing how to write bibliographies and knowing all the rules of capitalization and punctuation. Why? They think so because we always seem to do it right the first time. When we do demonstrations, we show our students how a task or process is to be done; we seldom demonstrate the trial and error nature of accomplishing tasks. To help fill that void, **Think Alouds** were originally discussed in the reading literature (Davey, 1983) as a way to help students with reading comprehension; their use has been extended to demonstrating the perils and pitfalls of any multi-step or obscure task. (Saphier, 1990)

Process
- Identify points you want to make with a **Think Aloud** prior to presenting it.
- Assume the role and talk out loud about your thinking and feelings as you attempt to do the task.
- Do not interact with the audience (your students).
- Model the following as appropriate:
  - **confusion** about what you are supposed to do
  - **failure to recall** all of the steps in the directions
  - **false starts**
  - **weighing alternatives**
  - **making predictions**
  - **reviewing** what you've done in **similar situations**
  - **remembering** what you've read or been told to do
  - **possible frustrations**
  - **thinking of places to get help**
  - **fix-up strategies**
  - **persistence and recognition of effective effort**
  - **feeling of success**
- When you are finished with the role play, **have students identify the strategies** you used in working through the task.
- Coach your students, or have students coach each other, in using the same process.

Lectures

Lecture (*n*) An exposition of a given subject before an audience.
Audience (*n*) A body of spectators, listeners, or readers of a work or performance.

Lectures are a mainstay of instructional practice. As the definitions at the top of the page indicate, the problem with lectures in isolation is that there is absolutely no guarantee of interaction between the lecturer and the audience. In *Leading the Cooperative School*, Johnson and Johnson state that one of the main problems with lectures is that, "**the information passes from the notes of the professor to the notes of the students without passing through the mind of either one.**" As educators, we must ensure that during a lecture the learners are purposefully interacting with the material and integrating it with their prior knowledge.

Uses of Lectures
- Introduce a unit
- Describe/present problem
- Share personal experiences
- Review most important ideas of unit
- Summarize a unit
- Provide information students cannot obtain any other way
- Clarify important concepts
- Input step in direct teaching of skills

Attributes of Good Lectures
- Addresses specific **objectives**
- Planned around a **series of questions** that the lecture answers
- Are **systematic, sequential**, and convey information in an **interesting** way
- Include **examples, stories, and analogies** that help learners relate new information to prior experiences

Potential Problems with Lectures
- Amusing anecdotes may entertain but teach little
- Lighthearted lectures may misrepresent the complexity of the material
- Incorrect or incomplete processing of content by students who mechanically write down whatever the lecturer says
- Students may be inattentive because of their roles as passive listeners and routine note takers
- Examples, references, and stories may have little or no meaning for students or may send students off on tangents in their thinking

Lecture Enhancements

Lecture Enhancements

To ensure that learners do the intellectual work of "making meaning," or organizing, summarizing, and integrating the new information with prior knowledge and experiences, include one or more of the following:

- Framing the Learning: Pages 57-61

- Discussion Partners: Page 67

- Processing Time: Pages 67 and 87

- Examples: Page 68

- Analogies, Metaphors, and Similes: Pages 70-71

- Stories: Page 72

- Written Outlines

- Graphic Organizers and other visuals: Pages 229-230

- Listening Logs

- Interactive Notebooks: Page 228

- Signal Cards: Page 154

- Podcasts

- PowerPoint Presentations: Page 82

- SmartBoards: Page 81

Technology Alert!

- A bad or inappropriate lecture accompanied by a PowerPoint presentation or using a SmartBoard is still a bad or inappropriate lecture.
- Reading PowerPoint slides and having students copy them is a digital version of writing notes on the chalkboard, reading them, and/or having students copy them. Neither is acceptable practice.
- See page 82 for guidelines in preparing and using PowerPoint presentations
- See page 81 for information about using SmartBoards to support lectures. As with PowerPoint presentations, it is essential that we understand that SmartBoards can really enhance learning or merely add digital glitz.

Lectures with Discussion Partners

One of the easiest ways to ensure that students are attentive and making meaning of the material being presented is to pause for processing. Since 75% of our learners are extroverted thinkers, partner discussions throughout the lecture make a great deal of good sense.

- Have students choose **partners** or assign partners.
- Present for small group discussion a **focus question** or **stem** which provides a set or direction for the lecture to come (4-5 minutes).
  - This discussion can focus learning, surface prior information, and/or promote predictions.
  - Focus questions or discussion topics can be on the board, a PowerPoint slide, or an overhead transparency as the students enter the area or room.
  - Process in large groups as you choose. While you may want to do that on occasion to ensure accountability, you probably would not want to use the time to do it after each small group discussion or you'll never have time for your lecture!
- Deliver the **first segment of the lecture** (10-15 minutes).
- Give the small groups the first **processing/discussion topic** (3-4 minutes). Possible processing points might be for students to summarize, react to, elaborate upon, predict, resolve differences, or hypothesize answers to a question posed by the input of new information.
- Deliver the **second segment of the lecture** (10-15 minutes).
- Give the small groups another **processing/discussion topic** (3-4 minutes).
- Continue **lecture segments and discussions** until the lecture is completed.
- Give the students a **final processing focus** (5-6 minutes). The purpose of this closure discussion is for students to process and make connections between the bits of information presented in the lecture and hook them all onto their own "velcro."

To ensure that students are discussing what you want them to discuss, you may need to model, to circulate, and listen in. Additionally, you may want to call on one or two pairs occasionally to share with the class what they have been discussing.

Using Examples in Lectures

Example (*n*) 1. one representative of a group; 2. a case or situation serving as a precedent or model for another one that is similar; 3. a problem or exercise that illustrates a method or principle.

Critical Attribute (*adj, n*) 1. a characteristic which is essential; 2. a quality which is basic or indispensable; 3. a component which is necessary in order for a concept to be.

Designing Examples to Teach Concepts and Generalizations

- Include the important characteristics and clarify what role these characteristics play in relation to the concept. We often point out or **highlight important information** about a topic without clarifying whether these points are **critical, essential, or merely interesting**.

- Help students recognize examples and non-examples of a particular concept **in isolation** (i.e., a mixed numeral or a democracy and to be able to notice the similarities and differences in two or more compared concepts or objects. For example, alligator and crocodile, Celsius and Fahrenheit).

- Use teacher or student generated examples to go beyond definitions. When teaching abstract concepts like democracy or romance we tend to rely solely on definitions. The problem with using only definitions is that **students often memorize the definition without understanding or making personal meaning of the concept**.

- When teaching **generalizations**, good examples must clearly identify the relationships and show the interaction between the **multiple concepts** contained in the generalization. If each of the concepts is not already well understood by the students, we must explicitly teach the concepts with their own definitions and solid examples before there is any chance that students can understand the generalization in a productive way.

- If the concepts being taught are ones that students will use as foundations or scaffolding for other concepts, and/or if the concepts are significant enough for students to remember five years from now, we need to identify or help them to **identify and isolate the concepts' attributes**.

Using Examples in Lectures

How to Identify Critical Attributes
- List as many attributes of the concept as you can think of.
- Cross out those which are obviously not essential but leave any that are questionable.
- Check the remaining attributes against your knowledge and other examples to ensure that the list is complete. Ask yourself if there are any examples you can think of which would meet these criteria but not be defined under the concept you are studying.
- Eliminate as many attributes as you can so that those remaining are truly essential or critical. The finished list might be only one attribute (i.e., mammals must have mammary glands) or a set of attributes (i.e., squares must have four equal sides and four right angles).
- The remaining attributes will help differentiate the concept you are studying from other similar concepts.

Using Analogies & Metaphors in Lectures

Analogy (*n*) demonstration of **similarity** in some respects between otherwise dissimilar things.

Metaphor (*n*) a figure of speech in which a **comparison** between two unlike things is made **without** using **like** or **as**.

Simile (*n*) a figure of speech in which a **comparison** is made between two or more unlike things **using like** or **as**.

Purposes

- Analogies allow students to work from a familiar area into a new area of study. Since understanding involves connecting new learning to something already understood, analogies can be really useful for some learners. It is important to emphasize the points of comparison so that other similarities and differences do not distract from student learning.
- Metaphorical thinking can cause the familiar to become strange or unique as well as promote divergent thinking. If the topic is one which students have studied before, and may suffer from "delusions of familiarity," a metaphor may be just the way to re-energize their thinking around the topic.

Creating/Identifying Useful Analogies, Metaphors, and Similes

- When reviewing textbooks or pieces of literature, watching television or movies, or participating in discussions with friends and colleagues, keep the idea of building a library of useful analogies in the back of your mind.
- Have students create analogies and save/record the examples that have future use.

Analogy Examples

1. Paragraphs and Hamburgers

A paragraph is a group of sentences that tell about one main topic. A good paragraph is like a good hamburger. It has a fresh bun on the top (a topic sentence), a fresh bun on the bottom (a conclusion), and a lot of meat/extras in between (details and transition words).

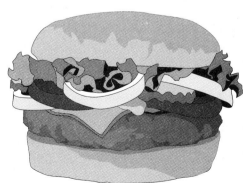

Using Analogies & Metaphors in Lectures

2. Bubble Gum and Muscles

What happens when you try to **blow a bubble with a fresh piece of bubble gum**? It pops, of course, or at the very best, a small bubble can be created. You have to **soften up the bubble gum** before it is pliable enough to form into large bubbles. **The same "softening up" is needed for your muscles** when you are getting ready for strenuous exercise in physical education class. It's important to "soften up" or warm up your muscles before making big movements...or you could pull a muscle and seriously injure yourself.

3. Direct Analogy (comparison of two objects or concepts)

How is the solar system like an orchestra?

4. Personal Analogies (description of yourself as the object or concept)

How would you feel if you were a computer? "Even though, as a computer, I am not alive, I do appear to have a mind of my own. I tell those interacting with me to, "Please Wait." I throw tantrums by ringing bells and flashing warning signs to those who try to force me to work faster than I can or to do a new task when I am already busy!"

5. Symbolic Analogies or Compressed Conflicts (a.k.a. Oxymorons...description of an object in which two words seemingly are opposites or contradict each other)

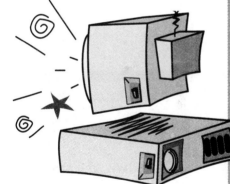

- What would be an example of thundering silence?
- What would a slow chase look like and why might it occur?

In addition to responding to teacher-created analogies, metaphors, and similies, students with modeling and instruction can learn to create their own.

Using Stories in Lectures

Story (*n*) 1. a narrative, either true or fictitious; 2. a tale, shorter and less elaborate than a novel; 3. a narration of incidents or events; 4. archaic, to tell the history or story of.

Essential Elements of a Story

Well-told stories hold our attention because we get "to be a part of the experience" and because they make points quickly. Whether you create stories to make points or build a library of possible stories for particular points you want to make, effective stories have these elements:

- a main character
- a problem or conflict
- a significant event, interaction, and/or insight which transforms or changes the main character
- a new condition, understanding, or perspective is reached

Variations

- short passages from literature
- quotes
- poems
- cartoons
- brief newspaper articles
- eye witness accounts
- imagery
- children's books

In the **study of a second language**, children's books in the target language are a rich source of language patterns and cultural tidbits. To find good books to use, spend an afternoon in the children's section at a library or a bookstore; the librarians or clerks in children's departments love to help!

Discussions

Discussion (*n*) 1. consideration of a question in open and usually informal debate. 2. informal group consideration of a topic 3. generally follows some input of information which may come from any source inside or outside the classroom.

Planning a Discussion

1. Decide on the purpose of the discussion and on the mastery objectives. There may be both academic and social objectives since students will be interacting. Possible purposes are:

   - **subject mastery** which includes definition of terms and identification of important concepts, application of the learning to other areas of study, and an evaluation of the author's arguments

   - **issue orientation** which includes an effort to increase one's understanding of others' beliefs and feelings about the subject being studied

   - **problem-solving** which requires strong background knowledge

2. Decide the format for the discussion. Will it be large-group/teacher-led, or small-group/student-led?

3. Consider the experience and skills of the students participating in or leading a discussion. If you are asking them to do something they have not yet demonstrated they know how to do, you may want to teach or model the skills you want to see.

4. Plan how long you will let the discussion continue. The objective, the importance and complexity of the issue, the product, and the discussion skills of the students will help you decide on how much time to allow.

5. Decide how the students will demonstrate what they have learned/processed during the discussion.

Online Discussions

- For information in setting up on-line discussions visit:
  - www.21classes.com
  - http://www.cwrl.utexas.edu/node/233
  - http://classblogmeister.com/
- For information on blogging and Wiki sites, examples from classrooms, and tips for teachers visit:
  www.my-ecoach.com/online/webresourcelistinfo.php?rlid=4992

Discussions

Implementation Tips

- Communication of the **purpose** of an upcoming discussion gives students focus for reading or other data gathering.

- **Announcement** of the **outcome/product/accountability factor** in advance generally causes discussion groups to stay more focused.

- Start with **short sessions** on topics of high interest so that you can assess student skill levels for being productive in discussion groups.

- To promote more participation, have students do a **brief reflective writing before the discussion begins**. That increases the likelihood that both introverted and extraverted thinkers are ready to participate.

- During discussions, teacher circulation from group to group listening in, clarifying as appropriate, and refocusing when necessary, is essential.

- Process the content, the students' responses to and questions about it, and the discussion process.

- What we call classroom discussions are often not discussions at all. They are really **recitations** during which teachers do most of the talking, calling on or giving permission to talk to certain students, asking low-level questions, and tending to limit length of student answers so that more students can participate.

- Be mindful of **which students participate** in large group discussions. If many of the students are silent observers, small group discussions would foster more participation by more students.

- To more tightly **structure discussions** and ensure **equal participation**, use active learning and/or cooperative learning formats.

Attributes of a Discussion

- Participants in the discussion present **multiple points of view** and are ready to change their minds after hearing convincing alternative viewpoints.

- **Students** must **interact with each other** as well as with the teacher.

- The majority of **comments** are **longer in length** than the three or four word answers often given during a teacher led recitation.

- **Most of the talking** is done by **students** rather than by the teacher.

Student-Led Book Discussions
Literature Circles

Harvey Daniels created Literature Circles as a way for students to lead and participate in small group discussions about books of their choice. He suggests that beginning groups use role assignments like those described below.

Discussion Director

Develop a list of questions for your group to discuss. Focus on the big ideas of the reading and on sharing your reactions to the text. The best questions come from your own thoughts, feelings, and concerns.

Connector

Make connections between the readings and your life beyond this assignment. You might focus on other classes, life beyond the school day, or other readings you have studied. Record any connections you make between this reading and other parts of your life.

Passage Master

Identify the most powerful, interesting, humorous, puzzling passages in the assigned reading. During the discussion, you decide how and when to have the segments brought to the attention of the group. You may decide to read them aloud, you may ask someone else to read a segment aloud, or you may decide to have all group members read the selection silently and then discuss its significance.

Illustrator

Draw, sketch, or find a visual that captures the essence of the assigned reading or of something you thought about as you read. Use your own artistic skills, graphics, visuals from the internet, or your photo or magazine collection to identify visual images that help paint a picture about the reading. You can explain how the visual works for you or ask group members to speculate on how the visual fits with the reading.

Summarizer

Prepare a two to three minute summary of not only the reading, but the discussion of that reading. You may ask group members to add to the points you make via a 3-2-1 summary or a reflective journal entry.

Visit www.literaturecircles.com for extensive information on organizing student-led discussion groups.

A Structured Small Group Discussion
Collaborative Controversy

Process
- Assign heterogeneous groups of four as pairs
- Assign each pair a perspective and give students supporting materials to read
- Students present conflicting positions to one another
- Students argue strengths and weaknesses
- Students take the opposite view without reading it
- Students drop assigned roles and work as a team of four to reach consensus on the issue

Teacher promotes controversy and thinking by
- Presenting contrasting viewpoints
- Playing devil's advocate
- Encouraging students to probe and push each other for rationale
- Monitoring how students process their actions
- Emphasizing rational and spirited discussion/argument
- Restating the question
- Asking for clarification, rationale, example, implications. A key question is "What were the best arguments you heard from the other side?"

Sample Topics
- Line item veto
- Protecting endangered species
- Balancing the federal budget
- Expense of space exploration
- Censorship of internet
- Need for instruction in cursive handwriting
- Dress codes in schools
- Usefulness of algebra

Through the Voice of...
Socratic Seminars

The Socratic method is a question-and-answer method of discussing subjects that was used by Socrates in his early discussions with Plato. This type of discussion does not revolve around the teacher but rather the purpose of this discussion is for students to discover "truths," understanding, and/or new knowledge through analytical discussion with one other.

"There is only one good, knowledge, and one evil, ignorance."
--Socrates

Preparation for the Seminar

- You will be given a work (literature, article, radio program, video, song) to read and study before the seminar. This will usually be completed as homework. Read and study it carefully. Make notes of interesting things. Also make notes of ideas or elements you don't understand.
- You will write your reactions and responses to teacher prompts on your Entry Ticket. These reactions will provide you with "food for thought and discussion" and will provide evidence that you have completed your reading in a thorough and thoughtful way.

Participation in the Seminar

- You must have a completed entry ticket to be a part of the discussion.
- The teacher will present the first question; it will usually be a part of the Entry Ticket assignment.
- Participants will ask questions and answer questions about the text or material you have studied.
- The teacher may intervene to remind participants to refer to the text -- "Where do you see that?" "What specific part of the story makes you feel or think that?"
- As a last resort, the teacher may occasionally offer questions to stimulate conversation, or direct the discussion toward pertinent information that has not been discovered by the participants. There will usually be no more than one or two teacher questions per discussion.

Visit www.studyguide.org for a high school English teacher's guidelines on Socratic Seminars.

Dorotha Ekx, Longmont High School, St. Vrain Valley Schools, Longmont, CO

Printed Text
Reciprocal Teaching

Predict   Clarify   Question   Summarize

Reciprocal Teaching is designed to help students develop expertise with the thinking and process skills of predicting, clarifying, questioning, and summarizing. It is a strategy that can be used with K-12 learners. It works equally well with literature and expository texts. Anne Marie Sullivan Palincsar developed **Reciprocal Teaching** as a variation of **Reciprocal Questioning (ReQuest)**, which was developed by Anthony Manzo. Both strategies have as their ultimate goal students independently setting a purpose for reading, asking questions throughout the lesson and summarizing.

These skills are best taught separately and then integrated into the model. The classroom teacher can model thinking aloud about each, use each of the process skills as prompts in **Think-Pair-Shares**, and as the focus of informal one-on-one discussions and quick checks for understanding.

There are several versions of the technique. In the original version, the teacher and a student take turns being the "teacher," hence the name. In this way the classroom teacher is able to model desired behavior, and the student "teacher" practices the processes immediately. Over time the strategy can be frequently used by a teacher working with a small group having students assigned various process responsibilities and different students functioning as the "teacher." In the elementary setting, small group guided reading sessions can be transformed into a reciprocal teaching structure. In the secondary classroom, the strategy can be used to structure small group work.

After students have developed familiarity with each of the four process skills, identify text to be read. Have students predict what the text will be about based on the cover, the headings, the first sentences, on what they know about this text or the author, or what has happened/been presented in previous chapters. Read a small section of material with the small group having the "teacher" clarify, question, and summarize. Have the students take turns being the "teacher" who leads the process. Continue the process alternating small sections of the reading material with pauses for predicting, clarifying, questioning, and summarizing.

Since the ultimate purpose is independent use of the process skills and strategies, in the most sophisticated version students would work in small groups with all students having prepared for the discussion by writing out their responses to each of the four processes. One student would be designated the "teacher" or leader of each discussion group and the classroom teacher would circulate around listening in on the discussions.

Printed Text

Unsuccessful Readers

- Have poor visualization skills
- Make little or inappropriate use of prior knowledge
- Do not make predictions or form hypotheses
- Do little self-monitoring of comprehension and use few, if any, fix-up strategies
- May form hypotheses but fail to evaluate and modify them on the basis of new information

Helping Unsuccessful Readers Be Successful

When students fail to re-frame their thinking around incorrect hypotheses
- Point out words with multiple meanings. Hammond's **Word Splash** is a good tool for helping students realize that words are being used in multiple ways. See pages 16-18.
- Point out the writing patterns of authors who use contradictions as a means of hooking new information onto old, incorrectly held ideas (i.e., "Most people think that..., but..."). The problem is that the topic sentence or the main idea is found in the middle or at the end of the paragraph or is never stated.

When students do not use prior knowledge and/or do not monitor comprehension
- Have students set their own purposes for reading rather than using teacher-imposed purposes for reading. For instance, rather than telling students to "read to find out why Jose was so excited about what was planned for after school," ask students to predict and speculate in their own words about what could be the cause of the excitement.
- Use **Three Column Charts** to help students focus on the reading. They are useful before, during and at the end of a reading selection. See page 113 for directions and the CD-ROM for a template for **Three Column Charts**.

When students fail to use productive strategies when reading
- Help students **figure out the sources of information** needed to comprehend the reading. Raphael suggests teaching students to ask themselves the following questions to guide reading comprehension:
  - Are all the parts to the answer in one sentence? Does the reader need to put together information found in various sentences and/or parts of the book?
  - Is the reader expected to combine information from the text with his own opinions and knowledge?
  - Is the reader to use his/her own experience and knowledge rather than information in the text to answer the question?

Printed Text

- Teach students not only reading strategies, but also **when to use** each strategy.
- Have students analyze the **effectiveness of the strategies** they use with teacher guidance and of those they use independently.
- Use **Reciprocal Teaching**, particularly with struggling readers. See page 78.
- Use **Think Alouds** as a demonstration of the thinking processes used by successful readers. See page 64 for information on Davey's Think Alouds.
- **Explicitly teach vocabulary**. See pages 16-19.
- **Teach text structure**. See pages 229-230.
- **Help students make connections**. Explicitly frame questions and prompts to cause students to make connections between what is being studied in class and their life beyond the moment, beyond the classroom, to the past and to the future. See pages 157-158 for guidance in framing questions.
- Use Marzano's high yield strategies. See page 3.

Through the Voice of...
Redefining Audio Visual: Going Digital

Using SmartBoards

SmartBoards have significantly changed the standard lecture. Instead of the familiar stand and deliver format, teachers can infuse their lectures with interactive games, video clips, and real life examples of their subject matter. This tool is essentially an interactive whiteboard. It has a touch sensitive surface that controls your computer. Your finger becomes a mouse that controls the computer's desktop. Any game that requires a mouse can become an interactive game on the SmartBoard. The software that is used to create lessons is similar to PowerPoint; the most significant difference is that the lessons are interactive.

SmartBoards are interactive, easy to use, and can help you design engaging learning experiences because you can bring the world into your classroom. They provide the means for you to show students real life examples of what they are learning. For instance, I was doing a lesson on scientific notation and found some interesting articles on new planets and solar systems. I incorporated the articles into my SmartBoard lesson. This made my lesson on scientific notation relevant and purposeful, not to mention more engaging. We also watched a short online video on scientific notation and took an online quiz.

They are the ultimate tools in teacher collaboration. It is easy for teachers to share lessons created using Smartboard software. After creating my lesson on scientific notation I shared it with several colleagues via email. Now, not only do they have the accompanying worksheets, but the entire presentation, complete with interactive examples and all of my web links. They could either use the existing lesson or modify it to meet their needs.

One capability of SmartBoard is for teachers to record their lesson plans using the SmartBoard software and a microphone. This makes preparing substitute plans a snap. I have done this on several occasions when I was out. I simply recorded my voice as I navigated through the files on my computer. Everything I did on my computer was recorded as a movie file. The substitute then played the movie for my students. It not only made the directions clear for my students, but for my substitute as well. I was at a conference one afternoon, but I still taught the first ten minutes of each of my classes using this Smartboard technology. All of the feedback I have received from my substitutes has been extremely positive.

Smartboard lessons can be posted online, either as a PowerPoint or PDF file. At the end of each day I save my Smartboard lessons as a PDF file. I then post these online for parents, or for students that were absent. Parents and students can view all my class notes and see the web links; in fact, they essentially have access to my whole lesson.

Stu Smith, Barker Road Middle School, Pittsford Central School District, NY

Redefining Audio Visual: Going Digital

Using PowerPoint

The good news is that PowerPoint presentations are widely used in classrooms today. The bad news is that they are not always used well. We are, unfortunately, replicating some of our bad habits with overhead transparencies and notes on the board in our use of this tool. One of the problematic issues is unreadable text, because it is too small, too crowded, or too dim. A second issue is asking students to copy the information on the slides into their notes without any opportunity to process and make sense of it. Another huge problem is notes read by the teacher to the students. In the worst situations we rely so heavily on the slides that we could have just emailed the presentation in and stayed home.

The good news is that help is readily available. To double check on your level of expertise, go to www.presentersuniversity.com/visuals.php for many easy to read articles on creating and effectively using PowerPoint presentations. The following are especially valuable:
- 9 Mistakes Presenters Make with Visuals
- Back to Basics: The Presentation Slide Show
- The Deadly Sins of Modern PowerPoint Usage

Timely Tips from the Field

- Begin with the end in mind. Identify the two or three key concepts or the essential understandings and plan how the presentation will focus on them.
- Avoid too much text. Use no more than six to ten lines with no more than seven or eight words per line on each slide.
- Avoid small text. The words should look oversized on paper. Use 40 or larger font size for headings and 24 or larger for body text.
- Avoid overpowering backgrounds, delayed transitions, visuals that do not support or enhance the content, all capital letters, PowerPoint templates, distracting sounds, and the use of all uppercase letters because they are hard to read.
- Be consistent but do not over do consistency to the point of being boring. Possible consistent components are: color, background, border, and fonts. Use one of two fonts providing variety with bold, italics, and color to emphasize key points.
- Use the B key. When the discussion takes an unexpected turn or questions arise, strike the B key to get a blank screen. When you are ready to return to the slides, strike B again.
- Jot down the numbers of key slides. When you want to return to one of them, press the number of the slide plus enter and you are there without scrolling through the slides.
- Use sans-serif fonts like Vag Rounded, Gill Sans, or Arial for ease of reading.

Active Learning

IV

TOP TEN QUESTIONS
to ask myself as I design lessons

The focus questions for this chapter are highlighted below.

1. What should **students know and be able to do** as a result of this lesson? How are these objectives related to national, state, and/or district standards?

2. How will **students demonstrate what they know and what they can do**? What will be the **assessment criteria** and what form will it take?

3. How will I find out what students already know (**pre-assessment**), and how will I help them access what they know and have experienced both inside and outside the classroom? How will I help them **build on prior experiences**, **deal with misconceptions**, and re-frame their thinking when appropriate?

4. How will new knowledge, concepts, and skills be introduced? Given the **diversity of my students** and the **task analysis**, what are my **best options for sources and presentation modes**?

5. How will **I facilitate student processing (meaning making)** of new information or processes? What key questions, activities, and assignments (in class or homework) will promote understanding, retention, and transfer?

6. What shall I use as **formative assessments** or **checks for understanding** during the lesson? How can I use the **data** from those assessments to **inform my teaching decisions**?

7. What do I need to do to **scaffold instruction** so that the learning experiences are productive for all students? What are the multiple ways students can access information and then process and demonstrate their learning?

8. How will I **Frame the Learning** so that students know the objectives, the rationale for the objectives and activities, the directions and procedures, as well as the assessment criteria at the beginning of the learning process?

9. How will I build in opportunities for students to make **real-world connections** and to learn and use the **rigorous and complex thinking skills** they need to succeed in the classroom and the world beyond?

10. What adjustments need to be made in the **learning environment** so that we can work and learn efficiently during this study?

Self-Assessment
Active Learning

Assess your practice around each of these strategies for engaging students in rigorous and relevant active learning.

Almost Always (A), Sometimes (S), Not Yet (N)

_____ **1.** I encourage students to express varied opinions as long as they support those opinions with data.

_____ **2.** I encourage students to think about how the information they are learning relates to other subjects and their lives beyond the school day.

_____ **3.** My students think critically and creatively because I ask questions that have more than one answer.

_____ **4.** I encourage students to think and discuss answers with a partner or a small group before answering in the larger group.

_____ **5.** I encourage my students to reflect on their experiences when learning something new and they often "mess with" new ideas before lectures or reading.

_____ **6.** I help students examine their own thinking and build on their ideas.

_____ **7.** I ask students what they already know about a unit before introducing it.

_____ **8.** I use essential questions and key concepts to help students organize new information in ways that make sense to them.

_____ **9.** Students share responsibility for generating their own vocabulary lists and the questions they want answered.

_____ **10.** Students resolve their differences by discussing their thinking.

_____ **11.** Class time spent on practice exercises and learning the facts leads to meaningful use of the skills and facts in the near future.

_____ **12.** I encourage students to try solving difficult problems, even before they learn all the material.

_____ **13.** Students are allowed to explore topics that excite or interest them.

_____ **14.** I design assessments around real world applications.

_____ **15.** Students help determine how they demonstrate learning and how they are assessed.

Adapted from _The Student Constructivism and Active Learning Environments Scale_ (The S.C.A.L.E.) by Bonk & Medury, 1991

I Forgot!

Ebbinghaus

When Hermann Ebbinghaus, a German psychologist, investigated memory using nonsense syllables, he found that **forgetting sets in very quickly**. Amazingly, of all that is forgotten during the first month after learning, **47 percent of forgetting occurs in the first twenty minutes** with 62 percent occurring within the first day. This research from the nineteenth century clearly indicates that the **prime time to process, discuss, and reflect is immediately after new information is presented (either in class or in independent study), before forgetting sets in**. This explains why we have problems deciphering notes we take during a lecture or presentation if we do not apply the information immediately.

Hermann Ebbinghaus, *Memory*. Columbia University Press, 1913.
First published in German in 1885.

H. F. Spitzer

In the 1930's, H. F. Spitzer analyzed the forgetting patterns of over 3,000 students. Spitzer, in this study which used textbook material, discovered that:

- The greatest amount of forgetting occurs rapidly, during the first day after material is presented. (This matches the findings of Ebbinghaus in the previous century.)
- Forgetting continues a quick pace for the first two weeks.
- **Forgetting slows down after two weeks**, but then again, **there is not much left to forget**.

Rate of Forgetting Textbook Material

After one day, 46% forgotten
After seven days, 65% forgotten
After fourteen days, 79% forgotten
After twenty-one days, 82% forgotten

H. F.. Spitzer, "Studies in Retention."
***Journal of Educational Psychology*, 1939, pp 641-656.**

10:2 Theory

Learners make sense of new information by integrating it with prior knowledge. During lectures or other presentations of new information, they take mental breaks to accomplish this task. Learners take these breaks even as more information is being presented. **Mary Budd Rowe** (1983) recommends that we provide short processing pauses at regularly scheduled intervals to accommodate these mental lapses.

Mental lapses occur when . . .

- **short term memory overloads** because too many new ideas are introduced in a given period . . . meanwhile, the discussion or lecture flows on!

- **an idea is not immediately grasped**. There is momentary confusion while a student tries to "make sense" of the information. If a suitable long-term "file" exists for the student, the transfer to long term memory occurs quickly. If, however, files have to be created or reorganized, the transfer takes longer . . . meanwhile, the discussion or lecture flows on!

- **different words or symbols are used by different sources** to identify the same chunk of knowledge. For example, a teacher might refer to a concept in one set of terms, a parent in another. The learner needs time to sort for similarities, differences, and patterns . . . meanwhile, the discussion or lecture flows on!

- **students are sent off on a mental detour** by something they hear in the discussion or lecture. This occurs when students are well versed in the content material. Even if the mental detour is an important mental exercise, they miss the content presented . . . meanwhile, the discussion or lecture flows on!

To reduce the information loss, Rowe recommends that we pause for two minutes at about ten minute intervals. . . hence the name, 10:2 Theory. **For every ten minutes or so of meaningful chunks of new information, learners should be provided with two or so minutes to process information.** Small groups share notes and/or discuss their current understanding and memory to fill in or supplement gaps.

Active Learning Strategies to Use
If You Want...

Students to work in pairs or in small groups

Think-Pair-Share - 112

Learning Buddies - 99-100

Discussion Partners - 67

Frame of Reference - 91

Graffiti - 92

Numbered Heads Together - 103

Sort Cards - 94

Collaborative Controversy - 76

Literature Circles - 75

Walking Tour - 116-117

Five Card Draw - 97

Jigsaw - 242-243

To gather pre-assessment data

Anticipation Reaction Guide - 110

Signal Cards - 154

Sort Cards - 94

Frame of Reference - 91

Line-Ups - 101-102

Think-Pair-Share - 112

Exclusion Brainstorming - 108

Three Column Charts - 113

Graffiti - 92

Stir the Class - 106

All Hands on Deck - 96

Take a Stand - 107

Students to access prior knowledge and make real world connections

Anticipation Reaction Guide - 110

Corners - 90

Stir the Class - 106

Frame of Reference - 91

Line-Ups - 101-102

Think-Pair-Share - 112

Graffiti - 92

Personal Opinion Guide - 111

Exclusion Brainstorming - 108

Three Column Charts - 113

All Hands on Deck - 96

Sort Cards - 94

To surface misconceptions and naive understandings

Anticipation Reaction Guide - 110

Personal Opinion Guides - 111

Three Column Charts - 113

Frame of Reference - 91

Line-Ups - 101-102

Think-Pair-Share - 112

3-2-1 - 114

Facts and Folklore - 109

To promote vocabulary development

Inside-Outside Circles - 93

Word Splash - 18

Three Column Charts - 113

Journals - 14

Tic-Tac-Toe - 98

Interactive Notebooks - 228

Graffiti - 92

Word Sorts - 17

Frayer Model - 18

Five Card Draw - 97

Six-Step Process - 19

Reciprocal Teaching - 78

Active Learning Strategies to Use
If You Want...

Students to set purpose for reading, listening or viewing

Walking Tour - 116-117

Three Column Charts - 113

Corners - 90

Line-ups - 101-102

Personal Opinion Guide - 111

Anticipation Reaction Guide - 110

Exclusion Brainstorming - 108

Take a Stand - 107

Think-Pair-Share - 112

Students to summarize their learning

3-2-1 - 114

Interactive Notebooks - 228

Three Column charts - 113

Scavenger Hunt - 104-105

Podcasts, blogs, etc. - 13, 73, 133-134

Journals/Interactive Notebooks - 14, 228

Graffiti - 92

Tic-Tac-Toe - 98

Ticket to Leave - 115

Connection Collections - 118

Think-Pair-Share - 112

ABC to XYZ - 119

To check for understanding

Signal Cards - 154

Line-Ups - 101-102

Slates - 156

Sort Cards - 94

Scavenger Hunt - 104-105

Think-Pair-Share - 112

I Have the Question...? - 95

Numbered Heads Together - 103

To have students "handle" their learning

Inside-Outside Circles - 93

Tic-Tac-Toe - 98

MI Kinesthetic Strategies - 128

Sort Cards - 94

Five Card Draw - 97

All Hands on Deck - 96

Connection Collections - 118

To build in movement

Scavenger Hunt - 104-105

Stir the Class - 106

Graffiti - 92

Inside-Outside Circles - 93

Line-Ups - 101-102

MI Kinesthetic Strategies - 128

Walking Tour - 116-117

Learning Buddies - 99-100

Corners - 90

1 Corners 2

Purposes

- To access prior knowledge
- To set purposes for reading, listening, or viewing
- To build in movement
- To promote critical thinking skills

Process

Pose a question that has multiple answers or asks students to rank order several options.

- Give students time to consider their own thinking about the topic, then have them move to a corner of the room that has been designated as the meeting place of all those holding the same opinion or view.
- In the corner meeting places, have students discuss why they think or believe the way they do. If the groups are large, have students divide into pairs or triads so that all can voice their opinions and their rationales.
- As appropriate, have selected students or volunteers report for their corner. Large group sharing can be oral only or the corner groups can also generate and share charts listing their rationales for choosing that particular answer/viewpoint.

Sample Topics

- CEOs of major corporations salaries should be....give alternative amounts, ratios, rationales for setting salaries.
- Which professions are most in demand now?
- Which character in the book would you most like to meet?
- What volleyball skill would you most like to develop?
- If you were the leader of your country/state, which issue would be your top priority...A, B, C, or D?
- How strongly do you agree or disagree with the statement, "All forms of violence should be censored on television."
- Predict the percentage of people who will respond affirmatively to stated survey questions.
- Name four inventions; which is most significant and why?
- Name four historical figures; who changed the world the most and why?

4 3

Used by permission of Kagan Publishing and Professional Development. All rights reserved.

Frame of Reference*

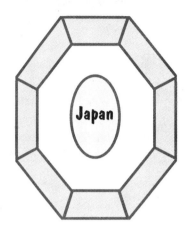

Purposes

- To gather pre-assessment data
- To access prior knowledge
- To surface misconceptions
- To help students make real-world connections
- To have students work in pairs
- To promote organizational and analytical thinking skills

Process

- The **topic or issue** to be discussed is placed in the center of the matted frame where a picture would be placed in a picture frame.
- Students are given several minutes to individually jot down **words or phrases** that come to mind when they hear or see the term "pictured." These words go in the "mat" area of their frame of reference.
- Students are then asked to jot down how they came to know what they know or think...that is the sources, people, events that have **influenced their thinking**. These reactions go in the "frame" area of the graphic.
- Following the individual reflection and writing, students are asked to share their "frames of reference" with a partner or a small group.

Variations

A variation of **Frame of Reference** can be used to process learning by having students place the name of a historical character in the center. The students then jot down how this person would describe his or her own life and times and then the events and people who influenced his or her thinking. Assigning different students different persons/perspectives can lead to powerful "in the voice of" discussions when the historical frames of references are completed.

Frame of Reference can also be used as an introductory and community building exercise. Students put their own names in the center, describe themselves and then cite those people and events that have shaped their thinking and lives.

* Access a template for Frame of Reference on the CD-ROM.

Graffiti

Purposes
- To gather pre-assessment data
- To access prior knowledge
- To have students summarize their learning
- To build in movement
- To promote critical thinking

Process
- Write problems, formulas, sentences to be translated, or ideas to brainstorm on pieces of large chart paper and post around the room. Students move in small groups from chart to chart.

    or

- Give each piece of chart paper to a group of three or four. Students work at their tables and the charts move from table to table. Kathy Anderson of New Trier High School, Winnetka, Illinois calls this version **Ready...Rotate**.

    In either case,

- each group works on a different question, topic, issue, or statement related to the concept being studied and writes responses or "graffiti" which can be short words, phrases, or graphics on their chart paper.
- After the allotted time period, have the students or the charts move.
- Repeat the process until all groups have reacted to all charts.
- Post the charts and have students react to the statements or topics, identify patterns, and/or make predictions based on what is written/drawn on the charts.

Variations
- This strategy can be used any time during a lesson or unit. At the beginning you and your students can find out what they already know and can do; in the middle it is a useful way for you and them to check on their learning. At the end of study, it can serve as a great review for an exam or even for predicting what might be on the exam.
- Individuals or groups can use different color markers to track contributions.
- See and Hear chart

Inside-Outside Circles

Purposes
- To have students teach each other
- To review
- To develop vocabulary
- To build in movement

Process
- On index cards, **write vocabulary words**, **math or science problems**, **or questions** about important points in the unit. Give a card to each student. Have students turn the cards over and **write the answer to their question on the back of the card**.
- Have the students number/letter off as "1s" and "2s" or "As" and "Bs". Ask one subset to stand and form a circle. When the circle is formed, have them face the outside of the circle. The other students then go and stand facing a student in the "inside" circle.
- **Have students ask each other their questions**. Advise them, if their partner does not know the answer, to immediately show them the question and the answer.
  - **As ask their questions of the Bs.**
  - **Bs then ask their questions of the As.**
  - **At the signal, students switch cards. Now the As have the Bs cards and vice versa.**
- Have the outside circle move to the left or the right until they reach the second or third person in the inside circle.
- These new partners quiz each other as before. Continue this sequence for as long as is appropriate.
- It is important to have the students **exchange cards** or they will get bored asking the same question over and over and won't learn nearly as much.

Variation on a theme...
Cake Walk
- Questions are written on the board or on an overhead transparency.
- Students form concentric circles.
- The teacher or a student plays music. While the music plays, the circles move in opposite directions. When the music stops, students in the outer circle turn to face students in the inner circle.
- Students discuss the question to which their attention is directed.
- Repeat the process for as long as it is appropriate.

Sort Cards

Purposes
- To gather pre-assessment data
- To check for understanding
- To review
- To access prior knowledge
- To develop selected thinking skills

Process
1. Students, working individually, generate words and short phrases that come to mind when they think of a designated topic. They record each idea on a separate index card.

2. Working in small groups, students:
   - share ideas
   - clarify similar ideas
   - eliminate duplicates

3. Students sort the ideas of the group into categories. The categories can be created by the students or the teacher can identify categories for student use.

4. When the sorting and labeling is completed, the students take a tour around the room to observe and analyze the work of other groups. One student stays behind at the base table to answer questions.

5. Groups return to tables to discuss what they observed and to revise or add new ideas/categories.

6. Groups use the generated ideas and categories as a basis of future study or discussion.

7. Ask students to do meta-cognitive processing; that is, have them process how they went about their thinking as they generated, sorted, categorized, labeled, and analyzed the work of others.

I Have the Question, Who Has the Answer?

Purposes
- To review concepts through active student participation
- To heighten attention and engagement
- To check for understanding

Materials
- **Two sets of index cards** or slips of paper. One set contains questions related to the unit of study. The second set contains the answers to the questions. **Hint: To keep students engaged, prepare more answer cards than question cards.**

Process
- Distribute **answer cards** to students.
- Place a stack of **question cards** face down in the middle of each of the student tables.
- Designate a student to turn over a question card. The student says "**The Question is...Who has the answer?**"
- All students check their answer cards to see if they have the correct answer or a possible one. If a student thinks he/she has an answer, she reads the answer. If it is a match, the student with the answer turns over the next question card, reads the question aloud, and the process continues.

Variations
- The whole group owns the answers distributed to individuals and they collaborate in deciding if they have a good answer.
- Start with just a few questions and answers for students and add to the collection as the unit progresses.
- Have students prepare the cards.
- Use the question/answer cards for individual/small group review.

All Hands on Deck

Purposes
- To promote participation by all students in a brainstorming process
- To focus students on topic/concept to be studied
- To find out what students know about the topic to be studied
- To access prior knowledge
- To gather pre-assessment data

Process
- Post chart paper listing subsets of the concept/unit to be studied around the room.
- Give examples of ideas that might be included in each category or on each chart.
- Provide each **group of students** with a **stack of index cards** with the same topic headings as found on the posted chart paper.
- **Each student takes one or two cards** (exact number determined by the number of students in each group and the number of subsets).
  - Each student has 60 to 90 seconds to brainstorm ideas about the subsets on their cards, with the expectation that each student will contribute at least one idea to each card.
  - When given the signal, cards are passed to the left and the next student adds ideas to the subset card just received. **Cards circulate** within the group until each student has written on each card.
  - A team reporter reads one contribution from their team for the selected chart on the wall in round-robin fashion. When one chart is completed, focus moves to the next chart.

Variation
Provide groups with sheets of paper with topics printed at the top and small **post-it notes**. Students write their ideas on the notes and stick them to paper. Large group sharing can be through **posting of the notes** and a **walking tour** of the charts. Each student in the small groups could be given a different color post-it note to further hold each student accountable for participation.

Card Categories
Five Card Draw

Purposes
- To place students in working groups
- To review/preview content specific vocabulary
- To have students practice categorizing skills
- To have students handle their learning

Process
- Prepare cards with vocabulary words, geographic locations, components of mathematical equations or formulas, or items from any set of categories. To fit the name, "**Five Card Draw**," identify **five items/cards for each set** and prepare the number of sets you need to have one card per student.
- As students enter the room, have them draw a card or have them draw (from a deck) as you circulate around the room.
- Students are to move around the room to find four other students who "fit" with the category represented by the item on the card.
- Once the groups have formed, students sit together and study/review material and categories represented by their cards. They are expected to figure out exactly how they fit together and prepare to present/explain their material to the class. Each member should be able to define, explain, or demonstrate all the concepts the group represents.
- The discussion and/or review can continue using one of several formats. To continue the random selection format, you could have students number off at each table, then spin a spinner or draw a straw, and have the selected student answer a question related to the material being studied.
- Other students could have listening logs, learning logs, or journals in which they are recording the information presented.

Possibilities
- Countries on a continent
- Types of numbers (prime, negative, ratios)
- Books in a genre
- Musical pieces by a composer or group
- Events in a decade

Tic-Tac-Toe

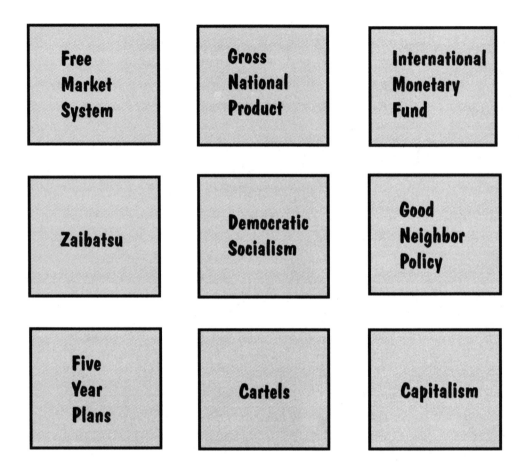

Free Market System	Gross National Product	International Monetary Fund
Zaibatsu	Democratic Socialism	Good Neighbor Policy
Five Year Plans	Cartels	Capitalism

Purposes

- To have students go beyond memorizing definitions and to look for patterns and **connections** embedded in the vocabulary words and concepts being studied
- To promote dialogue and debate

Process

- Place, or have students place, vocabulary words or important concepts on **index cards**.
- Give each student or group a set of cards.
- Have students shuffle their cards and deal out nine cards in a **3x3 format**.
- Ask students to form eight sentences each, including the three words straight across in a **row**, straight down in a **column**, or on the **diagonals**.
- Have the students or groups share the sentences that capture important **connections**, or "misconnections," between words and concepts being studied.

Learning Buddies*

Purposes
- To promote verbal fluency
- To build in movement
- To have students process their learning
- To peer edit and check work

Process
- Students can self-select another student with whom to do **10:2 processing** or **Think-Pair-Share**.
- The teacher announces a processing time. A focus question or process direction is given to define the task for the partners.
- To build in movement, have the partners stand together as they follow the teacher's directions or answer the question. The time for these processing discussions is generally brief; 2-4 minutes is the norm.
- Teacher circulation and listening in on the discussions provides a great deal of information about what the students are learning and/or are puzzled about. It also helps hold the students accountable for talking about the designated topic.

Variations
- Pairs can be carefully crafted by the teacher or randomly partnered by pulling names out of the hat, matching cards, counting off, etc.
- **Clock Buddies, Element Buddies, Parent Function Partners**, etc. are efficient, long term, content specific adaptations of this structure. Students are given a graphic with slots for ten to twelve "appointments." At each slot, two students record each other's name. This sign-up period takes about four to five minutes and provides an efficient way for students to interact during the next few weeks. Whenever the teacher announces a time for students to process learning, a partnership is identified and students meet with their partner.

Clock Buddies

* **See examples on following page and access multiple templates on CD-ROM**

Elements Buddies

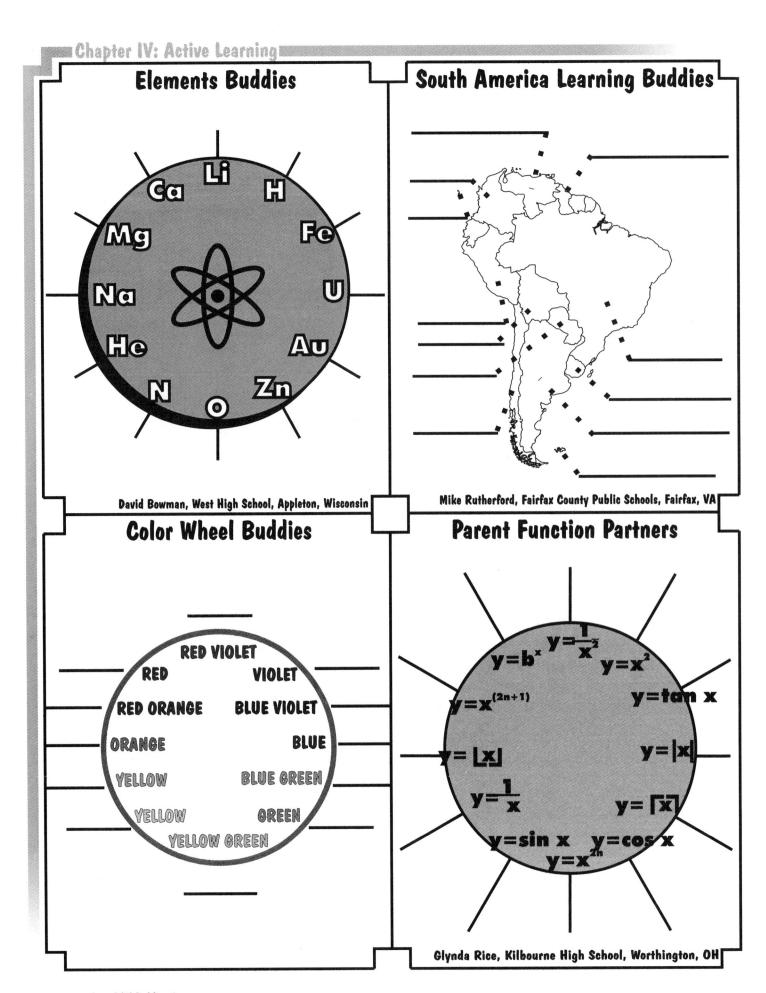

David Bowman, West High School, Appleton, Wisconsin

South America Learning Buddies

Mike Rutherford, Fairfax County Public Schools, Fairfax, VA

Color Wheel Buddies

RED VIOLET

RED   VIOLET

RED ORANGE   BLUE VIOLET

ORANGE   BLUE

YELLOW   BLUE GREEN

YELLOW   GREEN

YELLOW GREEN

Parent Function Partners

$y=b^x$ $y=\frac{1}{x^2}$ $y=x^2$

$y=x^{(2n+1)}$

$y=\lfloor x \rfloor$ $y=\tan x$ $y=|x|$

$y=\frac{1}{x}$ $y=\lceil x \rceil$

$y=\sin x$ $y=\cos x$

$y=x^{2n}$

Glynda Rice, Kilbourne High School, Worthington, OH

Line-Ups

Purposes
- To access prior knowledge
- To have students take and defend a position on a topic
- To evoke curiosity and heighten attention/focus during instruction
- To help students fine tune their estimation skills
- To help students develop their ability to articulate their rationale
- To check for understanding
- To set a purpose for reading

Process
- Have students **take a stand, make a prediction, or make an estimation** pertaining to the topic of instruction. Have them write their predictions on a small piece of paper or a post-it note.
- Designate one end of the room as the low end/beginning and the other as the high end/ending. Have students **line up in the order** of their predictions or estimates. Have students hold their written estimate where it can be seen and line up without talking.
- Have students **report their estimates** so that all students can see the wide range of responses
- **Fold the line** on itself so the person with the highest estimate or the end is facing the person with the lowest response. Or, find the center of the line and have the students move so that the person holding the highest estimate is facing someone with a mid-level response.
- The partners **share their estimates as well as the rationales and strategies** they used to determine their responses. Students can be asked to report on their partner's answers and rationale or on their own.
- If there is a correct answer, you may want to have them determine it or do research to find out the **answer** or the **opinions of experts** in the field.

Possibilities
- Sequence the steps in changing a tire. Place one step on each slip of paper and distribute randomly.
- How many hours of television do most 18 year-olds watch in one week?
- How much is spent on the marketing of a best-selling book?
- What is the life expectancy of the average female in the United States?
- Estimate the percentage of Americans (French) who exercise the right to vote.

©Just ASK Publications

Through the Voice of...
Metric Line-Up

You have received a card bearing the name (or abbreviation) of a unit of measure. When given the signal, you will have 2 minutes to **sort yourselves into 2 groups (either MASS or LENGTH). Then you must line up in order from largest to smallest unit**. (If both the name and the abbreviation are present, those two individuals should be side by side.) No talking!

After I have checked your group, list the units in order (abbreviations are okay). For each unit having a prefix, write 2 equivalencies in the form shown below:

ex: 1 kg = 10 ? g   &   1 g = 10 ?

Unit	Equivalence #1	Equivalence #2

Gillian Thompson, New Trier High School, Winnetka, IL

Numbered Heads Together

Purposes

- To check for understanding
- To develop verbal fluency
- To have students work in small groups
- To review

Process

- Have students form teams of 4 or 5.
- Have students within each team count off from 1-4 or 5 (depending on the number of group members). If teams are uneven, when #5 is called to answer, the #4 person on 4 member teams answers with the #5 people from 5 member teams.
- The teacher asks a question.
- **Students put their heads together** and collaboratively generate an answer.
- Members of the team make sure each member can answer the question.
- The teacher calls a number at random. All students assigned that number stand or raise their hands; one of these students is selected to answer the question.

Variations

- Using a spinning wheel, dice, or playing cards to identify the spokesperson makes this structure even more engaging.
- If the answer has several parts, #1 from one table can answer the first part, then another #1 adds the second part, etc.
- When a student gives a partially correct answer, another person with that number can be called upon to add to the response. Another variation is to have all teams put their heads together again to check understanding and supply the missing information.
- When divergent answers are the goal, use **Numbered Head Ambassadors** to have the identified group member move to the next table to tell that group what the ambassador's "home" group thinks.

Canada Scavenger Hunt

What do they call the leader of the Canadian Government? Sign. _____	What 3 oceans border Canada? Sign. _____	Name 4 French Explorers. Sign. _____	Which ocean does the St. Lawrence River empty into? Sign. _____	Which Great Lake does not border Canada? Sign. _____	What province has two official languages? Sign. _____
Which physical region of Canada is the largest? Sign. _____	List three ways the St. Lawrence Seaway is helpful. Sign. _____	What is the main job in the prairie provinces? Sign. _____	Where do most of the people in Canada live? Sign. _____	What river serves as a border between the US and Canada? Sign. _____	What is the difference between a territory and a province? Sign. _____
If you traveled west from Alberta, which province would you be in? Sign. _____	Winnipeg is the capital of ...? Sign. _____	Why don't many people live in the territories? Sign. _____	How do the Inuit make their homes? Sign. _____	What are the main jobs in the Atlantic Provinces? Sign. _____	Describe the tundra. Sign. _____
How do many people make a living in southern Ontario? Sign. _____	Name the largest province. Sign. _____	Which area of Canada is the warmest and why? Sign. _____	What body of water touches Quebec, Ontario, Manitoba and the NW territories? Sign. _____	Name the 3 Prairie Provinces. Sign. _____	What is the island of Newfoundland called? Sign. _____

Stacy Russotti, West Irondequoit School District, Rochester, NY

Scavenger Hunt

Purposes
- To jigsaw information
- To build in movement
- To develop verbal fluency
- To check for understanding
- To review, preview, and expand a topic
- To demonstrate to students that collectively they know a great deal

Process
- Prepare a set of questions on a topic.
- If students are not already in table groups or teams, they will need groups to discuss their work after the scavenger hunt.
- **Have students individually read** through the questions, **select one** on which they will be the expert, and **answer only that one** on their sheets. As an alternative, you may assign a specific question to each student or have them draw the question number out of a hat.
- You may wish to initial the answers before they start the hunt to ensure that a "virus" does not spread around the room, or you may wish to let students discover and deal with any errors.
- Students can use **all the people and materials** in the room as resources to obtain the rest of the answers. Students may only obtain one answer from each person they ask.
- **Answers can "flow through"** one person to another, but the "third party" and middle person should be prepared to fully explain the answer. The name the student lists as a resource is the person from whom they actually obtain the answer.
- When time is called, students return to their table groups or teams, verify answers, and complete any unfinished answers.
- Only unresolved issues need be discussed with the entire class.

Possibilities
- Book reports
- Vocabulary
- Math problems
- Objects by shape, color, size, texture

Stir the Class*

Purposes
- To gather pre-assessment data
- To access prior knowledge
- To develop verbal fluency
- To build in movement
- To have students share expertise and interests

Process
- Provide each student with a data collection sheet containing ten to twenty lines, or have them number their own sheets.
- Have each student write, as directed, three reasons, three causes, three points of interest, etc., about the topic/concept to be studied. Ask them to make the third one on their list unique.
- At a signal, students move around the room collecting/giving one idea from/to each student. Ideas received from one student can be passed "through" to another student.
- After an appropriate amount of time, students return to their seats. At this point, you can have students compare lists, prioritize, categorize, design research projects, etc.
- At this point, students can continue with a lesson format appropriate to the level of thinking you want them to do. They have had time to focus on the subject and to hear ideas from classmates.

Possible Topics
- Ways we use **AVERAGES** in daily life...
- Potential problems with a **FLAT INCOME TAX**...
- Significant pieces of **LITERATURE** you've read...
- Animals that live in **AFRICA**...
- Causes of **PREJUDICE**...
- Places you see or use **METRIC MEASUREMENT**...
- Primary causes of **EROSION**...
- Facts about **INUITS**...
- Effects of human behavior on the **ECOSYSTEM**...
- **HEROES, HEROINES, EXTRAORDINARY LEADERS, VILLAINS, GREEK GODS, COMMUNITY HELPERS, etc.**
- Spanish words related to **TRAVEL**...

* Access a template for Stir the Class on the CD-ROM.

Take a Stand

Purposes
- To motivate students through controversy
- To set purpose for reading
- To use students' experience base to involve them in new learning

Process
- Identify the **main points** students are to grapple with in a reading, video, or other source.
- Create five to ten **statements** related to those points. Some of the statements should be true and others false. Display the statements on an overhead, chart, or individual handouts.
- When each statement is read, either by the students or the teacher, the students record their responses on their statement sheet or use another means to express their **opinion**. Pam Lecy of Appleton, Wisconsin uses signal cards with "**AGREE**" on one side and "**DISAGREE**" on the other.
- After students have taken a stand on the statements, but before they read the material, discuss the pros and cons of each statement so that students hear **rationales** for varying positions.
- Students then consult the information source. As they work, students record information or note location of information that **refers to, supports, or contradicts** the position.
- The lesson can be continued in a variety of ways. In follow-up **discussion**, students can talk about what surprised them, what they learned, and continue to cite other sources of information that present different perspectives.

Variations...See the next four pages for directions.
- Exclusion Brainstorming
- Facts and Folklore
- Anticipation Guide
- Personal Opinion Guide

Exclusion Brainstorming

Purposes
- To predict and set a focus for learning
- To find out what students think they know about a topic
- To build skills for analyzing possible connections

Process
- Write a topic on the chalkboard. Under the topic, write a series of words, including:
    some words that clearly fit the topic
    others that clearly do not fit the topic
    and others that are ambiguous
- Students identify which words they think fit the topic by drawing a line through those that are not related and drawing a circle around those they think are related.
- Students then explain or discuss why they chose the way they did.
- Students then explore the topic by reading, viewing, or visiting.
- Students compare their predictions to their findings.

Hints
- This method is especially productive if the group is small or not yet skilled in the brainstorming process, because the teacher does the list-making and students systematically build skills.
- Students may learn to develop these lists for their classmates to respond to. This learning experience would be a good one as an extension and enrichment activity.

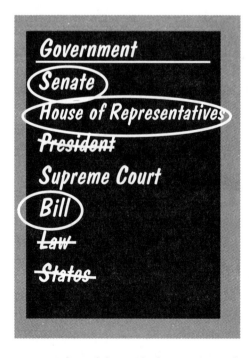

Adapted from Blachowicz (1986)

Facts & Folklore

Purposes
- To discover what students "know"...correctly and incorrectly...about a topic
- To differentiate between truth, fiction, and spin for concepts with much information in multiple forms
- To validate the existence of folklore

Process
- Have students list all they know about a topic. Encourage them to list folklore as well as facts. This can be done individually, in small groups, or in large groups.
- Have them identify which ideas they think are fact and which they think are opinion, fantasy, or political spin.
- Discuss with the students why they made their choices.

Examples
- **Facts and Folklore** is useful when beginning a topic widely covered in the media, such as a court case or a sport star, to help students learn to separate "hype" from "fact".
- Try **Facts and Folklore** when beginning a unit on a foreign country to see what the students' preconceptions are. For example, when studying Spain, students might respond: "They speak Spanish." "Spain is on the Iberian Peninsula." "They eat tacos." "They wear sombreros." or "Both Christian and Islamic influences are seen in Spanish architecture." When students share their current knowledge or thoughts, you can learn which topics or details you need to clarify as you teach.

Possibilities
- George Washington
- Substance abuse
- Difference in cultures
- Columbus
- Dinosaurs
- Metric system

109

Through the Voice of...
Anticipation Reaction Guide

Purposes
- To establish a purpose for reading, listening, or viewing
- To access prior knowledge
- To help students re-frame their thinking as necessary
- To promote critical thinking skills

Process
- Prepare a series of statements related to the reading or other input source.
- Have students, before reading, indicate whether they think the statement is true or false.
- Have students read the selection or watch the video or demonstration.
- Have students, after reading, answer the same questions again.
- Have students discuss where they found the information that changed their thinking.

Chemistry
Anticipation Reaction Guide

Directions:
1. Respond to each statement before you read.   T=true   F=false
2. Read section B.9, page 11.
3. Respond to each statement after you read.   T=true   F=false
4. Rewrite the statements that are false so that they are true.

Before Reading   **After Reading**

_____ 1. Many properties of elements are determined largely
         by the number of protons in their atoms and how   _____
         these protons are arranged.

_____ 2. Metal atoms lose their outer electrons more easily
         than do nonmetal atoms.   _____

_____ 3. Active metals can give up one or more of their
         electrons to ions of less-active metals.   _____

_____ 4. Stronger attractions among atoms of a metal result
         in higher boiling points.   _____

_____ 5. Understanding the properties of atoms does not
         help to predict and correlate the behavior of   _____
         materials.

Lynn Hiller, New Trier High School, Winnetka, IL

Through the Voice of...
Personal Opinion Guide

Purposes
- To set a purpose for reading
- To promote relevance
- To develop verbal fluency
- To have students use critical thinking skills

for *The Scarlet Ibis* by James Hurst

Before You Read: Work with a partner on this exercise. Read each statement below and put a + (plus) mark in the space under the Before Reading column if you agree with the statement, or put a - (minus) sign if you disagree with the statement. Use your personal experience, knowledge, and opinions to make your decision. After you have completed all statements, take turns with your partner and read each again. Explain why you agree or disagree with each other.

Before Reading		After Reading
_____	1. Pride is a wonderful thing.	_____
_____	2. Pride is a terrible thing.	_____
_____	3. Children can be cruel.	_____
_____	4. It's possible to like and dislike a person at the same time.	_____
_____	5. We should always be proud of our families.	_____
_____	6. Sometimes family members can be embarrassing.	_____
_____	7. A good deed is only worth doing if you get recognition for doing it.	_____
_____	8. Brothers and/or sisters are nothing but trouble.	_____
_____	9. It's uncomfortable to be around a handicapped person.	_____
_____	10. Feeling guilty is an awful burden.	_____

Read the piece of literature. Look for issues in the story that are relevant to these statements.

After You Read: Re-read the statement and mark your responses in the After Reading column. Tomorrow in class, you and your partner will compare your reactions and discuss your selections based on your interpretation of the story.

Mickie Froehlich, New Trier High School, Winnetka, IL

Think-Pair-Share

Purposes

- To provide processing time called for in 10:2 theory
- To build in wait time
- To provide rehearsal
- To enhance depth and breadth of thinking
- To increase level of participation
- To provide opportunities to check for understanding
- To provide time for teacher to make instructional decisions
- To provide time for teacher to locate support materials and plan the next question
- To allow the teacher to intervene with one or two students without an audience

Process

- Ask a question.
- Ask students to think quietly about possible answers to the question; this is usually only thirty seconds to one minute, unless the question is quite complex. (**think**)
- Have students pair with a neighbor or a learning buddy to discuss their thinking. The discussion usually lasts two to three minutes. (**pair**)
- Ask students to share their responses with the whole group or with a table group. Not all students have to share their answers with the large group. (**share**)

Some teachers use hand signals, pointers, bells, cubes, etc. to mark transition points during the cycle. When appropriate, students can write notes, web or diagram their responses during the "Think" or "Pair" time. Students can either explain their own thinking, that of their partners or the consensus they reached. Think-Pair-Share can be used 2-5 times during an instructional period.

Three Column Charts*

Purposes
- To access prior knowledge through brainstorming
- To identify areas of student interest or concern
- To aid the teacher in planning lessons as well as checking for understanding
- To track student learning throughout unit
- To identify areas for further student research/study

Process
- Use this strategy prior to, during, or at the close of any unit of study. The process can be done individually, in small groups, or as a class activity.
- Announce topic and column titles; post on charts or have students record in table groups.
- Have the teacher or students record student responses to the stems. The student who offers the idea tells the recorder which column to put it in.
- During the brainstorming phase, emphasize getting lots of ideas rather than debating or discussing the ideas as they are generated. Debates, clarifications, and discussion of ideas occur once the brainstorming is over. The teacher does not clarify any confusions or react in any way other than to record the data. Conflicting data may be recorded.
- During the lesson or unit of study points of misconception, confusion, or curiosity are addressed.

Possibilities
Choose any one of the following sets of column headings or create your own.

What I Knew	What I Now Know	What I Still Don't Know
What I Know	What I Don't Know	What I Wish I Knew
Productive	Somewhat Productive	Unproductive
Most Important	Somewhat Important	Not Important at All
Already Know	Want to Know	Learned
In Reading Vocabulary Can Read, Use in Writing & Use in Discussion	In Reading Vocabulary Can Read, But Don't Use It	Never Heard/Saw It Before

* Access a template for Three Column Charts on the CD-ROM.

©Just ASK Publications

3 - 2 - 1*

Purposes
- To have students process and summarize learning
- To promote relevance
- To surface misconceptions and confusion

Process
The 3-2-1 process provides a structure for student meaning making and summarizing of key points in a learning experience. The stems for 3-2-1 can be created to match the kind or level of thinking you want students to do about the material being studied.

3 most important events in this person's life

2 questions you would ask this person if you could talk with him/her

1 way in which you are like this person

At the end of a discussion, a reading, a video, or a field trip students might be asked to write:

3 things that really interested you

2 things you'd like to know more about

1 idea that you will write about tonight in your journal

Joanne Mayers-Walker, ESL teacher, Lee High School, Fairfax County Public Schools, Springfield, Virginia, asked her second language learners following a film on the Civil War to respond to:

3 important facts or events I would like to discuss

2 questions I have about the film

1 event similar to an event that happened in my country's history

* **Access a template for 3-2-1 on the CD-ROM.**

Ticket to Leave

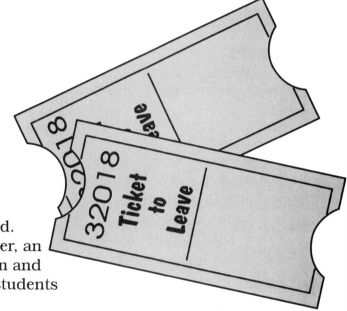

Purposes
- To have students summarize
- To have students make personal connections with the concepts studied
- To provide the teacher with formative assessment data

Procedure
- Use at the end of an instructional period.
- Have students use either their own paper, an index card, or a "ticket" you have drawn and copied for this purpose. Alternatively, students could draw or tell their thinking.
- Select an appropriate stem and provide time for students to write their responses. The stem will be determined by the kind of thinking you want the students to do.
- Stand at the door and collect the "tickets" as they leave.

Possible Stems
- List the most interesting thing you learned today and tell why you chose it.
- When you get home, what will you tell your parents you learned today?
- Write one reason why today's lesson may help you in the future.
- List as many occupations as you can that need the skills we practiced today.
- Describe one thing you accomplished that you feel good about today.
- Write one question you have related to the content studied/process used today.
- Write one question that would be a good test question on this material. Write the answer on the back.

Kathy Adasiak, a French teacher at Irondequoit High School in Rochester, New York, stands at the door as her students leave and has them use the target language to tell her such things as their birthday, favorite color, or age, or to use a simple sentence to identify or describe a picture she is holding. She finds that the flash cards for primary students available at teacher supply stores are useful for this process.

Walking Tour

Purposes
- To introduce complex texts, provocative ideas, or discrepancies
- To emphasize key ideas of content material
- To raise curiosity and increase speculation about a subject

Process
- **Compose five to eight charts** that represent the content material, pictorially or verbally. Use photographs of places or objects, direct quotes from the text, or other means to convey one idea per chart. For example, for a study of France, charts might contain postcards, phrases in French, and/or a map of France. *Hint*: **If the tour is used to introduce complex concepts or a complex reading, isolate the primary points and create one chart for each point**.
- **Post the charts** around the classroom and number each chart. Divide students into "touring groups" to fit the classroom space, age of students, and complexity of the material.
- **Assign one group per chart** as a starting point. Groups spend two to five minutes at that chart, taking notes on, and/or discussing the idea presented.
- **Rotate the groups** until all groups have "toured" each chart. When students return to their seats, allow some time for discussion and reactions.

Variations
- **Jigsaw Walking Tour** - If time to tour is limited, form groups made up of the same number of students as there are charts around the room (4 charts means there should be 4 members in a group). Have group members number off and send one representative to each chart. Students form new groups at the charts and react. They then return to their original groups to take turns reporting on the information on each chart and their reactions to it.
- Use student work as content to be studied during the Walking Tour.
- **Gallery Walk** - Pictures or other works of art are displayed around the room and the students move from display to display responding to questions or statements given as guidelines for analyzing the artwork.

Through the Voice of...
Art Treasure Hunt

Find the artwork that...(Write the title of the work, the artist, and date.)

repeats a shape	uses contrast to create interest	uses symbols
illustrates a fable or myth	has a rhythm like a song	is all about color
draws your eyes to one spot	makes you feel confused	is evenly balanced
really seems to move	uses line to create texture	captures a moment from history
tells a story	has very strong feelings behind it	seems to go back in space

Debbie Novak, Evanston Township High School, Evanston, IL
©Just ASK Publications

Connection Collections

Purposes
- To help students make personal meaning
- To connect learning to life beyond the classroom
- To promote creative thinking

Process
- Either the teacher or the students collect objects that represent literal or metaphorical connections to the content under study and place them in a bag, baggie, or box.
- Students identify the connections between the items and the content under study or make predictions about an upcoming study.
- The objects can be pictures or actual artifacts.
- Optional: Prepare five bags of five objects and call it **Facts in Five**.

Examples
- **The Renaissance**

  Joanne Fusare White, Rush-Henrietta School District, Henrietta, New York, used **Connection Collections** with her middle school students in their study of the Renaissance. She prepared bags of artifacts connected in some way to people like Michelangelo, the Medicis, and Leonardo da Vinci. She gave each small group a bag of artifacts. After they examined the artifacts they read short biographies of selected figures and determined which person was represented by the bag they had. When they had established the connection for their first artifact bag, they circulated the artifact bags until they had linked each artifact collection with a Renaissance person.

- **Books in a Bag**

  Linda Denslow, second grade teacher, Rush-Henrietta, New York used **Connection Collections** as a culminating activity for the books and stories she and her students had read during the year. She created a model connections bag for one of the stories, then asked students to choose a favorite story for which to create a bag. She wrote the directions so she could keep the bags to use the next year when she introduced each story.

- **Phoetry (photo poetry)**

  A third grade teacher in Chapel Hill, North Carolina, had her students create connections or artifacts bags as a prewriting assignment at the conclusion of a unit on poetry. They were given small brown bags and were asked to return the next day with a picture and two other items in the bag that related to the picture but were not actually in the picture. The students then wrote their poems about the item and the picture.

The End of the Lesson
ABC to XYZ

Purposes
- To have students process and summarize learning
- To promote various levels of thinking
- To have students think divergently and creatively

ABC -1

Randomly assign a letter of the alphabet to each student. Give them one minute to think of a word that summarizes the lesson or captures the essence of the concept being studied. Do a whip around the room to hear the words.

ABC - 2

Have students draw a magnetic letter from a basket. Each student must share a word that begins with that letter to summarize the day.

ABC - 3

Have students write the alphabet down the left hand margin of their paper and then work in small groups to think of words beginning with each letter of the alphabet related to the topic being studied.

Words -1

Have each student quickly jot down a word that captures the essence of the day's lesson. Have small groups combine their words, adding others as necessary, to make a complete sentence. The only rules are that it must be a complete sentence and they have to use all the words jotted down by individuals.

Words - 2

Give students a key word related to the topic being studied. Have students write it down the left margin of their paper one letter to a line. The task is for them to create an acrostic using each letter.

Words - 3

Write two to four nouns on the board. Students are to brainstorm how what they have studied today is like one of those objects. An object with moving parts adds to the possibilities. For example, "The U.S. Government is like a television because one channel often does not know what the other is doing."

Alternatives to...
Whole Class Question-Answer
...for a More Active & Productive Learning Environment

One of the most frequently used teaching strategies is the **Whole Class Question-Answer** strategy. The steps are as follows:

1. The teacher asks a question.
2. Students who wish to respond raise their hands.
3. The teacher calls on one student.
4. The student attempts to state the correct answer.

Recognize it? It often starts with **"Who can tell me...?"** Since this strategy, also known as a **recitation**, is used so frequently it is important that we ask ourselves just how effective it is. The bad news about this strategy is that the teacher is really the only one in the classroom actively engaged with all the questions and answers; many students may be simply putting in seat time while a few students answer the questions. For those students who are not auditory learners, the recitation may serve as background noise while they visualize who knows what.

It is time to eliminate this instructional practice from our repertoires!

Fortunately, there are many alternatives to **Whole Class Question-Answer**; they include manipulatives and signal cards, the active learning strategies described in this chapter, interactive notebooks, and cooperative learning structures such as jigsaw. If we want to engage learners, there are literally hundreds of ways to do so. **Whole Class Question-Answer** is not on the list.

Assignments

V

TOP TEN QUESTIONS
to ask myself as I design lessons

The focus questions for this chapter are highlighted below.

1. What should **students know and be able to do** as a result of this lesson? How are these objectives related to national, state, and/or district standards?

2. How will **students demonstrate what they know and what they can do**? What will be the **assessment criteria** and what form will it take?

3. How will I find out what students already know (**pre-assessment**), and how will I help them access what they know and have experienced both inside and outside the classroom? How will I help them **build on prior experiences**, **deal with misconceptions**, and re-frame their thinking when appropriate?

4. How will new knowledge, concepts, and skills be introduced? Given the **diversity of my students** and the **task analysis**, what are my **best options for sources and presentation modes**?

5. How will **I facilitate student processing (meaning making)** of new information or processes? What key questions, activities, and assignments (in class or homework) will promote understanding, retention, and transfer?

6. What shall I use as **formative assessments** or **checks for understanding** during the lesson? How can I use the **data** from those assessments to **inform my teaching decisions**?

7. What do I need to do to **scaffold instruction** so that the learning experiences are productive for all students? What are the multiple ways students can access information and then process and demonstrate their learning?

8. How will I **Frame the Learning** so that students know the objectives, the rationale for the objectives and activities, the directions and procedures, as well as the assessment criteria at the beginning of the learning process?

9. How will I build in opportunities for students to make **real-world connections** and to learn and use the **rigorous and complex thinking skills** they need to succeed in the classroom and the world beyond?

10. What adjustments need to be made in the **learning environment** so that we can work and learn efficiently during this study?

Self-Assessment
Assignments

Access your practice around each of these variables to ensure that the assignments you design are a good use of time and energy for you and your students.

Almost Always (A), Sometimes (S), Not Yet (N)

_____ I provide a clear explanation of the task so that students know exactly what they are supposed to do. To double check my clarity, I complete the task following the directions exactly as they are written.

_____ I provide the specific purpose for the task so that students know why they are engaged in the project or assignment.

_____ I explain the relation of the assignment or project to the learning outcomes, standards, key concepts, and essential understandings that provide the focus for our work.

_____ I clearly articulate the relevance of this assignment to life beyond the classroom.

_____ I consider who might be an audience (beyond my inbox) and have students complete the work with that audience in mind.

_____ I know and communicate to students the levels and kinds of thinking required by the task.

_____ I consider how to build student choice into the task and include choice as often as possible.

_____ I am purposeful in the selection and communication of the working conditions for student learning. That is:
- Individual and group work is identified.
- Roles are assigned as appropriate.
- Materials, resources, and equipment are identified and readily available to students.
- Administrative constraints are planned and communicated: time line, order of tasks, how to obtain help and answers to questions, etc.

_____ I task analyze so that I know who has the prerequisite skills and knowledge to successfully complete the task and then build background knowledge and provide scaffolding to those who do not have the needed skills and knowledge.

_____ I communicate exactly how students will know when they have successfully completed the task.

_____ I provide models of and/or practice with new behaviors, processes, and products.

_____ I ensure that students know what to do when they are finished with the assignment or project.

Project Power

Points to Consider

- Identify the **standards** and the **thinking skills** to be included.
- Consider how to appropriately integrate **technology** into the project.
- Distribute and explain **assessment criteria** to students at the beginning of the process.
- Decide whether to let students design projects based on their **interest** within the parameters established by the standards or to plan them yourself to match the standards.
- Decide whether students will work **alone or in groups** and what **choices** they will have about working conditions.
- Establish clear and reasonable **time lines**.
- Do a **task analysis** to identify potential problem areas and decide what to do to deal with these issues.
- Plan frequency of the **progress reports** based on the age, experience, and skill level of students. Design benchmarks where students check in with you or the project leaders. These can include not only what has been accomplished, but past and potential pitfalls, and plans for the next phase of the project.

Potential Final Product Problems

- **Oral Reports**: A series of oral reports can be deadly unless some clear elements of creativity are built into them. Consider having students make videos, podcasts, static displays, web pages, or newscasts.
- **Copy Work**: Rather than having students report on a given topic, have them react to or create something related to the topic. Tasks such as interviews, murals, debates, or presentations to other groups produce more thinking and more enthusiasm for the project.

Helpful Habits

- **Directions**: All multi-step directions are best communicated in writing.
- **Models**: Keep exceptional student projects from year to year to use as models...or videotape presentations to use as models.
- **Audiences**: As often as possible, have the students present or share their projects with audiences beyond the classroom.

See pages 135-140 for the **RAFT** format and **Chapter VII** for lists of potential products, perspectives, and audiences.

Through the Voice of...
Invention Convention

This English and math interdisciplinary project focuses on the problems of the first decade of the 20th century and is designed to provide struggling learners a task that is rigorous and relevant.

Purposes
- To integrate English and math skills into a real world project
- To engage learners in using basic skills in a meaningful project-based assignment

Process
- Students identify a task that is difficult for them or others to do.
- Students choose a project and solution that is realistic and acceptable for a school project.
- Have students brainstorm problems and possible solutions.
- Students may work with a partner or alone.

The Project
- Create a colorful, neat, schematic, **scaled drawing** of the invention on poster board.
- Create a **scale model** of the invention in a box no larger than that which would be used for Xerox paper.
- Write a **description of the invention** and how it works. Note any **math and/or physics** formulas and their applications.
- Write a **description of the benefits** of the invention (i.e., cost saving, time saving).
- Create a computer-generated full color **newspaper/magazine ad** for the invention. You can access graphics and layout designs on the Internet.
- Create and produce a **one minute television or radio commercial** for the invention.
- Write a **newspaper feature article** about the inventor(s) and invention.
- Prepare a **five minute speech** about the invention following the rules for speech making taught in class. An **outline for the speech** must be prepared and handed in prior to delivery of the speech.

Linda Karl and Ray Kropp, Polaris High School, District 218, Oaklawn, IL

Through the Voice of...
Unusual Units of Measurement

Throughout our short unit on the Customary Unit of Measurement (the measurement system used most often in the United States), we will be focusing on the units typically used every day. However, there are many **Unusual Units of Measurement** that are used by a variety of people in their jobs and/or hobbies.

Your research should answer the following questions

1. What is your unit of measure?
2. What does your unit measure (length, area, volume, capacity, weight, frequency, speed, amount, etc.)?
3. What specific item or purpose is it used for?
4. What is its size definition and/or relationship to other units?
5. What profession or person may use your unit of measure?
6. What are other interesting facts or history about your unit of measure?
7. List your resource (where you received your information).

Reporting Your Findings

- You may use any material available in school to report your research. You may use a computer to type your project (as long as you do the computer work). However, your final project should include written answers or diagrams to the questions 1-6 above.

- Materials available: chart paper, white and colored paper, construction paper, overhead materials... ask me and I'll see what I can do.

- Oral Report: Be ready to present on _____. Using the written part of your project, prepare a brief report (1-2 minutes) to the class based on your research on your unusual unit of measure.

Cord
Hogshead
Peck
Carat
Karat
Watt
Bolt
Barrel
Horsepower
Calorie
Rod
Furlong
Hand
Acre
Board Foot
Ream
Hertz
Gross Tonnage
Mach 1
Light Year
Jigger
Gill
Troy Pound
Knot
Quire
Gross
Bit
Nose
Magnum
Lux
Btu
Ampere
Volt
Dram
Rick
Hectare
Byte
Shot
Pica
RPM
Bushel
Mole
Fortnight
Eon
Fathom
Franc
Era
R Factor
Score
Pennyweight
Scruple
Decibel
Farthing
G Force

Chris Regelsberger, West Irondequoit Schools, Rochester, NY

Why We Should Use Multiple Intelligences (MI) Theory

The purposeful use of Multiple Intelligences (MI) Theory in the design of assignments we ask students to complete minimizes the need to differentiate instruction. When students spend a significant part of their day working in a comfortable learning environment, they are better able to work at other times during the day in situations that are less comfortable for them.

The use of Multiple Intelligences Theory causes us to:

- Put an emphasis on learning rather than teaching

- Hold a positive mental model of all students as capable learners

- Use more performance assessment

- Promote an enhanced sense of self-efficacy for learners

- Design lessons that promote relevance and enhance real world connections

If we do not think purposefully and broadly about the decisions we make about how we ask our students to process their learning, the chances are great that we will inadvertently default to our own learning style preferences. That simply will not work for many students. Use the suggestions and examples on the following pages to think carefully about the range of assignments you are asking students to complete.

Multiple Intelligences Surveys

http://www.ldrc.ca/projects/miinventory/mitest.html

http://www.accelerated-learning.net/learning_test.html

http://surfaquarium.com/MI/inventory.htm

Strategies for the Multiple Intelligences

Bodily/Kinesthetic

How can I involve the whole body or use hands-on experience?

- models
- skits or plays
- puzzles
- scavenger hunts
- dances or movement sequences
- labs
- projects
- manipulatives
- board or floor games
- learning centers
- sports/games
- simulations
- fieldtrips
- role playing
- environmental studies

Intrapersonal

How can I evoke personal feelings or memories, or give students choices?

- journals/diaries
- personal reactions to topic
- independent projects
- self evaluation
- visualization
- self discovery
- create own classwork schedule and environment
- relate topic to real life
- reflection periods
- goal setting

Interpersonal

How can I engage students in peer sharing, cooperative learning, or large group simulation?

- cooperative work
- diverse points of view
- interviews
- peer feedback
- teaching others
- outside resources
- plays & simulations
- field trips
- co-curricular activities
- group projects & presentations

Naturalist

How might I bring the outdoors and nature into the learning environment?

- scrapbooks, logs, and journals
- collections
- pattern recognition
- similarities and differences
- cultural artifacts
- drawings, pictures, photographs or specimens
- categorizations and data about objects or species found in the natural world
- outdoor lessons

Strategies for the Multiple Intelligences

Verbal/Linguistic

How can I
use the spoken or
written word?

- letters, poems, stories
- oral discussions
- interviews
- creation of story problems
- lectures
- audiotapes
- storytelling
- brainstorming
- journal writing
- mnemonics
- reading, reading, and more reading

Logical/Mathematical

How can I
bring in numbers, calculations,
logic, classifications, or critical
thinking skills?

- lists of facts
- logic problems
- data analysis
- story problems
- puzzles
- experiments
- hypothesizing
- graphic organizers
- classifications
- categories
- time lines
- outlines

Musical/Rhythmic

How can I
bring in music or
environmental sounds, or set
key points in a rhythmic or
melodic framework?

- musical vocabulary as metaphors
- song titles that explain content
- melodies that capture a mood or concept
- music associated with content or time period
- choral readings
- new lyrics to old song
- mnemonics

Visual/Spatial

How can I
use visual aids,
visualization, color,
art, or metaphor?

- charts, posters, graphs, diagrams
- videotapes
- collages
- use of color and shapes
- demonstration
- drawing
- map making
- visualization
- picture metaphors
- idea sketching
- graphic symbols
- manipulatives
- illustrations

Through the Voice of...
Formula Follies

🎵 **Sing to the tune of "Wheels on the Bus"**

Perimeter/Circumference

For **perimeter** of a figure you ADD THE SIDES,
ADD THE SIDES, ADD THE SIDES
For **perimeter** of a figure you ADD THE SIDES,
All the way around!

Circumference of a circle is π x d,
π x d, π x d,
Circumference of a circle is π x d,
π is 3.14!

Area

Area of a rectangle is LENGTH x WIDTH,
LENGTH x WIDTH, LENGTH x WIDTH,
Area of a rectangle is LENGTH x WIDTH,
only for this shape!

Area of a triangle is 1/2 bh,
1/2 bh, 1/2 bh,
Area of a triangle is 1/2 bh,
that's 1/2 times base times height!

Area of a circle is πr^2, πr^2, πr^2,
Area of a circle is πr^2, that's π x r x r!

Volume

The **volume** of a rectangle is lwh, lwh, lwh,
The **volume** of a rectangle is lwh, that's
length times width times height!

Sue Quinn & Joanne Fusare-White, Roth Middle School, Rush-Henrietta Schools, Henrietta, NY

Through the Voice of...
MI Book Reports

After you have read your novel, review this list of projects and select one. Fill out and return the attached contract to me no later than February 22. If none of the projects suit you, feel free to design one of your own. Don't forget to choose a project that showcases your strengths.

Kinesthetic

1. Make a life-sized paper-stuffed person found in your novel.
2. Draw a scale model of something from the novel you read.
3. Build a relief map of the setting of the story.
4. Construct a building from your novel.
5. Act out a scene from the novel you read.
6. Choreograph a dance that shows the theme, the development of a character, or a scene from the book you read.
7. Design and make a quilt/wall hanging that depicts your novel.

Verbal/Linguistic

1. Choose a major character from the book. Focus in on a crucial time in the book and create a diary that the character would have written.
2. Put together a cast for the film version of the book. Imagine the director-producer wants a casting director to make recommendations. Decide who would be the actors and actresses. Include photos and descriptions of the "stars" and tell why each is perfect for the part.
3. Write a collection of poems that show different aspects of the novel: the characters, the setting, the plot, the climax, the theme...
4. Write a newspaper article about an important event from your book.
5. Write the next chapter in the novel.

Logical/Sequential

1. Choose an automobile from the story you read. Find out as much as you can about the car, especially how the engine works.
2. Create a code that characters in the story could use to communicate.
3. Develop a logic puzzle or brain teaser based on something that happened in the book.
4. Set up a "what if" experiment to see what would happen if "this" didn't happen.
5. Make up a strategy game based on the book you read.
6. Create a flowchart/concept map that shows the major players.
7. Write equations that describe the characters in the story.

Through the Voice of...
MI Book Reports

Intrapersonal

1. Relate a character's development to your own life history. This can be done through writing, drawing or other means.
2. Relate a hobby or interest that you might have to the novel you read.
3. Create a project that "shows" your feelings about the book.

Rhythmic

1. Write a rap or a song about your book.
2. Create a discography that represents the book: the setting, the characters, the conflict, the plot, the climax, the theme.
3. What musical instruments would the characters play? What type of music would they listen to?
4. *The Outsiders*: watch the movie. If it were your job to change it to a musical, where in the story would singing be appropriate? Who would sing and what would the song be about? (*West Side Story*)

Visual

1. Think about the book you read. Find a comfortable place and doodle. Reflect on your doodles and see what story they tell about the novel you read. Report on your findings with a mini-exhibition.
2. Use a camera or camcorder to create a collage of the book.
3. Which geometric figures describe the characters in the book? Create something visual to represent these ideas.
4. What colors do the characters represent? Create an exhibition which shows the colors of the characters.

Interpersonal

1. Find a guest speaker to talk to the class about a topic addressed in the book you read.
2. Plan a party for a character in the novel. You need invitations, decorations, food, music, etc.
3. Mediate a problem between two characters in the book. What would your advice be?
4. Introduce one of your friends to one of the characters in the book. With which characters would your friends be comfortable? Why?

Wendy Govoni, Holderness Central School, Holderness, NH

Integrating Technology

WebQuests

Bernie Dodge, San Diego State University, created a model for web-based learning experiences. Access information and hundreds of examples of WebQuests at www.webquest.org. There are almost 2,500 WebQuests published and ready for use with K-12 students. One of the purposes of these web-based learning experiences is to maximize the time students spend using the information rather than spending time looking for the information. Additionally, the site includes templates and guidelines for teacher and student-made WebQuests.

CyberGuides

This amazing collection of lesson plans available at http://www.sdcoe.k12.ca.us/score/cyberguide.html includes ready-to-use standards-based lessons on virtually every piece of literature being studied in U.S. schools today. For example, there are CyberGuides for *Stellaluna*, *Two Bad Ants*, *Blue Willow*, *The Giver*, *Canterbury Tales*, *The Odyssey*, *Hamlet*, and hundreds more. There are also CyberGuides for 20 foreign language texts.

In the News

Kent Willmann, high school social studies teacher, St. Vrain Valley School District, Longmont, Colorado, has the three computers in his classroom on three different news sources such as CNN International, BBC, Reuters, or Aljazerra. Each day three students are assigned to read the current news about the region of the world they area currently studying. These web-based learning experiences provide up-to-the-minute relevance for the area being studied and provide students multiple perspectives on world events.

Podcasts

- Teachers and students all over the world are creating audio recordings and posting them online so that they can be listened to on computers or downloaded onto mobile devices like iPods or MP3 players. This allows teachers and students to create information for their own use as well as the use and enjoyment of others. In addition to creating original podcasts, thousands of podcasts are available at sites such as www.epnweb.org. Always review the podcasts before directing students to use them.
- If podcasts are a new instructional approach for you, listen to Kathy Schrock's podcasts at nausetschools.org/podcasts.htm for reassurance and information. The only equipment you need is a computer, access to the Internet, and an inexpensive microphone. Give students the assignment of creating podcasts and learn from them.

Integrating Technology

Make Music

- An orchestra teacher at Hammond Middle School, Alexandria City Public Schools, Virginia, uses an iPod to record individual students playing a particular piece of music. The audio files are then downloaded to a computer.
- The music department has software that will correctly play a piece of music.
- The student then listens to their rendition and the software version to pick up pointers and corrections.
- Since these are MP3 files, the student can then load these files onto their own iPod and listen to them whenever they want to do so.

Jeff VanDrimmelen, UNC Chapel Hill, in another posting on EduTechie.com recommends recording class presentations, creating and having students create instructional videos, and using class blogs.

Teacher and Student-Made Videos

- Record class presentations, both the lectures and demonstrations you make, as well as student presentations. Provide copies of these recordings to absent or struggling students for study at home or in the school media center.
- Have students create video projects and then post them online to send to family and friends or have them create videos for specific audiences like students in a younger grade or for senior citizens.
- Create instructional videos. Be constantly on the look-out for sites and events you can record and then use in the classroom. While students might not be able to go to the site, you can bring it to them.

Class Blogs

- Create a class blog and have your students record their reactions to literary or other assignments and post them on the blog. Use the blog to communicate with students and to have them communicate with you and each other. See a 4th grade example at http://marykreul.teacherhosting.com/blog/

Role
Audience
Form
Time*

The **RAFT** technique, which is explained in many journals and attributed to various sources, requires students to create scenarios about the content being studied. **RAFT** allows students to consider the information from a variety of perspectives and to use a wide range of formats to present information to limitless audiences. This brain-compatible approach causes students to rethink, rewrite, and discuss an event or concept in another place or time or through the eyes or voice of the famous or familiar. The lists of potential products and perspectives listed on pages 183 through 198 provide a multitude of possibilities.

You, as a fourth grade teacher, are to write test questions on the _____. Write one question for each paragraph, using either true-false, multiple-choice, fill-in-the-blank, or matching format. Provide the answers and sign your name. You will exchange questions with Mr. Oliver's class tomorrow.

You are a political cartoonist for the Washington Post newspaper. Design two cartoons that illustrate a "hot" issue related to our unit on Immigration. Prepare one to represent the issue in the early 1900s and one from a current perspective. Include captions and your signature as the artist.

Pretend you are a visitor from Ukraine. Write a three to five paragraph letter to your family back home describing how Chicago is like Kiev.

Assume that one of your classmates has been absent for all of our study of the circulatory system. Use the list of potential products to design a specific product that will describe in detail how the system works. Remember this student missed the entire unit! Spend some time thinking about what are the most important things to include.

*Access RAFT template on the CD-ROM

*The T can also represent the topic.

Through the Voice of...

Role
Audience
Form
Time/Topic

R ‐ You are a volunteer for the Bull Moose (Progressive) Party

A ‐ You are trying to attract Republicans to join the party

F ‐ Produce a campaign poster

T ‐ 1912 - Election Year

Bull Moose	President	Democratic
Teddy Roosevelt	William H. Taft	Woodrow Wilson

Joyce Nagle, West Irondeqoit Central School District, Rochester, NY

Through the Voice of...

TEEN HEALTH HABITS

Directions:

Imagine that you are a newspaper journalist for the **Rochester Democrat & Chronicle** and you have an assignment to do an article about teen health habits for the "**flipside**" column that appears in every Monday's paper. In order to do this, you need some research so...

Conduct a survey in which you will:

a. **Interview** 6 students not in this class.

b. Choose the students from **two different age groups**:

   10-12, 13-15, 16-18.

c. **Ask** the students privately, at a time when they can think.

d. You can ask the students and fill in their answers or you can have them **fill in the answers** for themselves.

e. After completing your survey, **show the main similarities and differences** by filling in the graphic organizer (Venn diagram) or making a spreadsheet on the computer.

f. Using the answers from your survey, **write an article** for "flipside" about teen health habits and what influences the health of teens in the '90s.

Judy White, Roth Middle School, Rush-Henrietta Schools, Henrietta, NY

Through the Voice of...
Ready! Set! RAFTs Away!

> Directions: Choose your **RAFT** and head out on an exciting adventure! You are invited to become a character from *The Hundred Dresses*.

RAFT 1:

You are **Wanda Petronski**. Write a **persuasive letter** to **Maddie** to convince her that she made the right decision when she vowed never again to stand by and say nothing when someone was being made fun of. You must convince her with three strong points.

RAFT 2:

You are **Wanda Petronski**. Write a **persuasive letter** to **Maddie and/or Peggy** to convince them that it is important to treat others with kindness and respect. You must convince them, with three strong points, to live by "The Golden Rule" and treat others the way you want to be treated.

RAFT 3:

You are **Maddie or Peggy**. Write a **letter to Wanda** asking for her forgiveness and ask her to come back to school. You must convince her that things will be different if she returns. You must **persuade** her to return using at least three good reasons.

RAFT 4:

You are **Maddie**. You have finally gathered the courage to write a **persuasive letter to Peggy** with the hope of convincing her to treat others with respect and kindness. You hope to show her that she will be a better person if she changes her ways. Persuade her to change her ways!

RAFT 5:

Create your own scenario. Take on **any role** you choose and identify your **audience**. The form must be a persuasive letter. You can base the situation on a classroom from today or fifty years ago like Room 13.

Michelle Flood, West Irondequoit Central School District, Rochester, NY

You are the proud owner of a sporting goods company that specializes in the manufacturing of **tennis rackets, basketballs, bicycles, and baseballs.** Your business is so successful that you also export goods to **France, Great Britain, Japan, and Russia.** Next month you are offering a special promotion of your goods. You want to make sure your prices are consistent in each of the countries where you do business. Use the **January 2008 Foreign Exchange Rates** to determine the prices for your goods.

Foreign Exchange Rates

(Value of 1 U.S. dollar January 2008)

Country	Value
France	.70 euros
Great Britain	.50 pounds
Russia	24.73 rubles
Japan	113.35 yen

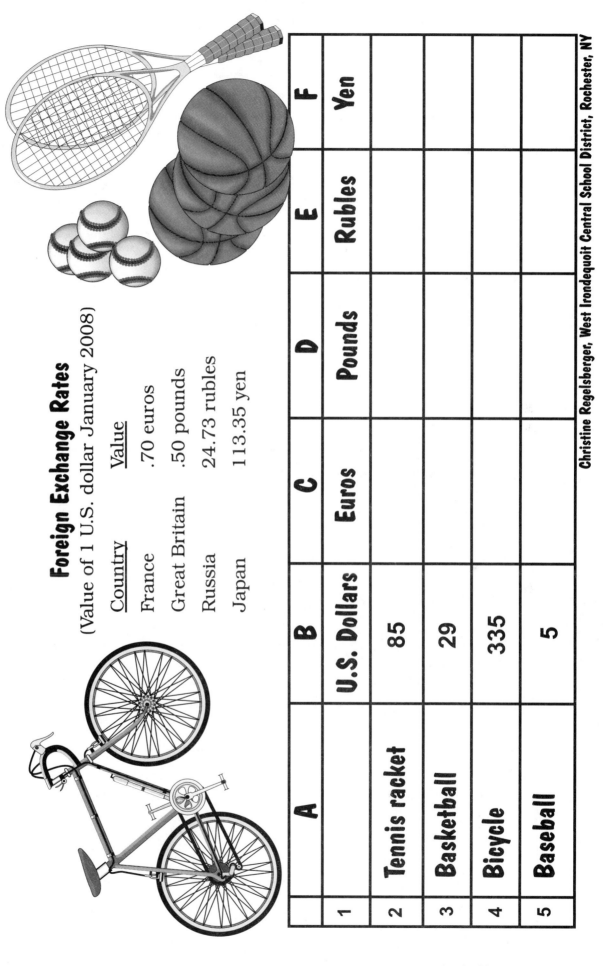

	A	B	C	D	E	F
1		U.S. Dollars	Euros	Pounds	Rubles	Yen
2	Tennis racket	85				
3	Basketball	29				
4	Bicycle	335				
5	Baseball	5				

Let's Go RAFTing!*

See Chapter VII for an extensive list of roles/perspectives students can assume, audiences for whom they can design their products, and products/forms they can create to process and demonstrate their learning. The RAFT format provides a straight-forward way to build in relevance, and with careful planning, rigor.

Role _____

Audience _____

Form (product) _____

Time _____

Role _____

Audience _____

Form (product) _____

Time _____

Role _____

Audience _____

Form (product) _____

Time _____

* **Access RAFT template on CD-ROM.**

Homework

homework (*n*): 1. carefully planned and meaningful work completed by students outside of the class period where it is assigned. 2. outside of class work for which students have prerequisite skills and are able to complete independently.

Categories of Homework Assignments

Practice Homework

helps students master skills and reinforce in-class learning; can be boring and repetitive. Unless we differentiate homework assignments, it is guaranteed that some students are wasting time practicing something they have already mastered and that some are trying to practice something they have not yet learned. Practice homework should be given only when it is clear that the learner can work with the skill independently. Avoid repetitiveness of practice homework by giving students the five most difficult problems to do. If they can successfully complete those, they do not need to do the easier problems. Better yet, let students identify the practice exercises they need to do; both teacher and student track the effectiveness of that practice and adjust as necessary.

Extension Homework

helps students take what they learn and connect it with real life. This type of homework often gives students the option to choose their method of gathering data, processing learning, and demonstrating learning.

Preparation Homework

prepares students for the upcoming lesson or unit. Reading a chapter on material to be covered in class is not good preparation homework. Reading research clearly indicates that comprehension is low if the students have no prior experiences with and/or discussions about the topic. Reading chapters is best assigned following classwork.

Creative Homework

helps students integrate multiple concepts (possibly from more than one curricular area); often presented in the form of long term projects. Students should be asked to react to rather than report on what they are learning. This promotes development of critical thinking and problem solving skills.

This classification system (Lee & Pruitt, 1979) makes it clear that most of the homework we assign falls in the practice and preparation categories. Common sense and our own experiences as learners tell us that extension and creative homework assignments are much more likely to engage students in the learning and minimize the ever present problems of incomplete or copied homework.

Examples of Each Category
Homework*

Practice
- most questions at the end of the chapter
- vocabulary drill
- memorization of (hopefully important) facts
- calculations

Extension
- RAFT assignments (pages 135-140)
- higher levels of Bloom's Taxonomy (pages 231-235)
- Williams' Taxonomy assignments (pages 236-238)
- daily journal writing from thought provoking stems
- interactive notebooks (page 228)
- locate real world situations where the knowledge and skills students are learning are used.

Preparation
- review of past related topics
- pre-tests
- surveys
- read the chapter prior to any discussion

Creative
- projects...especially involving student choice and interdisciplinary links
- performance assessment tasks

Practice/Creative Mix
- Have students complete a limited number of questions/problems.
- Then have them create several problems or questions using the same content or skills.

*Access a homework template on the CD-ROM

IN CASE OF STUDENT/TEACHER AGGRAVATION, CHECK FOR:

- Unplanned or irrelevant homework. Perhaps there is a homework policy and you feel compelled to assign something even when it isn't appropriate.
- Assignments given at the very end of class with no time for clarifying purposes or explanations of confusing directions.
- Assignments that seem like busy work and aren't moving students closer to competency with the standard on which they are working. They may already know how to do what they are being asked to do or this type of activity hasn't been productive in the past.
- Assignments which call for knowledge and skills not currently in the students' repertoire and there is little chance for success.

Meaningful & Productive Homework

- Include **choice** and **variety** in homework assignments.
- Review the assignment before giving it to students. Identify major concepts and important vocabulary. **Anticipate difficulties** and **prepare students** to deal with them.
- Design assignments that should yield a **success rate** of at least **80-90%**. If students have not mastered the basic concepts, do not give them an assignment that will send them home to work incorrectly.
- When students have difficulty with an assignment, **teaching has to take place** before they are asked to do more of the same work.
- Present assignment in such a way that there is time to **clarify instructions**.
- Give the assignment **orally** and in **writing**. Use a **consistent**, easily seen **location** to **post** assignments.
- Have students keep a **homework log** containing each assignment's directions, connection to the learning objective, completion time, or the reason why it wasn't completed.
- Have students keep a **learning log** containing a list of assignments, reflections on the learning process, and content. If the assignment is incomplete, have them enter what they tried and where the process broke down. Log entries may be accepted as an alternative to the regular assignment as a good faith effort to learn through trial and error.
- **Avoid assignments such as**:
  - *"Read Chapter 3"* (students may read the chapter without purpose or comprehension) and *"Read Chapter 3 and answer the questions at the end of the chapter"* (students may complete the assignment without comprehending a word).
  - Instead use "**Read Chapter 3 and identify the three most significant factors related to _____. Be prepared to discuss these factors and your rationale for selecting them as the most significant with your discussion groups at the beginning of class tomorrow.**" This communicates what success looks like and gives a purpose to the work outside of class.
- Give assignments for explicit instructional purposes, **not for punishment**. Do not excuse students from homework for good behavior.
- Plan homework assignments at least a week in advance and **give students a schedule for the week** so they can **allocate** their available **work time**.

Homework

Minimize the Grading of Homework

At the beginning of the instructional period, have the students work in pairs or groups to **reach consensus on practice homework**. When students cannot agree, they should circle any points of confusion or disagreement. You circulate and intervene with the small groups as necessary. Only mass confusion is dealt with in large groups. When papers are collected, they are all correct. The students have done the work and you have no papers to correct!

There is no need to "test" students on facts they have to memorize. Instead, have the students **draw the objects or some graphic representation of the facts** to be memorized as a homework assignment. Have the students exchange drawings and label those of a classmate. Students check each other's work. This practice can continue until the tidbits are memorized and can be used later for cumulative review. If drawing won't work, just have the students **create mini-tests or flash cards** to teach and test each other. There are no papers to grade!

When students **write a summary statement** of their thinking or of their readings as a homework assignment, have two students meet to **share their summaries** and to combine their thinking into one paper. **The consensus paper is collected.** The number of papers to be collected is cut in half!

When teaching a new operation in math, a new sentence structure, or a new science concept, have students **make up one to five problems that illustrate the new information as homework**. When they arrive in class, have them exchange problems or you can collect them at the door and redistribute them randomly. They work the problems they have received and the problems are returned to the creators for checking and correction. Once again, no papers for you to grade!

Through the Voice of...
2nd Grade Homework

The purpose of homework is to enhance learning through daily practice at home. Please encourage your child to develop good study habits by providing a quiet place to work and always taking time to do his/her best. Please check your child's work and sign your acceptance.

Monday

Language Arts:	Practice alphabetical order by putting this week's spelling words in your book in alphabetical order.
Math:	Do practice paper. Next, on the back of the worksheet, write a problem about the score of a game between two teams.
Reading:	Continue to read your mystery. When you finish one book, begin a new mystery. List the main characters and the main problem.

Tuesday

Language Arts:	Practice your spelling words by practicing writing good cursive with any ten words from the list.
Math:	Do practice paper, then write a problem on the back about the score between two soccer teams who scored a combined total of 7 goals.
Reading:	Before you continue your mystery, write a paragraph about what you think will happen next. Use examples from the book to tell why you predict what you do.

Wednesday

Language Arts:	Choose 5 spelling words to which you could add suffixes. Add a suffix to each word.
Math:	Do practice paper and then write a problem involving the use of money.
Reading:	Continue to read your mystery. Then choose 4 new words you have learned in this book and use each in a sentence.

Thursday

Language Arts:	Practice your spelling words by writing any 10 of them in cursive 2 times.
Math:	Do practice paper. Solve this problem on the back of your worksheet. First, you have to make up the data for the problem. Pete went to the store with $8.00. He bought two new books for school. How much money did he spend? Solve.
Reading:	Read your new chapter book for 20 minutes. Write a paragraph to tell how they are trying to solve the mystery.

Friday

Enjoy your weekend!

Pat Donegan, West Irondequoit Central School District, Rochester, NY

©Just ASK Publications

Through the Voice of...
4th Grade Reading Homework

Your monthly reading homework includes reading **two books and completing a project on each**.

Read a book of your choice for at least 30 minutes each day as time permits with other family activities. You may read more one day and less another. Choose books from a variety of different genres. Keep a record of your reading in your homework journal and hand it in each week on your assigned day.

You are responsible for completing two of the projects from the list of choices in your homework journal by the end of each month. New choices will be added each month. You may only use a choice once. This means that when you complete a book, you will choose one of the activities from the list, do the project, and hand it in. You will need to plan your time throughout the month so that you will be sure to complete the two required books and projects. One plan would be to do your reading during the week, and work on your projects on those cold, gray, winter days on the weekend. You will need to work out the plan that is best for you. (See next page for list of choices.)

If you have an idea for a project that is not on the list, let me know and we will discuss it.

If you would rather write responses to your reading in your journal as you have in the past, rather than do the projects, you may continue to do so.

Please cut off, sign, and return.

- -

I have read the homework assignment and discussed a plan for successful completion of the homework with my child.

Parent signature _____

Student signature _____

Jean Blakley and Karen Kessler, Honeoye Falls-Lima School District, NY

Through the Voice of...
4th Grade Reading Homework

Project Choices

- Imagine that you had an opportunity to **interview the author** of your book shortly after it was published. What questions would you ask? (Keep in mind that good interview questions encourage the person to "open up" and talk. Try not to ask questions that would only get one-word answers.) Write at least five good questions. After you have written the questions, write what you think the author might answer.

- **Choose the music** for an existing song or **write a song** using words that show the traits of one of the characters in your book. Record your song on a tape and include a song sheet with the words to the song. You can use a tape and tape recorder from school if you need it.

- A television spin-off is a new television show based on another show. One of the lesser characters from the original show stars in the new show. Pretend that your book is the original show and you have been asked to **write a spin-off series**. Think about the following when you write your ideas:
  - What is the name of the new show?
  - Which character will star in the show?
  - What new characters will be introduced?
  - What will the story of the first show in the series be about?

- **Make a poster** about the main character in your book. Put yourself in the character's place and decide what characteristics, likes and dislikes are important to show on the poster. You may choose to show these things in any creative way you choose. Be sure that when you are finished, someone who has never read the book will have an understanding of your character by looking at the poster.

- **Write a new ending** for the book you have read. In three different paragraphs, include these three things:
  - A brief description of what the book is about
  - Why you would like the ending to be different
  - How you would have written the ending

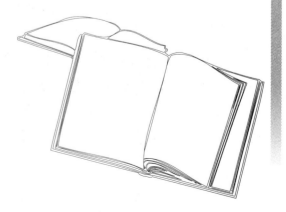

Jean Blakley and Karen Kessler, Honeoye Falls-Lima School District, NY

Through the Voice of...
Yup, It's Chemistry!

Organize these substances,
Create a data table,
Make a system,
Identify these unknowns,
Categorize these elements,
Classify this matter.

1. Be creative and find any **grouping of items** in your surroundings. That's right, look at your house, in your drawer, wallet, purse, or backpack. Ex.: shoes, desk drawer stuff.

2. **Lay the objects** out in front of you or draw pictures or take photographs to represent the various objects. You want to have the objects represented visually so that you can move them around and arrange and rearrange them.

3. **Arrange these objects both horizontally and vertically** (both across and up and down). This is similar to "the guys" you arranged in class, and remember how you drew in the secret agent.

4. There should be **at least two trends** or other criteria happening horizontally.
   Ex.: the "guys" bodies got thicker as you went across
         the "guys" had more hair as you went across
         the "guys" mouths went from a frown to a smile as you went across

5. There should be **at least two trends** or other criteria happening vertically.
   Ex.: the "guys" had the same body design in their column
         the "guys" arms increased by one arm as you went down the column

6. When you have arranged the objects, get poster board and glue and put either the objects or pictures of the **objects on the poster board in the order you decide**.

7. On the **back of the poster board, write a description of the order you chose** and share the reasoning behind your organization. Shhh...don't tell anyone the system you chose. See if they can determine the order on their own.

8. This project is worth **250 points** and **you have COMPLETE CONTROL**!

Laura Zboril & Lynn Hiller, New Trier High School, Winnetka, IL

The Assessment Continuum

VI

TOP TEN QUESTIONS
to ask myself as I design lessons

The focus questions for this chapter are highlighted below.

1. What should **students know and be able to do** as a result of this lesson? How are these objectives related to national, state, and/or district standards?

2. How will **students demonstrate what they know and what they can do**? What will be the **assessment criteria** and what form will it take?

3. How will I find out what students already know (**pre-assessment**), and how will I help them access what they know and have experienced both inside and outside the classroom? How will I help them **build on prior experiences, deal with misconceptions**, and re-frame their thinking when appropriate?

4. How will new knowledge, concepts, and skills be introduced? Given the **diversity of my students** and the **task analysis**, what are my **best options for sources and presentation modes**?

5. How will **I facilitate student processing (meaning making)** of new information or processes? What key questions, activities, and assignments (in class or homework) will promote understanding, retention, and transfer?

6. What shall I use as **formative assessments** or **checks for understanding** during the lesson? How can I use the **data** from those assessments to **inform my teaching decisions**?

7. What do I need to do to **scaffold instruction** so that the learning experiences are productive for all students? What are the multiple ways students can access information and then process and demonstrate their learning?

8. How will I **Frame the Learning** so that students know the objectives, the rationale for the objectives and activities, the directions and procedures, as well as the assessment criteria at the beginning of the learning process?

9. How will I build in opportunities for students to make **real-world connections** and to learn and use the **rigorous and complex thinking skills** they need to succeed in the classroom and the world beyond?

10. What adjustments need to be made in the **learning environment** so that we can work and learn efficiently during this study?

Self-Assessment
Classroom Assessment

Consider whether or not these statements represent your own professional practice.
A (Almost Always), S (Sometimes), N (Not Yet)

_____ I design summative assessments prior to planning the learning experiences for my students.

_____ I use pre-assessments to determine the knowledge, skillfulness, and depth of understanding of the class and individuals about upcoming areas of study and use that data to plan lessons and units.

_____ I task analyze so that I know the component skills and knowledge as well as the level of thinking required by each of the learning experiences and assessments I design/select for my students.

_____ I communicate precise assessment criteria and provide exemplars prior to students beginning the task.

_____ I use classwork and homework as well as student questions and answers in class discussions as formative assessment data and make instructional decisions based on that data.

_____ I use the patterns and trends in the body of assessment data I gather to inform my practice and to evaluate the effectiveness of the instructional decisions I made.

_____ I provide growth-producing feedback to students so that they know how their work is matched to the intended outcome and they know the next steps they need to take.

_____ I collaborate with other teachers to develop, use, and analyze common assessments so that we can identify best instructional practices and areas of our instructional programs that need modification.

_____ I use assessment tools and items that are matched not only to the standards but to the amount of time and emphasis placed on the material during instruction.

_____ I select assessment tools from a wide range of options including, but not limited to, paper and pencil assessments.

From Formative to Summative
An Assessment Continuum

The repertoire of assessment strategies can be arranged on a continuum as shown below. It begins with pre-assessment done prior to the learning experience through informal and formal formative assessments during the learning. It ends with summative assessments designed to allow students to demonstrate what they know and what they can do with the big ideas, key concepts, and essential understandings of the learning. In a standards-based classroom, even summative assessments become formative in nature because they inform us as to which learners need more work with what concepts and processes.

Pre-assessments: Page 153

Checks for Understanding: Pages 154-156

Observations/Anecdotal Records

Student Questions/Comments (In-Class and in Journals): Pages 14 and 228

Teacher Questions and Prompts (In-Class): Pages 157-158

Assignments (including Homework): Pages 141-148

Peer Assessment: Pages 162-163

Self-Assessment: Pages 162-163

Quizzes: Pages 159-161, 165-167

Tests: Pages 159-161, 165-167

Performance Tasks (Short and Long Term): Pages 168-180

Pre-Assessment

The good news is that many of the strategies we use to engage learners in active learning can be used as pre-assessment strategies. Even better news is that we do not have to do two exercises. We just need to pay attention to the assessment data that surfaces while we are accessing prior knowledge and surfacing misconceptions and naive understandings.

It is wise to do the pre-assessment a week or two before the beginning of a unit of study. That way there is time to locate the resources we need and to adjust the learning experiences we have planned for the unit.

Active Learning Strategies as Pre-Assessment Strategies

- Anticipation Reaction Guides   Page   110
- Corners (Kagan, 1994)   Page   90
- Frame of Reference   Page   91
- Graffiti   Page   92
- Journal Entries*   Page   14
- Line-Ups (Kagan, 1994)   Pages 101-102
- Signal Cards   Page   154
- Slates and White Boards   Page   156
- Sort Cards   Page   94
- Stir the Class   Page   106
- Three Column Charts   Page   113

* Use the essential questions for the upcoming unit as the prompts for journal writing.

Additional Sources of Pre-Assessment Data

Anecdotal Records provide a rich source of assessment data. Other ways to gather pre-assessment data include having students draw their understanding of, or create a graphic organizer about, the concept before the learning experience begins. If you have students complete another drawing or graphic organizer at the conclusion of the learning experience, they will have a clear representation of their learning. More formal ways of gathering and assessing student knowledge and skill prior to learning include pretests, standardized test information, portfolio reviews, and interviews.

Hands on Checking for Understanding

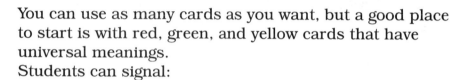

Signal Cards

Provide students with cards to signal understanding of concepts, or directions, or a sense of "I'm lost!", and you send the message that it is all right not to understand everything the first time around.

You can use as many cards as you want, but a good place to start is with red, green, and yellow cards that have universal meanings.
Students can signal:

- "Stop, I'm lost!" or "Slow down, I'm getting confused" or "Full steam ahead!"
- negative, positive, or zero
- complete, run-on, or fragments of sentences
- saturated, semi-saturated, or unsaturated

Whatever meanings you assign the cards, the possibilities are endless!

Gerry Zeltman, teacher of English at Rush-Henrietta High School in Henrietta, New York reports that his senior students are far more willing to admit confusion and ask questions when they have a set of cards with which to signal. Several elementary teachers suggest that library card pockets taped to the student's desk work well for keeping track of the cards. Pam Lecy, of Appleton Area School District in Wisconsin, reports that she uses narrow cards held together in a fan-like fashion with a brad, numbered 1 through 5. Students signal their responses to questions beamed to the entire class in response to stems such as "**If you think it is a mammal, signal 1.**" "**If you think it is a reptile, signal 2.**" "**If you are not sure, signal 3.**" Any meaning can be assigned to the cards.

Hands on Checking for Understanding

Manipulatives

Manipulatives provide **concrete props for abstract concepts** and objects for **kinesthetic learners** to handle. Elementary math teachers are masters at using math manipulatives and the usefulness of such tools is becoming more known across the profession. Using **index cards**, **strips of paper**, **or cut up transparencies** with words, phrases, events, steps in formulas, translations, etc. printed on them offer students the opportunity to demonstrate understanding of sequences and other relationships in a tactile way. Small globes, **miniature models**, straws, and other objects that can be moved and arranged are also useful in helping students process their learning and demonstrate their understanding.

Sort/Category Cards

A pack of index cards can work miracles in helping you and your students know who knows what! Paper cut to 3"x5" size can do the trick but these are much more likely to be torn or wrinkled beyond use in a very short time. Possible uses include:

- vocabulary terms and definition matching
- sequencing historical events or scientific processes
- categorizing
- "I know," "I sort of know," and "I haven't a clue" piles

In addition to their usefulness as a way to check for understanding, once the cards are made, they can be used in dozens of ways such as for **Inside-Outside Circles** or **I've Got the Question, Who Has the Answer**, as entries in class graphic organizers, and for student created games.

Checking for Understanding with Slates

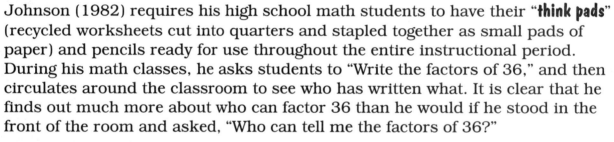

Students are provided with **slates, white boards, or pads of recycled handouts** cut into fourths on which to record their thinking during a lesson and given the appropriate writing tool.

At appropriate times students can "show" their thinking by holding up their slates for teacher review or the teacher can circulate around the room to check to see who understands or can use what information.

Johnson (1982) requires his high school math students to have their "**think pads**" (recycled worksheets cut into quarters and stapled together as small pads of paper) and pencils ready for use throughout the entire instructional period. During his math classes, he asks students to "Write the factors of 36," and then circulates around the classroom to see who has written what. It is clear that he finds out much more about who can factor 36 than he would if he stood in the front of the room and asked, "Who can tell me the factors of 36?"

This kind of checking can be done frequently throughout the explanation of any multi-step process. Asking for student responses after almost each teacher statement provides an opportunity to identify where and with whom the learning breaks down. While most often used in elementary classrooms, teachers of physics are also strong advocates for this active learning tool.

Checking for understanding in this way, before students do homework or other independent practice, helps ensure that the students are not practicing errors or experiencing frustration during their independent work.

As a variation, you can engage students in helping with the checking process by assigning the same problem to all students. As a student finishes, she signals for the teacher to check her work. If it is correct, this student and others who follow can join the teacher in checking the work of others. This shortens the process and gives all students a chance to successfully complete the practice problem before moving on to the next step.

Questioning

We ask questions to check for understanding...or at least knowledge about the topic, concept, or information under study. It is, however, considerably more complicated than that. While we want to be masters at checking for understanding, the results of carefully planned questions actually provide direction to the flow of learning and promote a productive classroom learning environment, which actually facilitates comprehension, transfer, and retention. The list below provides an extensive array of purposes of questions. Each student response tells us more about the experiences they bring to the learning and the level or type of thinking they are using. Until we have a mental script in our heads, we need to write out the questions which will facilitate the learning process.

We Use Questions at the Beginning of Learning Experiences:

- To initiate a discussion
- To pique student curiosity
- To focus students on a new concept or a different aspect of a concept
- To assess prior knowledge and experience
- To consolidate previous learning
- To surface misconceptions and naive understandings

We Use Questions During and Following Learning Experiences:

- To break down complex tasks and issues
- To promote transfer and retention
- To control shifts in discussions
- To keep discussions on track
- To invite student questions
- To elicit student opinions
- To promote student interaction
- To facilitate flexible thinking
- To challenge the obvious
- To check for understanding
- To help students confront their misconceptions and re-frame their thinking
- To focus on process
- To promote student evaluation of credibility of sources and strength of evidence
- To cause students to consider alternative viewpoints
- To help students make connections

Question Stems
to Promote Rigorous Thinking

When we ask students to recall information we are not checking for understanding. In order to have students analyze, apply, integrate, and evaluate new learning we have to have a strong repertoire of questions ready for use. The following stems work in any content area and at all grade levels.

- What do you need to do next?
- Based on what you know, what can you predict about ...?
- Does what ... said make you think differently about ...?
- Tell me how you did that?
- How does ... tie in with what we have learned before?
- Suppose ... what then?
- How does this match what you thought you knew?
- What might happen if ...?
- When have you done something like this before?
- What might ... think about this?
- How would you feel if...?
- How did you come to that conclusion?
- How about...?
- What if ...?
- What do you think causes ...?
- Yes, that's right, but how did you know it was right?
- When is another time you need to...?
- What do you think the problem is?
- Can you think of another way we could do this?
- Why is this one better than that one?
- How can you find out?
- How is ... different (like) ...?
- What have you heard about..?
- Can you tell me more?
- What else do you see?
- How does that compare with...?
- What do we know so far?

Variations on a Theme
Classroom Assessment

Designer Assessment

Create a bank of assessment questions or items. This assessment, which includes items totaling two to four hundred points, can be organized around levels of thinking or subsets of the topic being studied. Students choose questions to equal 100 points. Students could have complete free choice as to what to answer or you could designate a certain number of points from each section. Provide space in the margin so that students can keep track of the total points they have attempted to earn. This sort of assessment encourages students to build test taking skills, such as reading through the entire assessment before beginning, deciding what they know, and don't know, and planning use of time.

Front Page News

Put questions that are to be answered by all students on the first page. These questions would represent the most important information that all students need to know at the end of the unit of study. Put the next levels of questions on the following pages and then you and/or students decide which are to be answered. You may stipulate that in order to demonstrate competency students have to correctly answer all the questions on the first page, and failure to do so will result in re-teaching, restudy, and retesting on those particular points. If students are unsuccessful with the essential knowledge or understandings the teacher can see immediately not only what one student needs more instruction around but also can easily identify patterns and trends.

Differentiating the Big One

Design a comprehensive paper and pencil assessment and then circle or otherwise indicate which questions each student is to answer. For example, designate a certain copy of the test for Susan, then circle question numbers to indicate which questions Susan is to answer. You may want to offer Susan the option of trying other questions after she has attempted the teacher selected questions. Grading is done in terms of how Susan did with the questions she was supposed to complete rather than with the entire assessment. The student is set up for success and is simultaneously given the opportunity to stretch by trying additional questions. This method provides scaffolding and allows appropriate assessment of students working at different achievement levels without adding a huge amount of preparation time for the teacher.

Making Assessment a Learning Experience
Formative Assessment

What I Studied and You Didn't Ask

Include an assessment item that asks students to indicate what information they thought was important or especially interesting that you did not include in the assessment; the item is worth x points toward the total score. This builds in a relief valve for students, gives them a sense of efficacy, and gives the teacher important information about what students considered important or interesting.

Consensus Testing

Students work through problems individually and record personal answers. They then work in groups of two or three to compare answers and reach consensus about best answers or most important points to include. If you value assessment as a real learning opportunity for students, this method promotes that continued learning, and it simulates real-world situations in which students will have to listen to the ideas of others in "stressful" situations.

Best Test

Students create a test, complete with answers, for the unit of study. You and/or a committee of students review the tests and decide which one best assesses important ideas and is best constructed. The class takes the test and the test designers earn their grade for designing the test. For this method to be as productive as possible, some teaching about and study of test design is necessary. Time spent on applying these skills will help students better analyze test questions they encounter in the future and should have more impact on their learning than isolated mini-lessons on test-taking skills. Alternative uses of student generated questions are limitless. Individual questions can be added to later assessment as review items, or, if submitted on index cards, as game questions. Flash cards, story problems, language translations, etc. could evolve from the student generated questions.

The Answer Is

Provide a list of important concepts or vocabulary words from the unit of study. Have students generate three to four questions that could be answered with the word supplied. If your students have studied Bloom's and Williams' taxonomies, you can designate specific levels/kinds of questions you wanted them to use. This method helps students develop skill at predicting what questions might be included on future assessments.

Making Assessment a Learning Experience
Formative Assessment

Extra Inning

Collect test papers at the end of the period and announce that students will be able to have an extra inning tomorrow...ten minutes at the beginning of the period. They are to go home and study whatever they could not remember or figure out during the test. As promised, the next day they can work on their tests for an additional ten minutes. If you want to track what they struggled with have them use a different color ink or pencil. Do they get full points? Absolutely! We are into learning here and even those who had everything correct the first time are checking one more time!

David Brinley, St. Vrain Valley School District, Longmont, CO

Two Minute Warning

Two minutes or so before the end of the period announce that students can get out any materials they have with them to look up that nugget of information they need to support an argument or to clarify a point. Watch them get better at taking notes and knowing where to look in their texts and notes. Unlike during an open book test, when they have only two minutes they have to be really organized.

David Baker, St. Vrain Valley School District, Longmont, CO

2 x 2

Correct two tests simultaneously. Mark only those questions that both students answered correctly. Return the papers for the two students to go over. They have to discover if they are both incorrect or which one is correct and submit a new consensus answer to the problem.

David Baker, St. Vrain Valley School District, Longmont, CO

Chris' Test

The teacher designs a multiple choice test similar to the state or district test format. A fictional student named Chris takes the test. The teacher distributes copies of the test that Chris took to the students. Working in pairs, the students go through the test, question by question, and determine if Chris has answered the question correctly. In short, each pair of students grades the test. As they work together, they discuss content as well as test taking skills. This practice serves as a review of the content that the teacher has taught. The teacher administers almost the same test to the students the next day.

Brian Mandell, Thoreau Middle School Fairfax County, VA

Through the Voice of...
Peer & Self-Assessment

Please write your responses in complete sentences.

1. What did **you** do to **contribute** to the success of your presentation? **Be specific**.

2. List the names of your **group's members** and tell about their **contributions** to the success of your presentation.

3. What did you **learn about yourself** from doing this presentation?

4. What did you **learn about your group members** from doing this presentation?

5. What did you **learn about your topic** from doing this presentation?

6. What did you **learn about your community** and the available resources?

7. What grade would you give **yourself** for **your effort in the research and presentation** of your topic?

8. List the names of your **group's members** and give each of them a **grade for their effort** in the research and presentation of your topic.

9. What did you like **most** and **least** about your presentation?

Dan Struck, Jennings County High School, North Vernon, IN

Individual Participating Rating Sheet

First, rate yourself in each area. Then have each of your teammates rate your participation. If they agree with your self assessment, they need only initial the rating you recorded. If any teammate disagrees, that teammate should record the score and present the rationale on the back of this rating sheet.

	Almost Always 3	Often 2	Sometimes 1	Rarely 0
Team Participation				
Participated in discussions Did fair share of work Allowed others to work				
Group Process				
Helped plan how to accomplish task Helped identify and solve problems Summarized and clarified Praised efforts of others				
Responsibility				
Came to class on time Came to class with materials Did what I said I would do Made internal attributions				

Assessing with Balance

Performance assessments assess complex thinking and problem solving skills, and, because they are designed to be realistic, they are generally more motivating for students.

While performance assessments tell us how well students can apply their knowledge, more traditional assessments such as multiple choice, matching, true-false, etc. tests may be more efficient for determining how well students have acquired the basic facts and concepts.

Asking a student to perform an interesting or complex task/activity does not make it a good assessment. If the task is not one which when completed measures use of concepts identified as essential to know, it is worthless. Not only must the task be aligned with standards, it should be rigorous in that it causes students to demonstrate skills which transfer to other situations and problems.

Other issues of balance include a match with the learning time spent on the concepts/generalizations, the levels of thinking students were asked to do in class work and assignments, and with varied information processing styles. Unbalanced assessment unnecessarily creates frustration and failure.

The following pages describe assessment design elements and suggest best uses of each type of assessment.

Classroom Test Design

When selecting or designing a paper and pencil summative assessment it is essential that the test fairly and comprehensively represents the learning standards being addressed in the instruction, what was actually taught and processed, as well as the time and emphasis placed on the material during instruction. Current best thinking is that the assessment should be designed immediately after the standards and/or objectives are identified. Instruction is then planned to lead students to competency on the summative assessment.

There are two broad categories of paper and pencil assessment items. Each promotes and measures a different kind of thinking and gives the teacher different kinds of information about learning. One category requires the student to select the best answer from a list of alternatives or to recognize a correct or incorrect statement. The other broad category requires the students to supply or create an answer that may be short or long. The **Select the Answer** type item is efficient for measuring recall of facts and, when skillfully designed, can measure organizational, analytical, and problem solving skills with the topic being studied. The **Supply/Create the Answer** type item is not as efficient for measuring recall of facts, but is quite useful in measuring complex learning, promoting higher level thinking about the material being studied, and demonstration of what the student can do with what he/she knows.

Guidelines for the Design of Test Items
True-False (Select the Answer)
Uses
This type of test item is useful when there are not three or four plausible distracters to use in the design of a multiple-choice item.
Guidelines
- Avoid absolute words like all, never, always, and usually.
- Make sure items are clearly true or false rather than ambiguous.
- Attribute opinion statements to a source.
- State items in a positive, rather than negative, voice.
- Write all items at approximately the same length.
- Write approximately half true and half false items.
- Limit true-false questions to ten.
- Make each item focus on only one key concept.
- Consider asking students to make false questions true to encourage higher order level thinking.

Classroom Test Design

Matching (Select the Answer)

Uses

This type of test item is efficient at measuring competency with factual information when the emphasis is on the relationship between two components.

Guidelines

- Limit list to no more than ten. Use multiple sets of ten if necessary.
- State the basis for matching in the directions.
- Use homogeneous lists (Do not mix names with dates).
- Place directions and all items to be matched on the same page.
- Create more responses than stems.
- Consider the possibility that responses can be used more than once.
- Place responses in alphabetical or numerical order.

Multiple-Choice (Select the Answer)

Uses and Advantages

Multiple-choice items eliminate the prospect of random guessing that is inherent in true-false questions. This type of test item can go well beyond the recall of factual information. It takes thoughtful planning to write multiple-choice items that ask the learner to identify correct applications of facts and principles, to interpret cause and effect relationships, and to explain why a sequence or condition is the way it is. This type of test item allows the test designer to determine the level of discrimination required. Good multiple-choice items are the most difficult test items to write.

Guidelines

- Clearly state the problem or main idea in the stem.
- Avoid irrelevant information in the stem.
- When possible, state the stem in a positive voice.
- Use reasonable incorrect choices; make them plausible without creating "trick" questions.
- Make choices the same length.
- Avoid "all of the above," "none of the above," and "both A and B."
- Place one word options and short phrases in alphabetical order and numerical options in numerical order.

Classroom Test Design

Short Answer, Fill In the Blank, or Problems

Uses

This type item is useful in measuring knowledge of terminology, of specific facts, of principles, and of methods or procedures. It is also useful for measuring skills at making simple interpretations of data, at solving numerical problems, at manipulating mathematical symbols, and at completing and balancing chemical equations.

Essay

Guidelines

- When creating essay questions, focus on the key concepts and essential understandings studied during the unit.
- Use Bloom's Taxonomy to design items matched to the level of thinking cited in the benchmarks or indicators. See pages 231-235 for information on Bloom's Taxonomy.
- Decide whether to ask for an **extended response** or a **restricted response**.
  - An extended response asks students to respond in a more global way and requires them to use higher level thinking skills and decide what to include in the answer. They are often required to give a rationale for their decisions.
  - A restricted response requires a much more specific response like: "State two causes and two effects of deforestation." This kind of response does not require higher levels of thinking.
- Define point value and criteria for evaluation and communicate it to students before the test begins.

Potential Problems with Test Design

- ambiguous statements
- excessive wordiness
- difficult (or different) vocabulary
- complex sentence structure
- unclear illustrations or graphics
- crowded or cluttered presentation
- unintended clues
- lack of match to standards, benchmarks, or indicators
- level of thinking required by the test items is not aligned with the standards
- level of thinking required by the test items is not aligned with the assignments students have completed in preparation for the assessment
- students are asked to use processes they have not practiced

Why Use Performance Assessment?

Carefully crafted performance assessments such as products, performances, and portfolios that require quality responses:

- promote rigor and relevance
- support the conditions identified as being present in brain-compatible learning environments: varied sources of input; active, meaningful learning activities; and timely, appropriate feedback
- require students to develop literacy as they integrate reading/writing/speaking skills with content knowledge
- promote student engagement by providing tasks likely to match the multiple intelligences and various styles, aptitudes, and interests of the students
- require students to practice, refine, and revise in order to demonstrate learning
- assess the "essential to know" components of the concepts under study
- give students and teachers insights into student thinking, learning-to-learn strategies, and habits
- reflect growth in social and academic skills and behaviors that are not easily demonstrated in paper-and-pencil assessments
- encourage creativity and originality
- promote the use of processes and information from the world beyond the classroom and school. The tasks are authentic in that they are tasks that people engage in the world beyond academia
- cause school work to be more like the world beyond the classroom through use of the knowledge and skills listed in the **SCANS Report** and **Results that Matter: 21st Century Skills and High School Reform**
- demonstrates to the community what students are achieving

Through the Voice Of...
Performance Assessment

Espanol 1

Examen Final

In small groups you will write and produce the following production. Following script review and rehearsal, you will record your production using the class camcorder. Classmates and teachers will critique your production at our film festival.

You have been invited to a party on Friday night at 8:30. Call a friend and invite him/her to go with you. The friend accepts. Arrange for transportation and get directions to your friend's house.

You arrive at the party and greet the host/hostess who warmly welcomes you. You then pay a compliment to him/her.

While there, you get something to eat and discuss your food preferences.

You notice a new boy/girl and ask your host/hostess what his/her name is. You and your friend approach the new girl/boy and introduce yourselves. You ask where he/she is from and where he/she now lives. You talk about the weather and some likes and dislikes (maybe sports, movies, T.V. shows, famous personalities, etc.). You also talk about what school you attend and discuss some courses and teachers. Be sure to express what you think about these things.

You or your friend ask what time it is and announce that you must go home because it is late. You have to study for a Spanish test.

Before leaving, you ask your new friend if he/she would like to go to the movies tomorrow night. Discuss what's playing, what kind of movie it is, and when it begins. Your friend suggests a better movie and you all agree to go.

You then say goodbye to your new friend and the host/hostess.

Characters:	Hostess/Host
	Main Character
	Friend
	New Boy/Girl

Maureen Mugavin, Worthington Kilbourne High School, Worthington, OH

Espanol 1
Examen Final continued...

Function and Content

Before the party
___ call on phone
___ invite
___ accept an invitation
___ arrange transportation
___ give/get directions (2)

Arrival at the party
___ greet
___ welcome visitor
___ pay a compliment

Party talk
___ food preferences
___ ask name of new person
___ introduce self
___ ask where from
___ ask where lives now
___ talk about weather (2)
___ interest (3)
___ express opinions about courses
and teachers

Time to go home
___ ask/tell the time
___ announce need to go home
___ announce need to study for a test

Tomorrow's plans
___ ask about movies tomorrow night
___ discuss what movie to see
___ discuss when movie starts
___ suggest a movie
___ agree on a movie
___ say good-bye all around

Required Vocabulary
You must use at least 10 of these words.

Use at least 5 of these verbs in any form.

poder	querer
vivir	creer
asistir	deber
tener que	dar
llamarse	pensar
ir	venir

Use at least 5 of these words.
pelicula
tener ganas de
Que (noun) tan (adjective)
Me gusta (n)
empieza
Por que no?
De donde?
bienvenido
Hace (weather)

See attached rubric for assessment criteria. Note the x6 weighting of functions and content.

Maureen Mugavin, Worthington Kilbourne High School, Worthington, OH

Through the Voice of...
The USA since WWII
Class Portfolio

The final assignment of our year is intended to "**capture in pictures**" the history that has impacted the lives of your grandparents, parents, and yourselves. Form groups of 2 or 3. Each group will be assigned a time period of 4-5 years between 1946 and the present day. The following requirements and optional activities should be included in your portfolio:

1. **Identify 5-8 pictures that are vivid representations of the time period you have been assigned**. They should cover a wide range of topics and represent events/people/issues in the United States and around the world. Once each group has researched the assigned time period and has chosen the events, **the class as a whole will then create a Photo Story 3 portfolio in chronological order**.

2. Each group will submit a **detailed description of its pictures**. The "captions" should be typed single-spaced, and thoroughly explain the picture. Where, when, why, who, how, etc., should be answered for each. As your photo is shown on the screen, you will read your information to the class. Be ready to answer any questions and to explain why you selected the picture.

3. Each group is to turn in an **outline map** clearly identifying the location of each picture. Neatness counts! In addition to locating your events, the maps should also include any nearby cities or physical features. The use of color will greatly enhance your finished product and is recommended.

4. Each group is to write a **one page summary of your time period**. What was going on in the U.S.? What were the political issues? Which world events influenced U.S. society? How was life changing? etc. Do not merely restate your captions. Go beyond those events and explain the information that is crucial to these years.

5. **Interview** someone who lived during the years you studied. After introducing them in your opening, ask them which 5 events they most vividly remember. Where were they when they occurred? Why were they important? Did they directly affect their lives? Then, have them critique your choices. Do your pictures correspond with their memories or do they remind them of any forgotten events?

Pat Forward, Worthington Kilbourne High School, Worthington, OH

Through the Voice of...
The USA since WWII

Optional: The following could be added to your portfolio or substituted in place of one of the above. Please see me.

6. **Create a CD-ROM** or **add music to the Photo Story portfolio** that reflects the songs that people listened to during the years you researched. The tape should be 5 minutes in length and will serve as background music while you read your captions. Go to www.windowsphotostory.com for directions on how to add music to the Photo Story 3 portfolio.

7. Bring in **artifacts** from your family or friends that represent your time period. Please be careful, however, not to bring items of incredible value.

8. **Write a reflective paper** putting yourself into the years studied and tell whether you would have enjoyed being a teenager "back then." If you have a time period that you actually lived through, what do you think the next 10 years will add to history? Will life become easier, harder, or just different? What could your children's teenage years be like?

9. **Focus on the Future**: Add a segment to the class portfolio by capturing events or issues that you feel will impact the life of you and your classmates in the next decade. We will add your photos to the end of our class portfolio.

Years of Research

1946-1950	**1951-1955**	**1956-1960**	**1961-1965**
1966-1970	**1971-1975**	**1976-1980**	**1981-1985**
1986-1990	**1991-1995**	**1996-2000**	**2001-2004**
2005-2008	**The Future**		

Pictures can be obtained from the Internet, books, e-pals, newspapers, and magazines. If you are unsure about the clarity of an image, ask me.

Pat Forward, Worthington Kilbourne High School, Worthington, OH

Through the Voice of...
Calling All Travelers*

Second Graders!
This is your chance to show what you have learned about Ghana!

Essential understandings of the unit are:
- There are similarities and differences between and among cultures of people.
- People express their culture in many ways: writing, literature, architecture, celebrations, everyday tools and objects, etc.

You, a travel writer, are preparing a review on your recent trip to Ghana for the next issue of National Geographic for Kids. Bring a suitcase to school as if you just returned from Ghana. Include objects and symbols that represent the ways culture is expressed in Ghana. Think about it's geography, home life, schooling, foods, socializing, everyday tools, homes, and so on.

Write 2-3 sentences for each object in your suitcase describing the item, its importance in Ghanaian culture, and how it is used.

Be prepared to discuss the contents of your suitcase with a small group of listeners interested in visiting Ghana.

Include in your suitcase
- A map/globe showing Ghana's location in the world.
- Clothing appropriate for Ghana's climate.
- An African game, music, or art piece.
- A picture of the home where you stayed.
- Something you bargained for at the market.
- Something you would take to school with you.
- A short story you wrote down that someone in Ghana told you.

*Access the complete SBE Unit: Calling All Travelers on the CD-ROM.

Laura Cork, Newton Public Schools, MA

Through the Voice of...
Force & Motion
...the Science Behind Sports*

Welcome Sports Fans!

This is your opportunity to learn all of the "tricks of the trade" about your favorite sport! You and a group will:

1. Investigate a selected sport (from an extended list)
2. Relate it to Newton's Three Laws of Motion and other motion concepts
3. Choose a way to publish information
4. Publish it!
5. Set-up display
6. Present your findings in a school-wide sport symposium

You are to find as much information as possible about the mechanics of your selected sport. Each group is to keep a running log of the day's events, as well as a check on the types of information found. To guide you on this quest, see the attached list for some questions you should be able to answer as a result of your research. Be sure to record your bibliographic information. Keep your notes on the note cards as discussed in class. By the way, this list is only a framework! Try to go beyond these questions as you explore your interest in the sport.

From your research, it will be up to your group to design a show-board, highlighting your findings regarding the 12 questions, as well as any other important information that you may find. The showboard will be shared with class members during the symposium. In addition to the show-board, your group will need to publish your information in one of three ways:

- Create a webpage, outlining information and containing links to sport-related websites.

- Create a Power Point presentation, outlining information in a unique and creative way.

- Create a hard copy picture book or an electronic Photo Study portfolio and write narration to accompany it.

The publications will serve to teach a larger audience about the science behind certain sports. These publications and presentations will be made available to future classes at Dake for research purposes.

*Access the complete SBE Unit: Force & Motion... the Science Behind Sports on the CD-ROM.

Karen Finter, West Irondequoit Central School District, Rochester, NY.

Rubrics, Performance Task Lists, & Checklists
Assessment Criteria

Rubrics
- are a set of criteria expressed as a scale
- list and explicitly describe behaviors, processes, or products at each level of the scale
- are given to students as the assignment or performance task is introduced
- allow students to monitor how they are progressing and to make necessary corrections along the way
- can be either holistic or analytical in form; analytical rubrics are best used with formative assessments while holistic rubrics are often used with summative assessments. See examples on the following pages.

Rubrics are most effective in promoting student success when they are used in conjunction with models or exemplars of student work. Models should be developmentally appropriate yet vary in meeting the criteria. With older students, a professional model can also be included. Students learn to use the rubric to analyze the models, and, therefore, become even clearer about the requirements of the task before they begin work.

The process of creating rubrics is an ongoing one. If you do not have examples of student work at various levels of performance, it may be best to use a Performance Task List until you can obtain the examples. As soon as possible, collect student work samples for your own use as well as for exemplars for students.

Experienced rubric designers suggest that when creating a rubric, start with the **meets expectations** descriptors. To do that, ask yourself:
- What are my expectations or specific goals for this task?
- What behaviors will a student who has mastered the skill display?
- What level of performance do I hope all students will attain?

After that it is natural to move to **exceeds** and **does not meet** descriptors.

Rubrics, Performance Task Lists, & Checklists
Assessment Criteria

Performance Task Lists

Performance task assessment lists, developed by educators in Pomerang Regional School District in Connecticut, resemble the lists many of us used in the past to assess student projects or papers. We usually attached the criteria to the paper as it was submitted and marked the points on that paper. Performance task lists have several important characteristics not included in the lists we used in the past; specifically, the students are given the criteria and point values **before they begin work** and **students do a self-assessment before the work is submitted.**

Developing Performance Task Assessment Lists

- Identify the **standard** focus and determine clearly what students are to know and be able to do as a result of the unit of study.
- Design student **tasks that focus** on the **content knowledge** needed to demonstrate mastery and on the **process skills** and **work habits** students need in order to be successful.
- Do a **task analysis** both during and following task design.
- Make a **list of the components** of the performance task.
- **Assign points to each component** to match the significance of the component and the areas of need of the student(s).
- Provide/create **models** of both acceptable and unacceptable work.

When using performance task lists with **primary students**, the ratings may be "terrific," "okay," and "needs work." The educators in Connecticut recommend pictures such as smiling and frowning faces for an age appropriate rating scale. As the students mature, both the components and the ratings become more complex.

One of the powerful aspects of performance task lists is that they can be used to **differentiate instruction** by changing the components listed on the task list or by adjusting the number of points assigned to a specific component.

Checklists

Checklists are just that. A list of tasks to be completed or materials to be included. While rubrics and performance task lists provide more specific guidance there are times when a checklist is sufficient. Checklists, like rubrics and performance task lists, should be provided to the students before they begin.

Holistic Rubric
Foreign Language Writing Assignment

5   **Demonstrates High Proficiency**
-Well organized; ideas presented clearly and logically
-Few grammatical or spelling errors
-Wide variety of grammar, vocabulary, and sentence structures
-Few word-order errors
-Writing is appropriate to current level
-Thorough response to the question

4   **Clearly Demonstrates Proficiency**
-Loosely organized, but main ideas present
-Some grammatical or spelling errors
-Some variety of grammar, vocabulary, and sentence structures
-Some word-order errors
-Most of the writing is appropriate to current level
-Generally thorough response to the question

3   **Demonstrates Progress Toward Proficiency**
-Some attempts at organization, but with confused sequencing
-Many word-order errors
-Writing is below current level
-Partial response to the question

2   **Demonstrates Strong Need for Intervention**
-Lack of organization
-Significant and serious grammatical and spelling errors
-Lack of variety of grammar, vocabulary, and sentence structure
-Excessive word-order errors
-Writing is well below current level
-Insufficient response to the question

1   **Unacceptable**
-Response falls below the above descriptions or is inappropriate

Adapted from Ohio State Department of Education

©Just ASK Publications

Through the voice of...
Colonial Brochure Holistic Rubric

We Can't Keep 'Em Away

This brochure is truly exceptional in every way; it is sure to cause a steady stream of settlers to your colony!
Work shows evidence of outside research including technology.
Colony name is identified.
Colony founder is identified.

4 Map of where colony is found is labeled, colored, and includes a key.
Descriptions of political, economic, and social interests are supported by facts and details.
Complete sentences and paragraphing are used and contain no mistakes.
Brochure is neatly typed or written in ink.
Brochure is colorful and includes illustrations with explicit captions.

Lots of Interest

This brochure is right on target and will cause many curious travelers to come to call!
It meets all requirements or exceeds them.
The brochure shows evidence of outside research.
Colony name is identified.
Colony founder is identified.

3 Map of where colony is found is labeled, colored, and includes a key.
Description of political, economic, and social interests are mostly supported with facts and details.
Complete sentences and paragraphing are mostly used.
Brochure is neatly typed or written in ink.
Brochure is colorful and includes illustrations.

Occasional Traveler

This brochure may go to the bottom of the stack. You may get the occasional traveler to your colony.
The colony name is identified.
The founder is identified.

2 Map of where colony is found is labeled, colored, and includes a key.
Description of political, economic, and social interests are included but need some supportive details.
Complete sentences and paragraphing are used; there are however, errors in form.
The brochure is colorful, but lacks informative illustrations.
The brochure is generally neat and is typed or written in ink with some errors.

The Desperate Searcher

This brochure is incomplete, but may attract the desperate colonist!
Colony name is identified.
Colony founder is identified.

1 Map of where colony is found is included but may be lacking in labels, color, a key.
Description of political, economic, and social interests are lacking detail.
The use of complete sentences and paragraphing need revision.
Brochure hard to read with smudges and wrinkles.

Suzanne Blue, Rush-Henrietta Central School District, NY

Through the Voice of...
Bedroom Cleaning Rubric

Bed

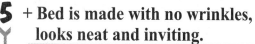

5 + Bed is made with no wrinkles, looks neat and inviting.
+ Bottom and corners of sheets and blankets tucked in.
+ Pillows are centered at one end of bed.

3 + Bed is made with some wrinkles, covers pulled up but not neatly.
+ Bottom and Corners not tucked in.
+ Pillows uncentered or thrown onto bed carelessly.

1 + Bed is not made or covers just thrown onto mattress.

Analytical Rubric

Floor

5 + No toys, clothes, papers, etc., on floor.
+ Floor is clean and vacuumed, even in corners.
+ Under the bed is clean.

3 + No toys, clothes, papers, etc. on floor.
+ Floor has not been vacuumed.
+ Under the bed is clean.

1 + Objects are out-of-place and on floor.
+ Floor is not clean or vacuumed.
+ Objects "hiding" under bed.

Closet

5 + The closet is neat overall, clothes are hung up in appropriate places.
+ Dirty clothes are in the laundry hamper.
+ Toys, blocks, games, and other objects are put away neatly.

3 + Clothes are hung up, but look messy or are misplaced.
+ Some objects scattered on floor or put away incorrectly.

1 + Both dirty and clean clothes are on the floor.
+ Toys and other objects look as if they were thrown in.

Total Bedroom Cleaning Score:

_____ out of __15__

Scott Perry, Linn Benton Lincoln Education Service District, Albany, OR
©Just ASK Publications

Through the Voice of...
Performance Task List for
Chemistry Mini-Lectures on Energy & Disorder/Reaction Rates

Guidelines

You will be working in a group of 3 or 4 to develop a mini-lesson on one of the following topics:

Enthalpy and Entropy   **Nature of Reactants and Concentration**
Free Energy and Standard States   **Temperature and Catalysis**
Reversible Reactions and Reaction Rate   **Reaction Mechanism**

All group members should be involved in the preparation and presentation. The presentation should be approximately 15 minutes long and include components listed below.

Your work will be scored according to the points assigned to each component.

You will view videotapes of previous presentations as models to evaluate.

The assessment of this material will be derived from the contents of the six group assessments. You may use any presentation notes and handouts on the test.

Components	Possible Points	Self Assessment	Teacher Assessment
Attention Grabber	5		
Supplemental Information (topic expanded beyond textbook)	5		
Transparencies or Handouts	5		
Visual Aids (poster, laser disk, pictures, model, etc.)	10		
Demonstration/Lecture	25		
Active Learning Strategies to Engage Class in the Topic	15		
Checks for Understanding (questions, problem, etc.)	15		
Assessment (5 questions typed with answer sheet)	20		
TOTAL POINTS	**100**		

Renee DeWald, Evanston Township High School, Evanston, IL

Products & Perspectives

VII

TOP TEN QUESTIONS
to ask myself as I design lessons

The focus questions for this chapter are highlighted below.

1. What should **students know and be able to do** as a result of this lesson? How are these objectives related to national, state, and/or district standards?

2. How will **students demonstrate what they know and what they can do**? What will be the **assessment criteria** and what form will it take?

3. How will I find out what students already know (**pre-assessment**), and how will I help them access what they know and have experienced both inside and outside the classroom? How will I help them **build on prior experiences, deal with misconceptions**, and re-frame their thinking when appropriate?

4. How will new knowledge, concepts, and skills be introduced? Given the **diversity of my students** and the **task analysis**, what are my **best options for sources and presentation modes**?

5. How will **I facilitate student processing** (**meaning making**) of new information or processes? What key questions, activities, and assignments (in class or homework) will promote understanding, retention, and transfer?

6. What shall I use as **formative assessments** or **checks for understanding** during the lesson? How can I use the **data** from those assessments to **inform my teaching decisions**?

7. What do I need to do to **scaffold instruction** so that the learning experiences are productive for all students? What are the multiple ways students can access information and then process and demonstrate their learning?

8. How will I **Frame the Learning** so that students know the objectives, the rationale for the objectives and activities, the directions and procedures, as well as the assessment criteria at the beginning of the learning process?

9. How will I build in opportunities for students to make **real-world connections** and to learn and use the **rigorous and complex thinking skills** they need to succeed in the classroom and the world beyond?

10. What adjustments need to be made in the **learning environment** so that we can work and learn efficiently during this study?

Potential Products

A

advertisement	apparatus	anecdote
advice column	aquarium	application
album	area graph	adventure
anagram	artifact collection	acronym
animation	audiotape recording	analysis
annotated bibliography	autobiography	

B

ballad	book jacket	business letter
ballet	book report	biographical sketch
banner	booklet	book
bar graph	bookmark	blog
biopoem	brainteaser	braille
bill of rights	brochure	business card
block picture story	bullet chart	
blueprint	bulletin board	

C

calendar	classification	constitution
campaign speech	list/system	conversation
cardboard relief	classified ad	costume
cartoon	clothing	couplet
CD cover	collage	coupon
celebrity profile	collection	critique
ceramics	column chart	crossword puzzle
charade	comedy act	caption
chart	comic book	conversation
characterization	commercial	children's book
checklist	comparison	commentary
choral reading	computer program	case study
cinquin	conference presentation	

Potential Products

D

dance	database	diagram
demonstration	description	dictionary
dialogue	diary	display case
diorama	display	DVD
documentary	dramatization	digital slide show
directions	debate	

E

editorial	e-scrapbook	equipment
essay	estimate	etching
exaggeration	experiment	explanation
error analysis	eyewitness account	exhibition
editorial cartoon	e-newsletter	email

F

fabric design	fairy tale	field manual
field trip	filmstrip	finger puppets
flag	flannel board	flash cards
flip charts	flow chart	food
free verse	friendly letter	furniture

G

gadget	gallery	game
gauge	glossary	gossip column
graph	graphic organizer	greeting card
guidebook	goal	gift basket

Potential Products

H

haiku	hand puppet	headline
handout	hat	hologram
hieroglyphic	history	
hypothesis	handbook	

I

icon	index	interview
imprint	invitation	interpretive dance
interview script	invention	instrument
inquiry	inquisition	
identification cards	illustration	

J

jigsaw puzzle	jingle	jukebox
joke	joke book	job description
journal article	jet ski	jewels

K

kit	kimono	kayak
kitchen tool	kite	kaleidoscope

L

law	lawyer's brief	layout
learning center	lecture	lesson plan
letter	letter of request	letter to the editor
letter of complaint	letter of support	limerick
list	lithograph	log
logic puzzle	lyrics	lab report

Potential Products

M

machine	meter	mime
marionette	mobile	model
metaphor	monument	mosaic
mnemonic	mural	music
monologue	musical instrument	myth
movement game	matrix	monograph
musical composition	manual	mp3
montage	map	multimedia
mask	memorandum	portfolio

N

newscast	newsletter	newspaper
newspaper ad	newspaper article	novel
nursery rhyme	notes	

O

oath	observation sheet	outline
origami	order form	obituary
operator's manual	owner's manual	online discussion group
	oral report	

P

painting	pamphlet	pen pal letter
patent	pattern	photo essay
pennant	petition	picture dictionary
photograph	pictograph	playing cards
pie chart	plan	prediction
poem	play	prototype
profile	poster	prophecy
puppet show	proposal	PowerPoint
portrayal	puzzle	presentation
podcast	parody	

Potential Products

Q

quatrain	quorum	quiz
question	quotation	
quarterly report	questionnaire	

R

rap	rationale	recipe
radio announcement	reproduction	research report
report	rewrite	rewritten ending
review	riddle	role-play
rhyme	request	reply
rubric	response	rebuttal
resume	re-enactment	recording
radio commentary	radio commercial	

S

satire	scenario	schedule
science fiction story	short story	scroll
sewing project	ship's log	skit
ship	slide show	sign
silk screen	song	slogan speech
soap opera	stick puppet	story
stencil	survey	symbol
solution	sculpture	script
simulation	summary	sketch

T

tall tale	taxonomy	telegram
television newscast	television sitcom	time line
transparency	travel advertisement	travel log
textbook	theory	3-D display
toy	translation	thumbnail sketch
task analysis	tribute	

Potential Products

U

UFO   utopia   urn
underwater scene   understudy

V

verdict   verification   videotape
video yearbook   visual aid   vocabulary list
voice-over   venn diagram   vase
virtual field trip   variety show   vibraphone
vinyl record   vintage fashion

W

wall hanging   warranty   webquest
warrant for arrest   web   wax sculpture
weather map   word game   window shade
writing   word search   web page
wanted poster   warm-up   website

X

x-ray   xylophone   xerox

Y

yardstick   year-in-review   yearbook

Z

zodiac chart   zoo guidebook   zen garden

Roles & Audiences
Potential Perspectives

A

artist	archaeologist	administrator
architect	anthropologist	aunt
actor-actress	animator	ambassador
author	astronomer	ambulance driver
astronaut	astrologer	activist
aviator	acrobat	athletic trainer
alien	attorney	assistant
actuary	accountant	appraiser
admiral	anesthesiologist	art therapist
atheist	acquaintance	analyst

B

baby	bully	bandit
brother	baby-sitter	beautician
basketball player	butcher	blacksmith
baseball player	blackjack dealer	bank robber
baker	bartender	biochemist
boat captain	botanist	bus driver
ballet dancer	boxer	biotechnologist
blogger	bellhop	businessman
bullfighter	bandleader	broker
boss	boy	

C

computer programmer	crossing guard	chairperson
cardiologist	case manager	committee member
comedian	chef/caterer/cook	comic strip character
composer	cartoonist	captain
customer services representative	cosmetologist	cowboy
	coach	cashier
custodian	clown	choreographer
carpenter	criminal/convict	concierge
college student	chauffeur	computer game designer
calligrapher	candidate	curator
counselor	Congressperson	

Roles & Audiences
Potential Perspectives

D

doctor	derelict	delegate
director	dog trainer	data analyst
demographer	drug dealer	dermatologist
dancer	daredevil	dietician
disc jockey	decorator	designer
dictator	dentist	dispatcher
drummer	diver	daughter

E

editor	exterminator	enemy
executive	educator	engineer
environmentalist	elephant trainer	epidemiologist
electrician	economist	e-business manager
EMT	emir	e-marketing manager
equestrian	emperor	event planner

F

firefighter	father	fashion designer
forest ranger	female	florist
football player	ferryman	FBI agent
fisherman	financier	film critic
friend	flight attendant	funeral director
farmer	furrier	forensic accountant
first lady	facilitator	frequent flyer
fitness expert	fictional character	foreign correspondent
fairy	falconer	fundraiser

G

gardener	gambler	grocer
governor	game warden	government official
giant	garbage collector	geographer
gymnast	gangster	graphic designer
grandparent	geologist	groundskeeper
general	ghost	gargoyle

Roles & Audiences
Potential Perspectives

H

hair stylist	housekeeper	headhunter
high jumper	hula dancer	harlequin
hero/heroine	hippie	healthcare worker
historian	hang glider	human resources
hunter	halfback	administrator
	historical figure	

I

ice skater	idealist	insurance salesman
ice cream man	idiot	interior designer
ichthyologist	illusionist	inspector
investment banker	illustrator	interpreter
iconographer	immortal	intern

J

juror	jazz singer	journalist
judge	jester	justice of the peace
janitor	jockey	juvenile
jeweler	juggler	

K

karate instructor	keyboardist	kickboxer
kid	kindergartner	kayaker
kleptomaniac	king	khan

L

logger	logician	lexicographer
lawyer	lady	literary critic
linebacker	lecturer	legal secretary
life guard	leader	loan officer
librarian	landscaper	locksmith

Roles & Audiences
Potential Perspectives

M

mail carrier	musician	manicurist
mentor	mayor	magician
military officer	mountain climber	marketeer
mother	machinist	monster
marriage counselor	mafioso	maid
mathematician	marksman	marine biologist

N

nurse	nanny	novice
neighbor	nephew/niece	navigator
newspaper carrier	neurologist	Nazi
night watchman	news anchor	naval officer
nun	newlywed	nursing aide
nanotechnologist	nomad	network
numerologist	nuclear physicist	administrator

O

optometrist	ornithologist	Olympian
organic agriculturist	opera singer	office manager
operator	official	orthodontist
orator	observer	obstetrician
oceanographer	officer	occupational therapist

P

president	psychologist	public defender
parent	priest	patron
principal	pianist	patriarch
producer	paleontologist	pauper
photographer	publisher	prosecutor
psychiatrist	puppeteer	politician
police officer	pirate	poet
professor	psychic	participant
pilot	pacifist	pharmacist
paratrooper	personal trainer	political cartoonist
painter	programmer	parking lot attendant

Roles & Audiences
Potential Perspectives

R

realtor	runner	refugee
reverend	rugby player	relative
rabbi	Rastafarian	recruiter
race car driver	rock star	radiologist
reporter	rebel	radical
researcher	receptionist	radio announcer
recreational therapist	referee	risk analyzer

S

sister	scientist	sailor
secretary	sculptor	soldier
senator	security guard	systems analyst
student	singer	school board member
senior citizen	stuntman	superintendent
soccer player	sales clerk	saint
systems engineer	sheriff	software engineer
surgeon	scapegoat	state trooper
seamstress	scholar	steel worker
superhero	social worker	sound engineer
stewardess	statistician	submarine captain

T

truck driver	tailor	transient
tourist	taxi driver	translator
tour guide	tax collector	traveler
travel agent	technician	trespasser
teacher	tenant	troll
toddler	terrorist	troubadour
tap dancer	therapist	troublemaker
telemarketer	technical writer	tutor
teller	townspeople	typist
tyrant	traitor	television star
tennis player	tradesman	train conductor

Roles & Audiences
Potential Perspectives

U

uncle	umpire	urbanite
urologist	union member	urchin
understudy	unicyclist	usher

V

veteran	violinist	villain
veterinarian	vampire	vegetarian
video game developer	vagabond	ventriloquist
vandal	vagrant	vendor
vice president	vocalist	volunteer
	volleyball player	videographer

W

writer	waif	weightlifter
witch	wallflower	welder
waiter/waitress	woman	wingwalker
webmaster	warden	westerner
worker	wrestler	web page designer

X

x-ray technician	xylophonist	xenophobe

Y

yachtsman	yeoman	yodeler
Yankee	yuppie	yogi

Z

zookeeper	zealot	zombie

Differentiation of Instruction

VIII

TOP TEN QUESTIONS
to ask myself as I design lessons

The focus questions for this chapter are highlighted below.

1. What should **students know and be able to do** as a result of this lesson? How are these objectives related to national, state, and/or district standards?

2. How will **students demonstrate what they know and what they can do**? What will be the **assessment criteria** and what form will it take?

3. How will I find out what students already know (**pre-assessment**), and how will I help them access what they know and have experienced both inside and outside the classroom? How will I help them **build on prior experiences, deal with misconceptions**, and re-frame their thinking when appropriate?

4. How will new knowledge, concepts, and skills be introduced? Given the **diversity of my students** and the **task analysis**, what are my **best options for sources and presentation modes**?

5. How will **I facilitate student processing** (**meaning making**) of new information or processes? What key questions, activities, and assignments (in class or homework) will promote understanding, retention, and transfer?

6. What shall I use as **formative assessments** or **checks for understanding** during the lesson? How can I use the **data** from those assessments to **inform my teaching decisions**?

7. What do I need to do to **scaffold instruction** so that the learning experiences are productive for all students? What are the multiple ways students can access information and then process and demonstrate their learning?

8. How will I **Frame the Learning** so that students know the objectives, the rationale for the objectives and activities, the directions and procedures, as well as the assessment criteria at the beginning of the learning process?

9. How will I build in opportunities for students to make **real-world connections** and to learn and use the **rigorous and complex thinking skills** they need to succeed in the classroom and the world beyond?

10. What adjustments need to be made in the **learning environment** so that we can work and learn efficiently during this study?

Self-Assessment
Inclusive Instruction

How is teaching advanced and struggling learners like and different? In reality, the same principles should apply to both. Compare and contrast your instructional approach with these learners.

Teaching Advanced Learners

How do you...

1. Discover and acknowledge what they already know.

2. Provide a balance of skill building and meaning making activities.

3. Plan and guide them in planning projects that capitalize on their interests.

4. Allow them some flexibility in the way they use their time.

5. Allow them to learn at a different pace than their peers.

6. Plan a variety of relevant learning experiences; both teacher and students monitor the effectiveness.

7. Help them to be aware of and use productive learning strategies.

8. Teach them to be self-sufficient; only do for them as much as you need to do.

9. Encourage them to demonstrate mastery in a wide variety of ways.

Teaching Struggling Learners

How do you...

1. Discover and acknowledge what they already know.

2. Provide a balance of skill building and meaning making activities.

3. Plan and guide them in planning projects that capitalize on their interests.

4. Allow them some flexibility in the way they use their time.

5. Allow them to learn at a different pace than their peers.

6. Plan a variety of relevant learning experiences; both teacher and students monitor the effectiveness.

7. Help them to be aware of and use productive learning strategies.

8. Teach them to be self-sufficient; only do for them as much as you need to do.

9. Encourage them to demonstrate mastery in a wide variety of ways.

Who Are Our Learners?

Our Successful Learners

- are motivated to learn and set learning goals
- think about what they know
- take responsibility for their own learning
- anticipate what they are to learn
- participate actively in their classes
- assimilate, consolidate, and integrate new knowledge
- are organized and try to manage their time well
- are persistent and are effective problem solvers
- seek comprehension and meaning
- monitor their own learning
- construct meaning

Our Struggling Learners

- are easily distracted
- tend to have short attention spans
- lack self-confidence
- demonstrate inappropriate communication and interpersonal skills
- have difficulty demonstrating empathy for others
- often have limited experience bases and range of interests
- do not know how to analyze the effectiveness of their efforts
- do not see cause and effect relationships
- appear not to learn from previous mistakes or errors in judgment
- avoid failure by avoiding tasks
- lack organizational skills
- appear to avoid responsibility and independence
- feel like they have no control over their behavior or lives
- have few, if any, productive strategies for dealing with stress and anger

Differentiation Non-Negotiables

We Must

- Be knowledgeable about and skillful with the **content** to be taught
- Acknowledge, understand, respect, and respond to the **differences** in, and **needs** of, the learners to be taught
- Hold and select purposefully from a deep and broad **repertoire of instructional strategies**
- Use **multiple sources of data** to inform decisions about instruction
- Realize that differentiation is not a set of strategies but is instead a **way of thinking** about the teaching and learning process
- **Not differentiate who will learn what but** rather, **how we will teach** so that all students have access to, and support and guidance in, mastering the district and/or state curriculum

Actions to Take

- Design learning experiences based on a task analysis that includes an analysis of the skills and knowledge embedded in the task plus an analysis of student readiness, background knowledge levels, interests, and information processing styles.
- Provide sources of information at various reading levels, in different languages, and in varying formats to match the needs of learners.
- Provide scaffolding as needed to ensure student success.
- Provide students precise and public criteria and guidelines prior to the beginning of the learning experience or assessment; include models and exemplars with the guidelines.
- Ensure that grouping is flexible so that students are working and learning with a variety of classmates.
- Orchestrate the learning environment so that the student is given both choice and responsibility around learning.
- Collaborate with colleagues and parents.
- Ask ourselves:
  - What will we do if some students do not learn?
  - What will we do if some students already know what we want them to learn?

Differentiating Instruction 3x3

Provide a range of and choice in

1 Sources

2 Processes

3 Products

Provide a balance of instruction and learning

1 Whole-class

2 Small-group

3 Individual

Variables to include in grouping and other instructional decisions

1 Readiness

2 Interests

3 Information Processing Styles

What Is Scaffolding?

Many of us probably think of a scaffold as a temporary framework that supports a building during construction. When the structure is sturdy enough to stand on its own, the scaffold is removed. In an educational sense, scaffolding, in the form of coaching or modeling, supports students as they develop new skills or learn new concepts. When the student achieves competence, the support is removed. The student continues to develop the skills or knowledge on his or her own.

Joe Banaszynski and Linda Starr

(http://www.educationworld.com/a_curr/curr218.shtml)

Guidelines for Effective Scaffolding

- Identify what students know

- Begin with what students can do

- Help students achieve success quickly

- Help students to be like everyone else

- Know when it's time to stop

- Help students be independent when they have command of the activity

Martha Larkin, CEC

What Does Educational Scaffolding Look Like?

Just as scaffolding is used to support buildings during the construction process, **educational scaffolding provides support systems for students during the learning process. Each of the following scaffolding tools can be used for all students or used to differentiate instruction.** Scaffolding is both planned in advance and provided in the moment based on available data. In order to provide scaffolding, teachers must expand their repertoires of scaffolding strategies and gather the materials and resources needed to build the scaffolding.

Fifty Ways to Scaffold Learning

- Adjust pace and rhythm of speech
- Assist students in building competency with key vocabulary especially academic/classroom terms and content-specific use of words
- Avoid small print on handouts, overhead transparencies, PowerPoint slides, and on boards
- Begin with recognition and move to generation of information
- Bookmark sites on the Internet
- Box key words
- Break complex tasks into simpler parts
- Build in movement with dance and Total Physical Response techniques
- Change and teach students to change paragraph text into bulleted lists
- Check for understanding on directions
- Give the student only one segment of the assignment at a time. When that segment is completed and checked for accuracy, give the next segment
- Have students use think-aloud paired problem solving
- Help students make real world connections
- Highlight critical attributes of concepts and have students learn to do the same using tools such as the Frayer Model
- Leave white space between items on handouts, overhead transparencies, and boards and/or use lines or boxes to clearly indicate segments of information
- Label objects in the classroom
- Label steps in operations and processes
- Label level of thinking required
- Limit choices on matching tasks
- Model note-taking with mini-lectures after which appropriate notes are displayed on overhead
- Model thinking aloud
- Monitor your use of language (academic/classroom terms, content specific meanings of words, slang, colloquialisms, figures of speech, idioms, jargon, out-of-date references, and the cultural context of learners)
- Outline necessary steps
- Present information in graphic organizers and teach students to use graphic organizers to organize information and their thoughts
- Provide basic facts so students can do higher level thinking and not be bogged down at the knowledge and recall level
- Provide checklists

Fifty Ways to Scaffold Learning

- Provide frequent opportunities for students to compare and contrast and note similarities and differences between past, present, and future information, processes, and concepts studied
- Provide models and examples of partially and completely finished processes and products
- Provide oral language rehearsals (alone with the teacher or in pair and small group work)
- Provide page numbers where answers can be found
- Provide picture glossaries
- Provide templates
- Provide timelines
- Provide word banks
- Re-teach/review key concepts and vocabulary before using again
- Teach error analysis
- Use tape recorded directions at centers and for homework
- Use songs, charts, and rhymes
- Teach (explicitly) reading strategies such as accessing prior knowledge, use of context clues, fix-up strategies when comprehension is difficult, etc.
- Teach students to highlight math operational signs
- Teach students to create rebus (pictures that capture the meaning of unknown words)
- Teach text structure
- Teach time management skills by having students estimate how long it will take to complete a task, track the time, and note for future use
- Teach students to use removable highlighting tape, erasable crayons, sticky notes, colored sticker dots, typing correction tape, etc., to take notes/make notations in texts
- Use color to call attention to important information, key words, and directions
- Use concrete to semi-abstract to abstract approaches to introduce new information and concepts
- Use and have students learn to use mnemonics
- Use props and realia
- Use known and practiced learning strategies to introduce new information and concepts. Use known information and concepts to introduce a new learning strategy
- Use visuals

Using Modalities to Reach More Learners
Visual, Auditory, & Kinesthetic

To Emphasize Visual Learning
- Write directions on the chalkboard, as well as giving them verbally. Give a copy of assignments in written form, weekly or daily.
- Use flash cards printed in bold colors.
- Supplement lectures with colorful transparencies shown on the overhead projector. Also use models, charts, graphs, and other visual aids.
- Allow students to read assignments rather than depending on oral presentations.
- Use and teach students to use graphic organizers.
- Have students take notes on important words, concepts, or ideas.
- Provide a written copy of board work if student has difficulty copying.

To Emphasize Auditory Learning
- Record assignment directions on tape or cassette so that the student can replay them as needed.
- Give verbal as well as written directions.
- Tape textbook materials for the student to listen to while reading. Tape only the most important information and simplify or explain the vocabulary.
- Give an oral rather than written test or allow tests to be administered by the special education teacher in the resource room.
- If practice is needed, student can use tape recorder to recite and then play back. A student can practice aloud with another student.
- Substitute oral reports or other written projects for written assignments.
- Have another student read important information to the student.

To Emphasize Kinesthetic or Tactile Learning
- Use frequent classroom demonstration and participatory modeling.
- Allow student to build models, draw pictures, make a display or a video, do an experiment, or give a dramatization.
- Use role-play and simulations.
- Provide a lecture outline for the student and give note taking instructions.
- Allow the student to move about, for example, to another seating area during class.
- Use manipulative objects, especially when teaching abstract concepts, such as fractional parts, measurement, and geometry.

Reaching More Students through
Analytical & Global Learning
Preferences

Analytical thinkers prefer to think and work in these ways:

- process through intellectual lens
- structured/planned
- control feelings
- sequential
- logical
- remember names
- rational
- solve problems by breaking them apart
- time-oriented
- auditory/visual learner
- prefer to write and talk
- follow spoken directions
- prefer T/F, multiple choice, matching
- take fewer risks
- look for differences
- think mathematically
- think of one thing at a time
- judge objectively

Global thinkers prefer to think and work in these ways:

- process intuitively
- spontaneous
- let feelings go
- creative/responsive
- more abstract
- remember faces
- more likely to act on emotions
- solve problems by looking at whole
- spatially oriented
- kinesthetic learners
- prefer to draw and handle objects
- follow written or demonstrated directions
- talk to think and learn
- "picture" things to think and learn
- prefer essay tests
- take more risks
- look for similar qualities
- think simultaneously
- judge emotionally

Three Key Points

- Provide learners with opportunities to work in their "comfort zone" and opportunities to stretch their thinking and develop skills at working in ways that are not as natural for them.
- To help students maximize efforts be aware of which students are comfortable/uncomfortable with the tasks they are doing.
- We have a tendency to ask students to work and think in ways that are comfortable or productive for us so it requires careful planning to include learning experiences for all learning preferences.

How I'll Show What I Know*

To demonstrate what I have learned about _____ I want to:

____ write a report   ____ do a photo essay
____ compile a scrapbook   ____ build a model
____ put on a demonstration   ____ do a statistical chart
____ set up an experiment   ____ design a mural
____ produce a videotape   ____ write a song
____ develop an interactive computer presentation
____ create a series of sketches, diagrams, or graphic organizers
____ other _____

This would be a good way to demonstrate understanding of this concept because:
_____
_____

To do this project, I will need help with:
_____
_____

Action Plan: _____
_____
_____
_____
_____

The criteria/rubric that will be used to assess the finished product is:
_____
_____
_____

My projected completion date is _____

Student Signature _____ Date ___/___/___
Teacher Signature _____ Date ___/___/___

*Access template on the CD-ROM

Through the Voice of...
2nd Grade Fire Safety Project

Plan with your family the procedure you should follow should there be a fire in your home. Your plan must include the points listed below, which we talked about and practiced in class. You may record your plan to present to the class using a **video**, **diagram**, **model**, **song**, **written report**, **or photo essay**.

Include the following points:

1. Check closed doors before opening.

2. Stop, drop, and roll.

3. Stay down, close to the floor.

4. Have two ways of evacuation.

5. Know what to do if both ways are blocked.

6. Establish a family meeting place.

Nancy Reece, West Irondequoit Central School District, Rochester, NY

Through the Voice of...
General Science Space Project

Choose one of the projects
listed below to further explore space
and to demonstrate what you have learned
during our space unit.

1. The school newspaper is doing an article on space exploration and the editor has asked you to create a **timeline** to go along with the article. Your timeline is to include major events in space exploration and discovery from the time of Sputnik until the present. Each event should have a brief explanation and a **visual** of some sort.

2. You are a realtor selling vacation condos on an orbiting space station. Create some sort of **advertisement** that will be seen across Indiana to convince people why they would want to buy a space station vacation condo. Your ad can be for a magazine, newspaper, or TV.

3. You are an astronaut on the space shuttle. Write a **letter** home to your family detailing how you get by doing day-to-day activities without gravity and with Newton's laws in full effect. Include in your letter **pictures** of where you go about these activities.

4. Mr. Wizard is doing a TV show on space exploration. You are to write a **song** to be performed on the show about all of the important explorations into space since Sputnik.

5. Create a new **board game** (you may use any available game board) about the history of the space program. The board game will be played in class as a review activity of the space chapter.

6. You are a TV news anchor doing a series on how the space program has impacted the lives of everyday people. **Research** man's first landing on the moon and the Challenger disaster. **Interview** some people on how those two events impacted their lives. In some way, recreate the interview for your classmates to see.

Jeanne Galbreath, Jennings County High School, North Vernon, IN

Through the Voice of...
A Look at the Theater

Choose two or more of the following projects for your further study of the theater.

Project Possibilities:

1. Write an original play or TV drama of your own.

2. Study a playwright. Suggested authors:

   Lorraine Hansberry: *Raisin in the Sun*   **Neil Simon** (free choice)
   Carson McCuller: *Member of the Wedding*   **Andrew Lloyd Webber** (free choice)
   Arthur Miller (free choice)   **Thornton Wilder:** *Our Town*

   Read two plays written by the playwright, a biographical sketch, and either a play review or a feature story about the author. Write a 4-5 page paper on his or her contribution to the theater.

3. Attend a play. Write a critical review or prepare and present a radio or television review.

4. Read and analyze a play by Shakespeare and see the movie version. Design a project that compares the two versions.

5. Research the history of the musical comedy in the U.S. Write a paper or prepare a multi-media presentation for the class.

6. Read a play concerning a famous person and compare it to a biography of that person. Use a paper, oral report, or artistic presentation to make your comparison. Suggestions:

   Clarence Darrow: *Inherit the Wind*   **Helen Keller:** *The Miracle Worker*
   Anne Frank: *The Diary of Anne Frank*   **Franklin D. Roosevelt:** *Sunrise at Campobello*

7. Read a book that is a source of a musical. Study the musical and give a written, oral, or artistic presentation comparing the two. Suggestions:

   Anna and the King of Siam and **The King and I** or *Don Quixote* and **Man of LaMancha** or
   The Once and Future King and **Camelot** or *Oliver Twist* and **Oliver** or *The Matchmaker* and
   Hello, Dolly!

9. Read the live theater sections of the newspaper for a month. Clip reviews, feature stories, and advertisements of plays. Make a handbook of local theater offerings, including a brief commentary about each clipping.

10. With others, give a puppet or marionette show. Write a script and make the puppets.

11. Adapt a favorite short story, book, or comic strip into a play or musical. Write a script or songs or choreograph dances or design sets and costumes for the production.

12. Write a paper on the history of drama, including the Greeks, medieval pageant plays, and modern theater. Use correct research form and at least four sources.

Adapted from unknown source.

Through the Voice of...
Revolutions Unit Test

Directions: Choose one project from part A and one project from part B.

Part A:

Choose one of the following Revolutions and complete one of the three assignments.

Scientific Revolution or Enlightenment   **Glorious Revolution**
French Revolution   **Industrial Revolution**

1. **Political cartoon w/caption** - Draw a political cartoon explaining the viewpoint of one of the sides involved in the revolution you have chosen.

2. **Newscast** - In news format, chronicle the events that occurred during this revolution. You may use visuals to enhance your newscast. You are required either to perform it for the class or to videotape it for me in order to get credit (Computer-generated visuals are acceptable).

3. **Flip Chart** - Chronicle the major historical events of this revolution by using a flip chart of graphics and facts. (Computer-generated are acceptable.)

Part B:

Choose one of the following V.I.P.s from a revolution other than the one you chose above (i.e., if you chose the French Revolution, you may not choose Napoleon, Robespierre, or Louis XVI), and complete one of the three assignments below.

Any Philosopher	**Louis XVI**	**Napoleon**	**Marie Antoinette**
Oliver Cromwell	**James I**	**Charles II**	**William and Mary**
Adam Smith	**Robert Owen**	**Karl Marx**	**Sir Isaac Newton**
Robespierre			

1. **Biopoem** - Write a biography of your chosen leader by writing a poem about their policies and/or accomplishments. Enhance your poem by including personal information as well.

2. **Job Application** - HELP WANTED: Seeking person with revolutionary ideas. Develop an application that would ask all pertinent questions to find the perfect person for the job. Then choose one of the people above to fill out the application. Answer it in the voice of the person, based on what you have researched about him/her.

3. **Wanted Poster or National Hero Poster** - Draw (do not download photo) your chosen leader and, in advertisement format, tell why this person is/was considered a villain or a national hero. Use factual information. This is similar to the mini-wanted posters we have done, only more information is required.

Lynn Butler and Lorraine Fusare, Rush-Henrietta School District, Henrietta, NY

Interest Grouping

Giving students a voice in how they will access and process new learning, and how they will demonstrate that learning, appeals to their ever changing interests and to their need for independence. If these decisions have been entirely teacher-centered, you can start with a limited array of choices and gradually increase the options as students are independently able to choose productive learning experiences for themselves.

> You can interview students, use interest inventories, and just listen in and observe to gather data about what choices might be of interest to them. Your knowledge about multiple intelligences theory, as well as the extensive list of potential perspectives and products found in the chapter on assignments, should make this match up between student interest and assignments an easy one to accomplish. The form *How I'll Show You What I Know* can serve as a template for students to use in identifying their preferences.

If you want to be explicit about gathering some data about influences and interests, these questions can provide a starting point:

1. What books, movies, or television programs make you think? Why do you think that is so?
2. If you could live in another place, where would you live and why?
3. What is the best/most exciting/most memorable moment you have had so far in your life?
4. If you could meet three famous people, who would you want to meet and why? What would you want to ask them?
5. If you could live in another time period, what time period would it be and why?
6. If you could choose any person in the world to have dinner with, who would you choose and why?
7. Given five choices, have students rank order any of the following: classes, recreation activities, times of the year, toys, vacation sites or activities, sporting events, best places to eat or live, school activities, television shows, or movies.

No matter what questions you choose, **patterns of interest** will begin to emerge. This information will enable you to design individual choices and plan group assignments around similar interests, as well as plan meaningful stories and examples to use in instruction.

Top 10 List
Jigsaw Research

Interest Grouping

If, when you do a task analysis you discover that many of the students lack the background information they need to make sense of material they are about to study, the necessary information can often be generated by the students.

Have the students **generate a list** of what they would like to know about a topic, time period, region of the world, concept, etc. The **Three Column Chart** or **All Hands on Deck Brainstorming** can be a useful tool in this process.

Have the media center staff prepare a **book cart** for use in the classroom, raid storage closets, and have students bring in any materials they have at home related to the topic to be studied.

Assign or have each student select a sub topic; this is a great opportunity for **interest grouping**! Ask each student to prepare a list of ten things they learned about their topic in their research.

Cluster students by topic and have them share their individual lists. Have the groups then generate their group's **Top Ten Lists** of facts about the information they have gathered. Provide large pieces of chart paper and markers to each group so they can write out their lists complete with pictures, charts, graphs, and/or artifacts as appropriate.

These can be shared with the entire class by posting and having students do a **Walking Tour** or by **group reports** on the background information.

By taking the time to do this gathering of background information up-front, students will have a foundation on which to hang the more complex information you want them to learn during the unit.

Anchoring Activities

Anchoring Activities are the activities students work on as they enter the classroom, when they are finished with other assigned work, or at any other potential "down time." These activities "anchor" students to continuous learning if the activities are matched to standards and district guidelines.

Points to Note

- These activities can be done individually or in small groups.
- Use old materials (cut up worksheets and workbooks, assignments you no longer use, etc.) in a new way to avoid massive teacher preparation.
- Think about how the anchoring activities can be translated into a second language or have the emphasis shift from math to science to language arts with a slight change in the directions.
- Change the target audience (younger children, classmates, parents, pen pals, etc.) to completely change the nature of the assignment.
- **Design anchoring activities that match your state and district standards or program of studies**, the learning styles, and interests of your students. Create exercises for remediation or extension purposes, or let the students select from or create a new menu.

Possibilities

- Journaling
- Creative writing
- Supplemental readings related to concepts being studied
- Enrichment/extension packets with self-checking keys
- Remedial packets with self-checking keys
- Interest packets
- Learning centers
- Multiple Intelligences preference work
- Vocabulary development games
- Making or listening to podcasts

Anchoring Activities

Spelling Spectacular

Make a list of all the spelling words students of this age (or studying this subject) should know or of the words it would be fun to know how to spell. Words can be used for a variety of classroom activities such as cooperative spelling lessons, categorizing by known spelling rules, by parts of speech, by similarities or differences, etc.

Standardized Test Preparation

Identify standardized test areas (SAT, ACT, SRA, IGAP, ISTEP, Iowa, Terra Nova, Regents, etc.) and prepare independent packets for shoring up weak areas or areas not emphasized in the standard course of study.

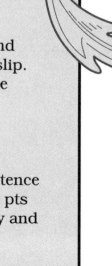

Research Race

Contest Rules:

- In the fishbowl, you will find dozens of folded slips of paper. Each slip contains a question about the world around us. Multiple resources are available around the room to help you locate the requested information.
- Choose a slip from the fish bowl and answer the question found on the slip.
- Use 5"x7" index card for writing the answer.
- Use the question as the title.
- You can earn 50 points for each information card you complete.
  - Each grammatically correct sentence (no more than six sentences) 5 pts
  - Quality of information: accuracy and completeness 10 pts
  - Neatness of product 5 pts
  - Bibliography information presented in correct format 5 pts

All Month! Learning! Fun! Prizes!

Through the Voice of...
Plate Tectonics
Tiered Assignment

Complete a total of four assignments from the list below. For the first three, choose one assignment from each level. Be sure that each choice is a different letter. The fourth assignment is your choice, but it must be a different letter than the other three. Scoring is based on total points scored out of a maximum 100 possible points.

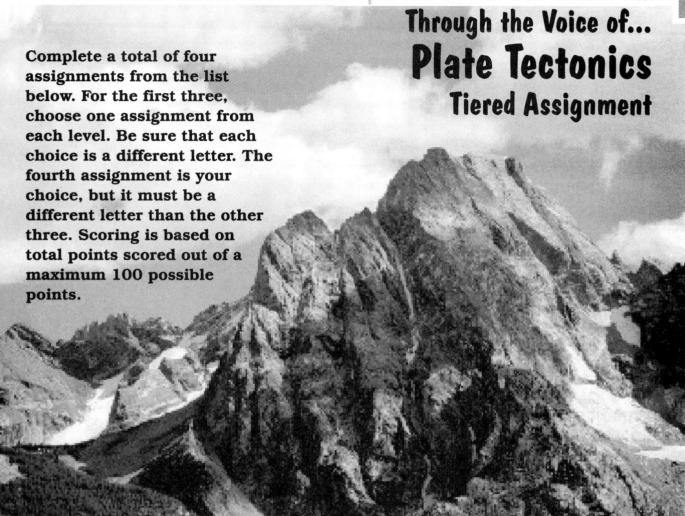

LEVEL ONE

A. Describe the stages of mountain development and the characteristics of each stage. Give one example of the location of mountains at each stage.

B. Construct a diagram of the complete rock cycle; compare and contrast each of the three (3) types of rocks according to a written list of three (3) of your own criteria.

C. Investigate and provide an imaginative explanation for the simile: The rim of the Pacific Ocean is like a "ring of fire."

D. Write a letter to a friend expressing your thoughts and concerns about a recent 7.0 magnitude earthquake that occurred in her city at a longitude opposite of yours. Provide for her a "scientific" explanation for the cause of the earthquake. Also explain why you did not feel it.

Each choice from this level is worth a possible 10 points.

John Banker, Rush-Henrietta High School, Heneritta, NY

Through the Voice of...
Plate Tectonics Tiered Assignment

Remember: Complete a total of four (4) assignments. Choose one (1) assignment from each level. Be sure that each choice is a different letter. The fourth (4th) assignment is your choice, but it must be a different letter than the other three.

LEVEL TWO

A. Construct a poster of a cross-sectional diagram of at least five (5) sedimentary rock layers. These layers formed within the same geologic era but are of different absolute ages; they are also intruded with a dike and a sill. The age and type of each rock layer must be shown.

B. Develop a hypothesis that explains the relative and absolute ages of the Hawaiian islands. Support your hypothesis with at least three (3) lines of scientific evidence.

C. Develop a design for an "earthquake-proof" high rise building or bridge. Or speculate on the likelihood of a major earthquake occurring in Southern California. Describe the earthquake's cause and ways damage might be controlled or reduced.

D. Suppose you are an old, lifelong, wilderness resident of the north slope of Mt. St. Helens. The date is May 16, 1989. Write a diary entry describing your decision to stay, or leave, the mountain. Include at least three (3) reasons for your decision.

Each activity at this level is worth a possible 20 points.

LEVEL THREE

A. Construct a chart showing and explaining three (3) types of plate boundaries and describing the features found at such areas that result from plate movement.

B. Research the Himalayan Mountains. Develop a classification system based on their characteristics and process(es) of formation. Identify other mountain ranges that fit your classification system.

C. Speculate on the scientific validity (relative to that period in history) of Alfred Wegener's original theory of continental drift. Add to it at least two (2) explanations of more current discoveries that will serve either to support or refute the theory.

D. Imagine that you are a geologist working in a seismology lab at the University of Rochester. Develop some imaginary earthquake data and an analysis of that data to calculate your distance for the earthquake's epicenter. Describe what you do and how you feel when you locate the epicenter near the residences of two of your closest friends or relatives.

Each choice from this level is worth a possible 35 points.

John Banker, Rush-Henrietta High School, Heneritta, NY

Thinking Skills
for the 21st Century

IX

TOP TEN QUESTIONS
to ask myself as I design lessons

The focus questions for this chapter are highlighted below.

1. What should **students know and be able to do** as a result of this lesson? How are these objectives related to national, state, and/or district standards?

2. How will **students demonstrate what they know and what they can do**? What will be the **assessment criteria** and what form will it take?

3. How will I find out what students already know (**pre-assessment**), and how will I help them access what they know and have experienced both inside and outside the classroom? How will I help them **build on prior experiences**, **deal with misconceptions**, and re-frame their thinking when appropriate?

4. How will new knowledge, concepts, and skills be introduced? Given the **diversity of my students** and the **task analysis**, what are my **best options for sources and presentation modes**?

5. How will **I facilitate student processing** (**meaning making**) of new information or processes? What key questions, activities, and assignments (in class or homework) will promote understanding, retention, and transfer?

6. What shall I use as **formative assessments** or **checks for understanding** during the lesson? How can I use the **data** from those assessments to **inform my teaching decisions**?

7. What do I need to do to **scaffold instruction** so that the learning experiences are productive for all students? What are the multiple ways students can access information and then process and demonstrate their learning?

8. How will I **Frame the Learning** so that students know the objectives, the rationale for the objectives and activities, the directions and procedures, as well as the assessment criteria at the beginning of the learning process?

9. How will I build in opportunities for students to make **real-world connections** and to learn and use the **rigorous and complex thinking skills** they need to succeed in the classroom and the world beyond?

10. What adjustments need to be made in the **learning environment** so that we can work and learn efficiently during this study?

Self-Assessment
21st Century Thinking Skills

Consider whether or not these statements represent your own professional practice.
A (Almost Always), S (Sometimes), N (Not Yet)

_____ I ask students to go beyond the factual level and think at the conceptual level.

_____ I pose questions and create learning experiences that cause students to challenge their current thinking and consider alternatives.

_____ I ensure that when technology is used as a learning tool, the learning experiences are designed to include the use of a wide array of thinking skills as students access, respond to, communicate, and create information and ideas.

_____ I design learning experiences in which thinking processes are named, modeled, and practiced in a variety of situations.

_____ I ask students to reflect on and monitor the effectiveness of their thinking.

_____ I structure the learning environment so that all skill building and information input leads to opportunities to make personal meaning and connections to life beyond the classroom.

_____ I provide opportunities for students to respond to and ask thought-provoking questions.

_____ I consider the levels of Bloom's Taxonomy when planning instruction and build on Bloom's in ways that promote rigor and relevance.

_____ I build decision making and problem solving situations into learning experiences.

_____ I set up situations where students use collaborative thinking and communication skills and then analyze and reflect on the effectiveness of actions.

Thinking Skills for the 21ˢᵗ Century

Creative Thinking is
- open-minded
- fluent
- flexible
- innovative
- adaptative
- visualizing
- done with future-oriented lens
- synthesizing
- metaphorical
- responsible risk taking

?

Metacognitive Thinking
(thinking about your thinking)
- set goals
- have repertoire of thinking skills
- know which skills to use when
- monitor effectivness of efforts
- monitor results
- assess processes and products

Conceptual Thinking
(includes creative, critical, and metacognative thinking)
- examine facts
- connect facts to prior knowledge
- seek and see patterns
- form conclusions or generalizations
- transfer understanding across time and situations

(Erickson, 2008)

Aha!

Introspective Thinking
(knowing self)
- know own preferences for processing information and the world
- self-assess and self-adjust
- recognize own emotions
- recognize own world lens, perspective, and bias
- aware of own strengths and weaknesses

Thinking Skills for the 21st Century

Systems Thinking
(organizational, social and technological systems)
- understand systems
- monitor and correct systems performance
- improve and design systems

(SCANS Report, 1992)

Collaborative Thinking
- read environment
- be empathic
- understand social context
- know when to lead and when to follow
- know what to say and not to say

Critical Thinking
(Skills apply to the acceptance, use, and creation of information and conclusions.)
Determine
- criteria to be used to assess information
- accuracy and relevance of information
- credibility of sources
- reliability and validity of the data used to support the information or conclusions drawn

Identify and reconcile
- inconsistencies
- lack of data to support conclusions
- missing/omitted information
- bias or prejudices of source

Navigate unpredictable situations

Aha!

Analytical Thinking
- note and remember facts and details
- grasp key points
- identify critical attributes
- sequence steps and events
- compare and contrast
- note similarities and differences
- identify patterns and trends
- determine cause and effect
- use data to make predictions

Through the Voice of...
Top 10 Historical Changes
from the Age of Transition

A RAFT

You have been hired to edit a new history textbook. Your boss, the publisher, wants a rank ordering of the top ten historical changes during the Age of Transition.

Your publisher has given you a list of ten events that occurred during the Age of Transition. Your job is to rank order these events according to your group's criteria for which event is more important than another. Use the process described on the next page.

Age of Transition Events

- Machiavelli's *The Prince*

- Gutenberg's invention of the printing press

- Galileo's findings with the use of the telescope

- Martin Luther's posting of the 95 Theses

- Columbus' discovery of the New World

- The Commercial Revolution and the invention of capitalism

- Henry VIII's creation of the Anglican Church

- Calvin's predestination

- Rebirth of Greek and Roman ideas and culture

- The theory of mercantilism

Tamara Lipke, Irondequoit High School, Rochester, NY

Through the Voice of...
Age of Transition

Process

1. Discuss each event in your group's list and use the attached sheet to

   a. List the event.

   b. Write an explanation of the impact this event had on history (both short term and long-term). Remember the most important information for your group's ruling will come from your assessment of the impact of each event.

2. Discuss the criteria you will use to decide which event ranks first, second, etc.

   a. Using the criteria sheet, list the priorities you will use. Example: When I asked myself what reasons I would use to rank one event higher than another, I thought that maybe events that had an effect on the largest number of people might be valued higher than ones that affected a limited region or area.

   b. Possible criteria include, but are not limited to, the following

- What reasons will I use to decide which event ranks first, second, etc.?
- How will I decide which events had the most impact on history?
- Will I rank the events that had the most positive effect on man's life first... or the events that had the most economic impact...?
- What criteria will I use to decide which event ranks first, second, etc.?

3. As an individual, rank the ten events, using the sheet provided

   a. Use your criteria to guide your placement of each event.

   b. Be sure you have a rationale (reason) for placing the events in the order you have rated them.

   c. Be prepared to share your reasons with the class during a class discussion/activity.

Tamara Lipke, Irondequoit High School, Rochester, NY

Technology Alert

Check out Intel's Visual Ranking Tool at
http://educate.intel.com/en/ThinkingTools/VisualRanking
Karen Finter, Director of the Teaching Learning Center for West Irondequoit Central School District, Rochester, New York, says that this tool, available free at the above site, makes learning tasks like this one even more rigorous and relevant for today's learner.

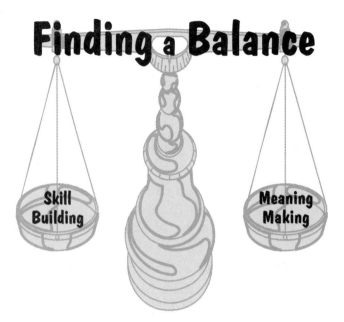

Explicit Thinking Skill and Strategy Instruction

Just because learners use a skill doesn't mean they know which skill they are using. We need to be explicit about teaching the names of the skills they are using. This is a part of the academic vocabulary development process.

They need multiple opportunities to reflect about and label the skills they are using. Ask students to analyze assignments and projects to identify the skills required.

Just because students use a skill doesn't mean they recognize where else that skill can be used! They not only need to use skills in a variety of situations, they need to focus on where else they might be able to use that skill both inside and outside the school setting. This is essential if we want them to become independent users of the skills.

Just because learners can name and define the skills they are using does not mean they know how to use those skills well or efficiently. Have them keep a running record of skill use and perhaps even use a longitudinal rubric to track their level of expertise with the skill or strategy.

Learners also need to reflect on the usefulness of each of the skills, and analyze what actions or behaviors were the most effective and why. As students develop their repertoires of skills and strategies, they should be given opportunities to analyze and reflect on which works best when, and why that is so.

Skill Building & Meaning Making for Me*

Directions for student: Use this form at the beginning of each unit to maximize your own learning experiences. These are questions you need to ask yourself whenever you are trying to learn or make meaning of something.

1. What should I know and be able to do at the end of this lesson/unit or experience?

2. What do I already know that will be useful in learning this new material or working in this way?

3. How are this knowledge and these skills important in the world outside of school?

4. When are the important checkpoints and deadlines?

5. How will I be able to tell when I have done a really outstanding job?

*Access template on CD-ROM.

4ᵗʰ Grade Learning Log*

for the week of _____

M O N D A Y	Things I Learned 1. 2. Opinion of My Day Something on Which I Want to Work Harder and What I Plan to Do
T U E S D A Y	Things I Learned 1. 2. Opinion of My Day Something on Which I Want to Work Harder and What I Plan to Do
W E D N E S D A Y	Things I Learned 1. 2. Opinion of My Day Something on Which I Want to Work Harder and What I Plan to Do
T H U R S D A Y	Things I Learned 1. 2. Opinion of My Day Something on Which I Want to Work Harder and What I Plan to Do *Access template on CD-ROM.

Stacy Holahan & Margie Cawley, Sherman School, Rush-Henrietta School District, Henrietta, NY

4th Grade Reflections for the Week*

Name:_____ Week of: _____

What I Learned This Week:

How I Can Use It:

Areas in Which I Am Making Progress:

I Need to Improve In:

My Goal for Next Week:

What I Enjoyed Most This Week:

Parent's Signature and Comments:

***Access template on CD-ROM.**

Stacy Holahan & Margie Cawley, Sherman School, Rush-Henrietta School District, Henrietta, NY

Interactive Notebooks

One of the most exciting innovations to promote student processing of new learning is the **Interactive Notebook** described in Addison Wesley's **History Alive!** and widely used by teachers of history and other social sciences. The uses of the **Interactive Notebook** extend to all areas of study because the structure and potential contents capture the essence of active participation, multiple intelligences, and the variables of the brain-compatible classroom.

To get started with the **Interactive Notebook** process, ask students to purchase and bring to class each day an 8½ by 11 inch spiral notebook with at least one hundred pages and a container holding a pen, a pencil with an eraser, at least two felt tip pens of different colors, and at least two highlighters of different colors. Other desirable equipment includes a small pair of scissors and a glue stick. If the cost is prohibitive for some students, create classroom supply kits.

Students are taught productive methods of notetaking during lectures, readings or other presentations that they record on the **RIGHT side of their notebooks**. They are encouraged to vary size of letters, boldness of letters, use of capital letters and lower case letters, indentations, underlining, bullets, colored markers, and highlights in the notetaking process.

The **LEFT side of the notebook** is reserved for student processing of the information recorded on the **RIGHT** side. Students can be asked to review and preview, draw maps, think of a time when..., summarize in a sentence, create graphic organizers, create a metaphor, respond to "what if" questions, or take a stand. Additionally, encourage them to add newspaper clippings or political cartoons, drawings and illustrations, or other such personal touches. The use of color and visual effects is highly encouraged! The **LEFT**, or processing side, can be completed in class or as homework.

Visit uweb.txstate.edu/teachamhistory/lessons/notebook.pdf for a social studies example.

Text Organizational Patterns

Almost all nonfiction books are presented in one of, or a combination of, these five text structures. Teach students to recognize the structure and to use the graphic organizer that is best for organizing the information presented in the text.

Classifications and taxonomic listings

focus on information about different concepts/facts that are classified according to a specific set of criteria. Signal words are "there are several types," and "one subset of this issue is...." The visual that looks like an organization chart or family tree is a useful graphic organizer for this pattern of text.

Sequential and chronological text patterns

present a series of events in chronological order, or the sequential steps of a process. Information in history texts is often presented chronologically, while information in science is often presented as a sequence of stages. Signal words for this text structure are "first," "next," "then," and "following that." Flow charts are best for capturing the important bits of information in this text structure.

Compare and contrast text patterns

identify items with similarities and/or differences. Signal words for this text structure are "similarly," "likewise," "contrary to," and "unlike." Venn diagrams and matrices are useful graphic organizers with this pattern.

Cause and effect text patterns

are used when two events or items are related to each other, with some causing an event and some resulting from the event. Signal words for this pattern include "as a result of...," "consequently," and "therefore." The graphic organizer with the "event" in the middle, with causes flowing into the event and the effects flowing out, is useful with this pattern.

Expository or descriptive text patterns

present a series or list of facts, ideas, or variables that may not immediately seem to be related to one another, or may seem to jump from one point to another. Mind maps or semantic maps and webs are useful in clustering the information.

Graphic Organizers

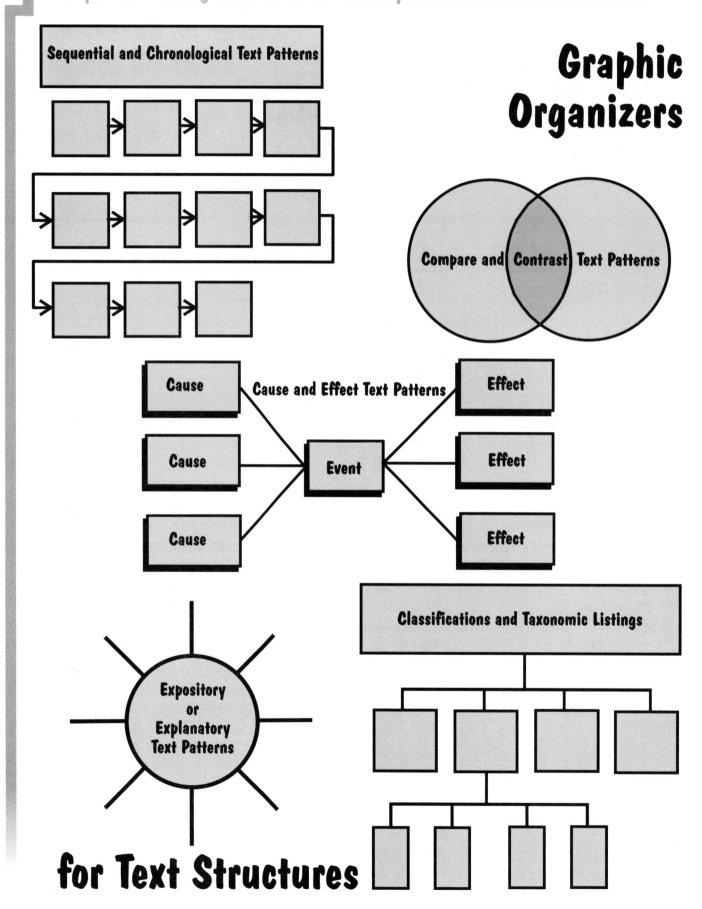

Sequential and Chronological Text Patterns

Compare and Contrast Text Patterns

Cause and Effect Text Patterns

Cause — Event — Effect
Cause — Event — Effect
Cause — Effect

Expository or Explanatory Text Patterns

Classifications and Taxonomic Listings

for Text Structures

Bloom's Taxonomy

Evaluation
Examine all parts of a concept in order to evaluate or assess it. Judge the significance of a problem.

Read an article and evaluate the author's argument. Listen to debate and judge which side presented the best argument.

Synthesis
Combine a new concept with what you already know in order to construct new knowledge. Compose, design, rearrange, plan.

Combine the ideas presented in several readings about the death penalty with your ideas to develop your argument.

Analysis
Able to separate the new concept into its parts and understand their relationships. Compare, contrast, analyze, identify. Recognize patterns.

Identify the author's 3 main arguments in an assigned article. Analyze a song by separating it into it's parts.

Application
Able to use the new concept to solve problems. Able to apply the concept in a situation that is different from that in which the concept was first learned.

Develop a chart showing 5 things computers can do but people cannot. Use the Spanish verbs you just learned in 5 sentences.

Comprehension
Able to explain or restate ideas in own words. Translates and interprets. Able to use the new concept as a building block for further learning.

Summarize the author's point of view. Restate the poem in your own words.

Knowledge
Recognize and recall facts. Able to repeat what was learned or follow rules. Material learned in this manner may be remembered long enough for a test, but until understood, it can't be used as a foundation for further learning.

Recite the periodic table. Memorize ten Latin nouns. Define metaphors.

Bloom's Taxonomy
Question & Task Design Wheel

speech
photograph
diagram
graph
own
statement

model
conclusion
implication based on idea
causal relationships
summary

analogy
outline
compare

tape recording
drama
skit
cartoon
story

match
restate
paraphrase
rewrite
give example
express
illustrate

explain
defend
distinguish
summarize
interrelate
interpret
extend

map
project
forecast
diagram
illustration
paper that follows
an outline

events
people
recordings
newspapers
magazine articles
television shows
radio
text readings
films/videos
plays
filmstrips

describe
memorize
recognize
identify
locate
recite
state
label

select
list
name
define

Comprehension

organize
generalize
dramatize
prepare
produce
choose
sketch
use

apply
solve
show
paint

solution
question
list
project
drama
painting
sculpture

Knowledge

Application

conclusion
self-evaluation
recommendation
valuing
court trial
survey
evaluation
standard
compared
standard
established
group discussion

judge
relate
weigh

criticize
support
evaluate
consider
critique
recommend
summarize
appraise
compare

Evaluation

Analysis

compare
analyze
classify
point out
distinguish
categorize
differentiate
subdivide

infer
survey
select

questionnaire
argument
parts of
propoganda
word defined
statement identified
conclusion checked
syllogism
broken down
report
survey
graph

Synthesis

compose
originate
hypothesize
develop

design
combine
role play
construct
produce

plan
create
invent
organize

article
invention
report
set of rules
set of standards

game
song
machine
alternative course
of action

experiment
play
book
formulation of
hypothesis
question

E V A L U A T I O N

S Y N T H E S I S

A N A L Y S I S

A P P L I C A T I O N

C O M P R E H E N S I O N

K N O W L E D G E

To promote student thinking at various levels of Bloom's Taxonomy, use the inner ring to identify the level of thinking and then select a verb from the middle ring. Link the verb selected from the middle level with a product listed in the outer ring to construct questions and assignments.

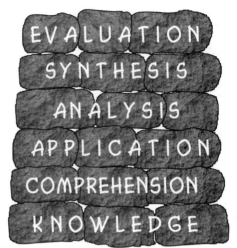

EVALUATION
SYNTHESIS
ANALYSIS
APPLICATION
COMPREHENSION
KNOWLEDGE

Bloom's at Work!

Identify the level of each of these tasks.

_____ List the departments of the Executive Branch that are headed by cabinet level positions.

_____ Based on our research, discussions, and your own personal knowledge, how might the cabinet be reorganized to function more efficiently?

_____ Compare and contrast the areas of responsibility of the Secretary of State and the Secretary of Defense.

_____ Select three cabinet level departments and summarize the primary responsibilities of those positions in your own words.

_____ Justify or criticize the suggestion to eliminate the Department of Education.

_____ Using the information you obtained in your readings, create a graphic organizer that shows the organization of the Department of the Treasury.

Bloom's Taxonomy
Don't underestimate the power of the knowledge level!

1. The higher levels of the taxonomy are not necessarily "better" than the lower levels. Evaluation without knowledge and comprehension can lead to faulty decisions. Do not underestimate the importance of the knowledge level. Learners need to master the following as part of the educational process:

Knowledge of Concepts

Knowledge of Specific Facts

Knowledge of Terminology

Knowledge of Principles and Generalizations

Knowledge of Theories

Knowledge of Trends and Sequences

Knowledge of Universals

2. Higher level questions are not necessarily more difficult than lower level questions. For divergent thinkers focusing on the details required for knowing and comprehending can be a difficult task; they would prefer to create new versions or render judgments about the information.

3. The use of certain process words will not necessarily guarantee a particular questioning level. If you have told them "why" and then ask them "why," the question is at the recall or knowledge level.

4. Don't get "too hung up" on the particular level of the question so that you lose sight of the overall value of the need for different levels of questioning. There is clearly overlap in the levels because one builds on the other. Analysis and application require solid knowledge and comprehension.

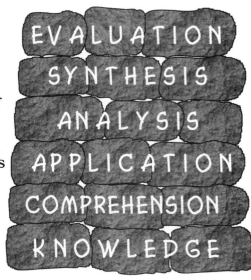

EVALUATION
SYNTHESIS
ANALYSIS
APPLICATION
COMPREHENSION
KNOWLEDGE

Building on Bloom's Taxonomy

This text uses the original Bloom's Taxonomy as a major component of the study of thinking skills. It is important to note, however, that in 2000, Loren Anderson, David Krathwohl, and others revised Bloom's Taxonomy of the Cognitive Domain. In their revision these former colleagues of Bloom's reversed the order and placed synthesis above evaluation in terms of complexity. They also changed the level names from nouns to verbs. The changes are:

Knowledge	to	Remembering
Comprehension	to	Understanding
Application	to	Applying
Analysis	to	Analyzing
Evaluation	to	Evaluating
Synthesis	to	Creating

It is possible that in the near future this revision will replace the original Bloom's Taxonomy; for now, it is important that all educators know the original because many curriculum documents are based on it.

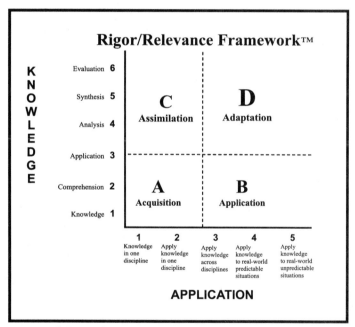

© International Center for Leadership in Education   www.leadered.com
Used with permission. All rights reserved.

As mentioned in Chapter I, the International Center for Leadership in Education has created the above Rigor/Relevance Framework for use in designing tasks, projects, and assessments that go far beyond what we usually ask our students. Willard Daggett and his colleagues at the Center have combined Bloom's Taxonomy with an Application Taxonomy. When we design tasks that ask students to apply knowledge to real-world unpredictable situations, we are providing them with the skills that Partnership for 21st Century Skills has identified as essential for the future.

Through the Voice of...
Teachers' Guide to Williams' Taxonomy

Fluency

Name as many _____ as you can in 60 seconds.

Flexibility

Classify the _____ listed in the fluency exercise. Use a unique classification system.

Originality

Think of a unique way to...

Elaboration

Explain what you think it would be like today if...

Risk-Taking

If you compared yourself to a _____, what kind of _____ would you resemble?

Curiosity

If you could meet a/an _____, what would you want to know about...?

Complexity

Describe or design an object or machine that you could make from _____.

Imagination

Imagine that _____ could talk. What would they say to/about...?

*Access template on CD-ROM.

Mary Ackley, Rush-Henrietta Central School District, NY

Williams' Taxonomy
of Divergent Thinking & Feeling

Fluency

is a thinking skill that allows a learner to generate many ideas.

Flexibility

is a thinking skill that allows the learner to adapt everyday objects to fit a variety of categories by taking detours and varying size, shape, quantities, time limits, etc.

Originality

is a thinking skill that allows the learner to seek a unique or not so obvious use or twist by suggesting unexpected changes.

Elaboration

is a thinking skill that allows the learner to expand, add on, enlarge, enrich, or embellish a list of ideas in order to build on previous thoughts.

Risk Taking

is a state of mind and skill that allows the learner to explore the unknown by taking chances, experimenting with new ideas, or trying new challenges.

Complexity

is a competency or skill that allows the learner to be "multi-tasked," to deal with intricacies, competing priorities or events, and to create structure in an unstructured setting or bring logical order to chaos.

Curiosity

is a way of thinking that allows the learner to follow a hunch, to inquire, question alternatives, ponder outcomes, and wonder about options.

Imagination

is the capacity to fantasize possibilities, build images in one's mind, picture new objects, or reach beyond the limits of the practical.

Williams' Taxonomy at Work!

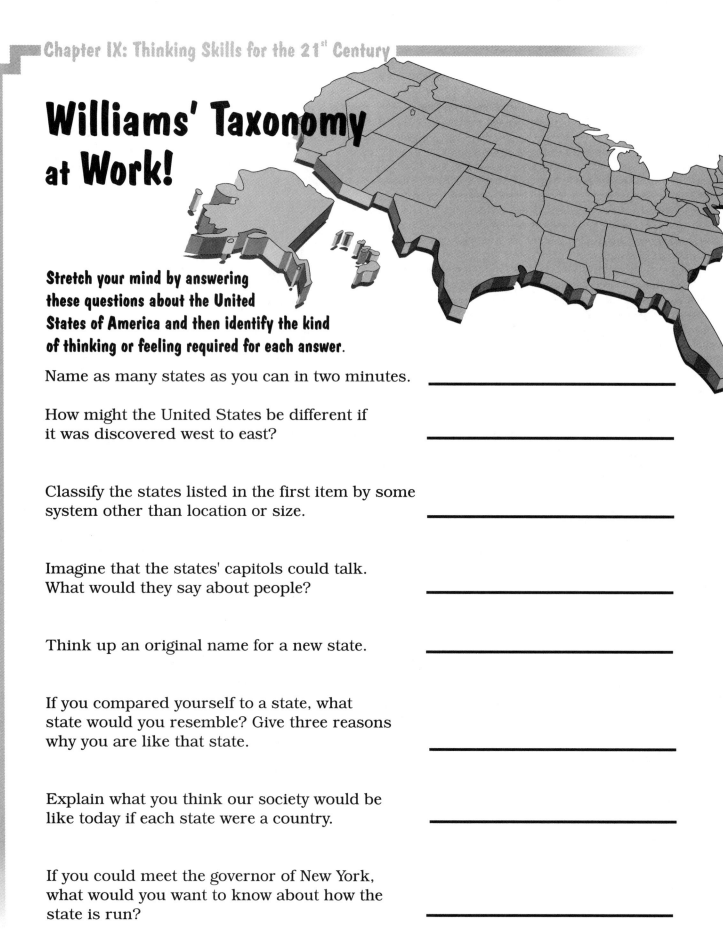

Stretch your mind by answering these questions about the United States of America and then identify the kind of thinking or feeling required for each answer.

Name as many states as you can in two minutes. _____

How might the United States be different if it was discovered west to east? _____

Classify the states listed in the first item by some system other than location or size. _____

Imagine that the states' capitols could talk. What would they say about people? _____

Think up an original name for a new state. _____

If you compared yourself to a state, what state would you resemble? Give three reasons why you are like that state. _____

Explain what you think our society would be like today if each state were a country. _____

If you could meet the governor of New York, what would you want to know about how the state is run? _____

Stacey Russotti, West Irondequoit Central Schools, Rochester, NY

Convergent & Divergent Thinking

Questions that have more than one correct answer are **divergent** questions. Questions with only one correct answer are called **convergent** questions. We want to use a balance of these two types of questions in our instructional programs.

Mark the following questions about music with either a "C" for Convergent or a "D" for Divergent.

_____1. Leonard Bernstein based the musical "West Side Story" on what play by William Shakespeare?

_____2. How would you describe the music of Andrew Lloyd Weber?

_____3. What are the sections of a symphony orchestra?

_____4. How did the Beatles influence music in the '60s?

_____5. How are marching bands and drum and bugle corps different?

_____6. Why is the piano a member of the percussion family?

_____7. How is a jazz combo like a football team?

_____8. Who composed "Appalachian Spring?"

_____9. Who followed Arthur Fiedler as conductor of the Boston Pops?

_____10. What contributions did George Gershwin make to American music?

_____11. What effect does MTV have on American popular music?

_____12. When was the electric keyboard invented?

Concept Attainment Model

Purposes
- To develop inductive thinking skills
- To practice identifying patterns and forming hypotheses

Set-Up
- Identify the concept to be studied.
- Locate positive and negative examples of the concept. A minimum of twenty sets of examples is recommended with at least two-thirds positively representing the concept.
- Sequence the examples starting with several positive examples.

Procedure
Phase One:
- Inform learners that they will see positive and negative examples of an idea you want them to discover.
- Present data to the learners in pairs and label the data sets as positive or negative examples.
- Ask students to develop hypotheses about what attributes or patterns they are seeing. Prompt them to try out several hypotheses and extend their thinking by focusing attention on specific features of the examples.
- Track and record on the board or chart paper the possibilities they generate and delete those proven incorrect by the presentation of additional examples.
- Have students name the concept and the rules or definition of the concepts according to their attributes. If the students do not know the name of the concept, provide the name in phase two when student hypotheses are confirmed.

Phase Two:
Students confirm their thinking about the concept by:
- correctly identifying additional unlabeled examples of the concept as positive or negative
- by generating their own positive examples

Phase Three:
Students analyze the processes and strategies they used, what they did when strategies did not work, and whether or not they explored more than one hypothesis at once, etc.

Hilda Taba's
Inductive Thinking Model

Stage One: **Concept Formation**

Phase One: Creating and listing of data set
Phase Two: Grouping of data
Phase Three: Labeling and categorizing of data

Stage Two: **Integration of Data**
(Interpreting, Inferring, and Generalizing)

Phase Four: Identifying relationships
Phase Five: Exploring relationships
Phase Six: Making inferences

Stage Three: **Application of Principles or Ideas**

Phase Seven: Predicting consequences and hypothesizing
Phase Eight: Explaining and/or supporting the predictions and hypotheses
Phase Nine: Verifying predictions

Implementation Guidelines

- Teachers may organize the data set or have the students create and organize the data set. If time is limited, the process can be shortened by teacher preparation of the data.
- During the process, teachers ensure that the stages occur in the right order. It is common for students to try to label the categories and then try to force items into their prenamed/predetermined categories.
- Teachers plan and ask questions designed to help students move to the next stage at the appropriate time.
- When first using the process, the teacher decides when to move on to the next phase; as students gain experience with the model, they can make decisions about when to move on to the next phase.
- Props, or other visual cues, help to focus students on the topic to be studied. For example, when the lesson is based on current events, the covers of news magazines can be posted to remind students of specific events and of the kinds of events that make the news as they generate the data set.

Jigsaw Cooperative Learning

Set-Up

1. Identify content that could be divided into segments and taught by students to other students.

2. Divide the material to be studied into meaningful chunks. Identify the number of segments of material to be learned and place the same number of students in each base group (Three to five segments/students in a group is workable).

3. Assign a segment of the material to be learned to each person in the base groups. Each person in the base group has different material to study.

Student Tasks

4. Each student studies his/her material independently (This can be done in class or as homework, depending on the material and age of the students).

5. Students meet in "expert" groups to study the material and to plan how to teach it to their base groups (All the 1s who have independently studied the same material meet together, the 2s meet together, etc.). This segment is crucial because you want to be sure that the "expert" groups are identifying important/significant points; it is often helpful to prepare "expert sheets" for the groups to use in their planning.

You can build in requirements for visuals and planned checks for understanding.

6. Students return to their base tables and teach the material they studied independently and in their expert groups to their base group.

Jigsaw Cooperative Learning

Assessment and Individual Accountability

7. Ensure individual accountability by some means. This can range from a traditional quiz to Numbered Heads Together to a random oral check for understanding.

Helpful Hints

If this process is completely new to your students, use it first with simple content. A general rule of thumb is to avoid, when possible, introducing complex material and complex processes at the same time.

Analyze the interpersonal/communication skills needed for your students to work successfully in this way. Identify which skills they have and which you will need to explicitly teach prior to their working in two different cooperative groups.

Provide opportunities for the students to discuss, not only their learning about academic content, but how they worked together in their groups.

Decisions! Decisions!

In column 1, list three **situations** in which you made a choice today.

In column 2, tell what your **choice** was.

In column 3, give the **reasons** why you made that choice.

In column 4, tell whether you think you made the **right choice or not**.

1 Situation	2 Choice Made	3 Reason	4 Evaluation

Decisions! Decisions!

1. Define the problem: _____

_____

2. List the Alternatives:	3. State the Criteria:			

4. Evaluate the alternatives: Place a (+) opposite each alternative and under each criteria that you believe is desirable. Place a minus (-) opposite each alternative and under each criteria that you believe is undesirable. Place a question mark (?) opposite each alternative and under each criteria that you believe is neither desirable nor undesirable.

5. Make your decision: Write your decision and the reasons for the decision below.

_____

_____

_____

Inquiry/Problem Solving Model

Steps in the Inquiry Model

- Identification of a content-based question/problem
- Presentation of the question/problem
- Formation of hypotheses
- Gathering data
- Analysis of data and formation of conclusions

Putting the Inquiry Model to Work

Identification of a Content-Based Problem

The **problem/question** that serves as the basis of an inquiry lesson may surface as a result of ongoing study, or it may be identified by teacher and/or students as an appropriate focus of study. Teachers and students working in a **standards-based classroom** often organize their study on **essential questions** that are complex and, more often than not, have more than one "right" answer. This process is a powerful one for focusing student learning on the essential questions.

Presentation of the Problem

- The use of an **anticipatory set** or **props** helps students focus the problem. This increases the likelihood that students will make connections between this problem and their life experiences.
- Present an explicit statement of the problem/question orally and in writing.

Formation of Hypotheses

Students may spontaneously volunteer **hypotheses**, as well as respond to questions or prompts from the teacher or the student leading the process.

Inquiry/Problem Solving Model

Gathering Data

- In many instances, the teacher organizes the **data-gathering** process. As students build skills in organizing the process, more responsibility can be turned over to them.
- Who does the gathering of the data depends on the age of the students, the complexity of the problem, and the amount of time the teacher wants to spend on the **inquiry process** as compared to the time spent on the **content**. Teacher gathering of data can make the problem-solving process seem easier to the students than it really is, but that may be a small price to pay if it allows the teacher to add inquiry learning opportunities to his/her instructional repertoire.
- The data gathering may take place in the classroom setting, or it may be completed individually or in small groups outside the classroom. Data gathering outside the school setting helps promote the idea that inquiry and problem-solving are not just school work, but are rather the work of real life.

Analysis of Data and Formation of Conclusions

- This is a difficult task and students may need **modeling** and/or **coaching** in order to get the most out of this phase.
- The data can be organized in a variety of ways. Students can be taught to use **graphic organizers** to organize data so it can be evaluated and patterns identified.
- Original hypotheses need to be revisited, revised, and perhaps eliminated, if the data does not support original conclusions.

Points to Ponder
21ˢᵗ Century Thinking Skills

Literacy in the 21ˢᵗ century will mean the ability to find information, decode it, critically evaluate it, organize it into personal digital libraries, and find meaningful ways to share it with others. Information is a raw material - students will need to learn to build with it.

Thomas Friedman, *The World is Flat*

In any symphony, the composer and the conductor have a variety of responsibilities. They must make sure that the brass horns work in synch with the woodwinds, that the percussion instruments don't drown out the violas. But perfecting those relationships - important though it is - is not the ultimate goal of their efforts. What conductors and composers share - what separates the long remembered from the quickly forgotten - is the ability to marshal these relationships into a whole whose magnificence exceeds the sum of its parts. The boundary crosser, the inventor, and the metaphor maker all understand the importance of relationships. But the Conceptual Age also demands the ability to grasp the **relationships between relationships**. This meta-ability goes by many names - systems thinking, gestalt thinking, holistic thinking, I prefer to think of it simply as **seeing the big picture**.

Daniel Pink, *A Whole New World*

The SCANS Report for America 2000 listed **systems thinking** as one of the five competencies needed to "learn a living" in the 21ˢᵗ Century. It reported that our students needed to not only understand **organizational, social, and technological systems** but to be able to monitor and correct performance and improve or design such systems. Written in 1992, the report stated "Look beyond your discipline and classroom to the other classes your students take, to the community, and to the lives your students lead outside of school. Help your students connect what they learn in class to the world beyond the classroom and school walls."

The SCANS Report, U. S. Department of Labor

As educators, we must take our cues from our students' 21ˢᵗ century innovations and behaviors. We need to pay attention to how our students learn, and value and honor what our students know. We must remember that we are teaching in the 21ˢᵗ century. This means encouraging decision making among students, involving students in designing instruction, and getting input from students about how they would teach. Teachers needn't master all the new technologies. But we must find ways to incorporate into instruction the information and knowledge that students acquire outside class in their digital lives.

Marc Prensky, "Listen to the Natives," *Educational Leadership*

The Learning Environment

X

TOP TEN QUESTIONS
to ask myself as I design lessons

The focus questions for this chapter are highlighted below.

1. What should **students know and be able to do** as a result of this lesson? How are these objectives related to national, state, and/or district standards?

2. How will **students demonstrate what they know and what they can do**? What will be the **assessment criteria** and what form will it take?

3. How will I find out what students already know (**pre-assessment**), and how will I help them access what they know and have experienced both inside and outside the classroom? How will I help them **build on prior experiences**, **deal with misconceptions**, and re-frame their thinking when appropriate?

4. How will new knowledge, concepts, and skills be introduced? Given the **diversity of my students** and the **task analysis**, what are my **best options for sources and presentation modes**?

5. How will **I facilitate student processing** (**meaning making**) of new information or processes? What key questions, activities, and assignments (in class or homework) will promote understanding, retention, and transfer?

6. What shall I use as **formative assessments** or **checks for understanding** during the lesson? How can I use the **data** from those assessments to **inform my teaching decisions**?

7. What do I need to do to **scaffold instruction** so that the learning experiences are productive for all students? What are the multiple ways students can access information and then process and demonstrate their learning?

8. How will I **Frame the Learning** so that students know the objectives, the rationale for the objectives and activities, the directions and procedures, as well as the assessment criteria at the beginning of the learning process?

9. How will I build in opportunities for students to make **real-world connections** and to learn and use the **rigorous and complex thinking skills** they need to succeed in the classroom and the world beyond?

10. What adjustments need to be made in the **learning environment** so that we can work and learn efficiently during this study?

Ways to Communicate High Expectations
for Student Learning

Assess your practice around each of these strategies for letting students know you believe that they are capable of achieving a high level.

Almost Always (A), Sometimes (S), Not Yet (N)

Do you...

_____ 1. **Communicate clear expectations**. Include criteria for success such as rubrics, task performance lists, and exemplars of good performance.

_____ 2. **Model enthusiasm** for what is to be learned, the work to be done, and for student effective efforts and successes.

_____ 3. **Organize the learning environment for thinking**. Carefully plan questions, craft examples, stories, and activities that promote transfer and retention.

_____ 4. **Monitor student attributions and use attribution retraining** with those who make external attributions.

_____ 5. **Provide feedback from multiple sources** so that learners are able to learn from the feedback and make adjustments in their future work.

_____ 6. **Design a brain compatible classroom** through the use of active learning, feedback, and varied sources of input in a safe environment.

_____ 7. **Coach students** in setting challenging yet attainable **goals** and in designing and implementing **action plans** for attaining those goals.

_____ 8. **Include opportunities for all categories of thinking** in discussions with and assignments for low performing students. Teach students to think **about their thinking** and to learn what kind of thinking is required in which situations.

_____ 9. **Promote and teach effective effort strategies such as**
- task and error analysis
- choice of sources, processes, and products
- focus groups for skill development
- graphing of progress
- interactive notebooks
- journal/log entries (cause and effect of effort)

_____ 10. **Scaffold instruction** so that all students have the appropriate levels of support and structure they need to achieve success as learners and withdraw the scaffolding when students are to learn more independently.

The Classroom IS the Real World!

When twenty to forty people of any age spend 180 plus days together in a relatively small space, careful attention must be paid to how property, space, time, and human interactions are handled. First, think of the issues facing any group of people spending that much time together and consider the instructional pieces after you've clarified how this society should function.

Use all you have ever learned about etiquette, group process, conflict resolution, problem solving, personality types, safety, time management, etc. when considering how to set up the learning environment. The classroom should be as much like life beyond the classroom as possible. The students are real people, who just happen to be a little younger than the teacher, and who have been ordered to report to your care. If you are inclined to set up a dictatorship, be prepared to deal with stealth attacks and/or revolutions; if, however, you are interested in establishing a more democratic type setting, be clear what the parameters are. Not only must you be clear, you must clearly communicate those boundaries to the students as all of you collaborate to create an effective and efficient learning environment.

Tips for Surviving and Thriving Together

- Use inclusive pronouns; i.e., "our" classroom not "my" classroom.
- Become a world-class listener!
- Learn how to send assertive messages...and teach students to do the same.
- Be aware of all that is going on but make thoughtful decisions about when and how to react to inappropriate situations.
- Use and teach students to use processes for decision making, problem identification and solving, and conflict resolution.
- Keep both feet on the ground. You are the adult! As Fred Jones says, "It takes one idiot to backtalk; it takes two to make a discussion out of it."
- Practice what you preach!
- Catch them being right!
- Remember that kids are people too. Sometimes they are simply acting their age rather than like the "little adults" we think we want them to be.
- View discipline problems as human relations problems and react accordingly.

Attribution Theory

Development of the intrapersonal intelligence causes one to examine the effectiveness of one's effort. Teaching students to assess what works and what doesn't work for them in the learning process may be the most important thing we teach them. Younger children believe ability and hard work combine to promote success. As students get closer to adolescence, they tend to believe that those who succeed are smart or are just plain lucky; one thing they know for sure is they do not want to be caught trying, because if they fail, everyone will know they are dumb! This perception for them is a reality that greatly impacts their willingness to expend effort. **Attribution retraining** can make a huge difference in the lives of our students.

	Internal	External
Stable	ability	task difficulty
Unstable	effective effort	luck

-Weiner, 1970

Attribution Retraining

A learning environment where students learn how to learn includes opportunities for students to reflect on their efforts and to learn from their errors. Successful adults know that it is the effectiveness and efficiency of effort that determines how well we reach the goals we set for ourselves. Our tendency is to tell students this "fact of life" rather than systematically teaching them by our modeling and by insisting that they analyze their own work.

The single most effective way to respond to students who say the task was too hard, or they were unlucky, or they are just too dumb is to say, "Given that you believe/think/feel that..., what might you do about it?" The least effective response is to try to confuse them with logic by pointing out how unclearly they are thinking; they will not buy it. Allow them to see the world as they see it AND create conditions that cause them to consider how they might do something to improve the results in the future. For example, catch them being right and point out that effort must have played a part, mention that you work hard to prepare interesting and challenging lessons, and include recognition of effective effort in your verbal and written praise.

Through the Voice of...

Error Analysis

You may correct your quiz and earn back at least 1/2 of the points you missed. Follow the steps below. Do all of your work on your own notebook paper. This is due: _____.

1. Write the problem and/or the word you missed.

2. Find the correct answer and write it down under the problem and/or word you missed. Write a brief statement about how or where you found the correct answer or solution.

3. Analyze why you missed the problem or work originally. Write a statement about your reasons.

4. Write 1 or 2 sentences explaining how you can prevent this mistake in the future.

Example

1. JARGON: I gave an incorrect definition of this word.

2. JARGON is defined as being a vocabulary specific for a particular field of study. I found this definition in my notes from class.

3. I believe that I missed this word because I didn't study correctly or enough. I also think I get a little nervous when I take a test and can't remember some of the things I studied.

4. I think that I need to go through my notes and make a list of all the words that I don't really know and the words my teacher has indicated might be on the quiz. I need to then give myself a "practice test" on those words. I might need to make flash cards of the words I have trouble remembering. If I still have problems with tests or quizzes, I will see my teacher for help.

Lynne Gronback, McDougle Middle School, Chapel Hill-Carrboro Schools, Chapel Hill, NC

Error Analysis Chart*
Multiple Assignments

Name _____

Period _____

Date	Assignment/ Assessment	Score	Added Wrong	Multiplied Wrong	Used Wrong Operation	Dropped a Negative Sign	Did Not Distribute Number	Copied Incorrectly	Mistake in Formula	Did Not Follow Directions	Incomplete	Cancelled Wrong	Skipped the Problem	Other (Specify)

Directions:
For each assignment or assessment completed, write the name of the assignment and the date on the lines to the left. Check as many types of errors in each row as apply.

*Access template on the CD-ROM.

Contract for Improvement Points*

Name:

Class Period: _____ Date:

Title of Work to be Improved:

I, _____ agree to re-work/re-write the work named above. I will improve the work by addressing the following specifics agreed upon by my teacher and myself. The points I might earn have been assigned and I understand that I must complete the work according to the contract requirements in order to receive full credit.

Specific Improvements	Points Possible
1.	
2.	
3.	
4.	
5.	
6.	

Date Improved Work Due: _____ Total: _____

Signatures:

*Access template on the CD-ROM.

Lynn Gronback, McDougle Middle School, Chapel Hill-Carrboro Schools, Chapel Hill, NC

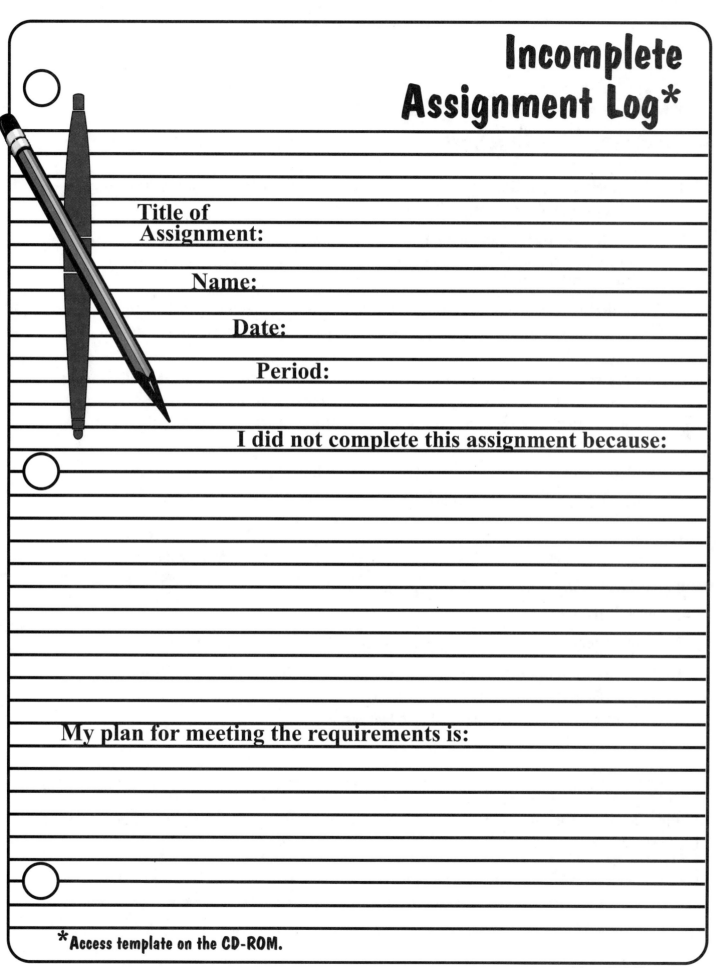

Incomplete Assignment Log*

Title of
Assignment:

Name:

Date:

Period:

I did not complete this assignment because:

My plan for meeting the requirements is:

*Access template on the CD-ROM.

Top 10 Questions
for Secondary Teachers

1. What **choices** do students have around **sources of information, processes for making meaning, and for demonstrating their learning**?

2. How often do **students feel in control**, and in charge of themselves? What causes them to feel in control? Think beyond "They decide whether or not to get involved and to do the work."

3. What **decisions** that really count are students allowed to make? Consider issues like pacing, contracts, order of study, and depth and breadth of particular areas of study.

4. What structures are in place to help students learn how to be **responsible for their own learning**? Think of issues like error analysis, lessons to be learned from errors, rubrics, self, peer and group assessment, time management and study skills lessons, and reflections.

5. How do your students know (**beyond grades**) when they have pleased you?

6. How do you know when **you have pleased them**?

7. How purposeful are you in planning and asking questions that have more than one right answer? **How often do the students ask you and each other complex questions**?

8. How often do students feel important in your classroom? **What makes them feel important**?

9. How often do you and your students share laughter and pleasure?

10. How do the students react when they walk into your classroom? Happy? Calm? Safe? Excited? Assured? Afraid? Bored? Sorry? **What goes on in this learning environment that contributes to that reaction**?

"In all my 25 years of teaching secondary students and training teachers, I have never known teachers who are having trouble with discipline or motivation to say that their students have choices, control, or true responsibility for their own schooling."

Carolyn Mamchur, "But... the Curriculum," *Phi Delta Kappan*, **April 1990**

Orchestrating the Learning Environment

Stop the Stoplight!

No more names on the board! No more names in lights! No more student's hearts in and out of the teacher's heart! What were we thinking when we engaged in such humiliating practices? Just imagine how we would feel if the principal or workshop leader wrote our names on the board when we arrived late, forgot our materials, had a side conversation, or some other infraction. If that response would make us feel bad, it has to be true for children as well. Yes, we should communicate clear expectations and have attitude adjustment chats with students, but we should have them privately. Nagging and public humiliation does not work in international relations and it does not work in the classroom. We want to provide students growth-producing feedback on both academic and behavioral issues and then provide scaffolding so that they can be successful.

Stop the Pop Quizzes!

We should not use assessment as a management tool. The purpose of assessment is to help the students and teacher know what is being learned and to provide feedback on the effectiveness of the instructional program.

Design a Strong Instructional Program!

Rather than focusing time and energy developing and implementing an elaborate control and compliance system, spend your time and energy on designing a strong instructional program. Humans, young and old, tend to act out when they are frustrated or bored. Given clear and realistic expectations along with engaging and relevant learning exercises, we will almost always join in the learning process with enthusiasm.

So, what do you do when clearly communicated and realistic expectations are not met? See the next two pages for alternatives to public humiliation and the gotcha' game of pop quizzes.

The best management program is a strong instructional program!

Dealing with Unmet Expectations
in a productive & positive learning-centered environment

- Focus on finding fault. Instead, catch students being right!
- Use rewards for good behavior. Students begin to work for the reward rather than because the work is interesting or the behavior is the right thing to do.
- Ask students to make promises. They often promise anything to get us off their backs.
- Nag, scold, and threaten. These may lead to immediate compliance, but there is high potential for resentment and frustration.
- Chastise in public. Names on the board is not acceptable practice!
- Blame the parents. We do not teach the parents. We have the next generation of parents in our classes today. If we miss the chance to influence difficult students, they may become even greater problems in our society later, as parents and citizens.
- Be overly concerned about your own authority base. Real authority comes from knowing what you are talking about and modeling respectful behavior.
- Use double standards. The same standards should apply for students and teachers.

- Identify causes of inattentive or disruptive behavior and match your response to the perceived cause.
- Clearly communicate the expectations for work and behavior.
- Focus on future behavior rather than on past behavior.
- Establish a relationship based on trust and mutual respect with each child.
- Wait to hold discussions about inattentive or disruptive behavior, or unmet expectations, until both of you are calm.
- Use logical consequences directly related to the behavior. Logical consequences are designed to get students back to work.

Beyond survival our
Basic Needs:
To Belong
To Gain Power
To Be Free
To Have Fun

William Glasser, 1986
Control Theory in the Classroom

Dealing with Unmet Expectations
in a productive & positive learning-centered environment

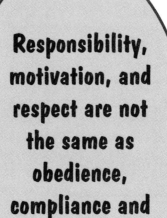

Do

- Teach that fairness has to do with equity rather than equality. That is, you get what you need when you need it rather than everyone getting the same thing at the same time.
- Distinguish between the behavior and the person exhibiting the behavior. Build self-efficacy by focusing on what effort is needed.
- Admit your own mistakes.
- Work for responsibility, motivation, and respect...not obedience, compliance, and fear.
- Remember that responsibility is taught by giving responsibility. Include students in developing procedures for handling inappropriate behavior or unmet expectations.

Responsibility, motivation, and respect are not the same as obedience, compliance and fear.

Kohn, 1996

When The Going Gets Rough...

- Stay calm, move slowly, get close, be quiet, and relax.
- Make eye contact.
- If you must talk, lower your voice rather than raising it.
- Try to keep the situation in perspective. Don't overreact and escalate minor incidents into major confrontations.
- Avoid public confrontation. An audience for a confrontation escalates any differences.
- Avoid threats you can't or don't want to carry out.
- Keep both feet on the ground emotionally! It is easy to get knocked over if you try to balance on one foot!

Space, Time, & Procedures
for a Productive Learning Environment

Space

Arrange the space to reduce barriers between you and the students and to help them see and hear one another. Match the room arrangement to the instructional objectives and to the interactions you wish the students to have.

> ### Room Arrangements That Maximize Learning
>
> - Small group/cooperative work: Tables or clusters of desks or chairs with teacher circulating
> - Class discussion: Circle or horseshoe with teacher seated as part of the group
> - Test taking: Rows with teacher circulating
> - General overall best arrangement: Horseshoe or double horseshoe with teacher seated at the front of the group
>
> The teacher's desk is a barrier and should be avoided during class.

Time

Give students time to process and time to think before calling on someone or before responding to a student response. Too often, we are uncomfortable waiting for a response and want to hurry on to the next question. As a result, many students realize that they can just watch the action and do not even attempt to participate; others with word retrieval problems often find themselves at least one question/comment behind. **Learning is not a spectator sport.** This means that we need systems for purposefully building in time for students to think. See the time templates on following pages.

Procedures

Procedures/routines that are not followed are simply **dreams** and routines that are blindly followed become **ruts.** Constantly check to see how expensive your classroom procedures are in terms of time and energy. Maximize your efforts by honestly assessing what needs to be changed, added, or deleted.

Time Templates

"Learning is the constant; time is the variable."
...Vermont teacher

Wait Time

Review Mary Budd Rowe's extensive research on wait time on the next page.

10:2 Theory

Pause after small meaningful chunks of information for student processing. Have pairs or trios discuss the most important points, confusing points, connections, etc.

Sequence

We remember best that which occurs in the first few and last few minutes of instruction. Maximize that time. Create lots of beginnings and endings. The information just after the middle of a list is the hardest to remember. When possible, reorder the list to place the difficult items at the beginning or end.

Movement

Legitimize movement. The brain can only absorb what the rear end can endure. Have students stand for the two minute processing in 10:2. Have students move to meet with a partner or use various signals to indicate understanding or agreement.

Practice

Divide new skills into the smallest meaningful chunks and mass short practice sessions at the beginning of new learning. Always move to real and meaningful use of the skills as soon as possible.

Forgetting

Most forgetting occurs within just a few minutes of learning. Build in recitation, review, processing, and practice immediately.

Notice

Warn students of upcoming transitions. Think of the "two minute warning" before the end of football games and do the same in the classroom.

Wait Time

Mary Budd Rowe's research indicates that slowing down the questioning pace actually speeds up the pace of learning. We tend to rush through question and answer sessions because "We have so much to cover!" and because we fear that moments of silence will lead to off task behaviors. She recommends that **we pause for three to five seconds before calling on students to answer the questions we pose and before responding to their answers to our questions.** This sounds easy, but it takes determination and practice!

One tip for remembering to incorporate this quality thinking time is to ask the question from the front of, or from one side of the classroom, and walk slowly to the opposite side before selecting a student to respond. A way to deal with "blurters" is to acknowledge students who indicate that they wish to respond by signaling each of them a number in order of recognition. When most students have indicated their readiness, select a number at random and call on the student who was assigned that number.

To engage all students in thinking about and responding to important questions, you might use **Think-Pair-Share**, as described on page 112, since the think time is built-in wait time. Many teachers have found that the use of **slates, think pads, or white boards** or **signal cards** helps reprogram them and their students to pause for processing.

What Wait Time Accomplishes

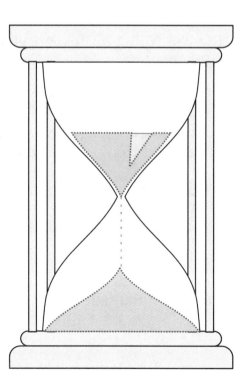

- Students ask **more questions**.
- Student to student **interaction increases**.
- The length and number of **student responses increases**.
- **Contributions by "low performers" increase.**
- The need for **management actually decreases** because more students are engaged.
- **Failures to respond decrease.**
- **Teachers ask more higher level questions and ask more follow-up questions.**

Procedure Potpourri*

Planning procedures and evaluating the effectiveness of those procedures for conducting the business of the classroom is crucial in creating a productive learning environment. Read through the regularly occurring events listed below. Think about the procedures currently in place in your classroom and rate their effectiveness. In rating, consider the time and energy each is costing you and the students, as well as the results achieved. If the record keeping or the "nag factor" is too time and energy consuming, then either the procedure or the process for implementing the procedure needs to be adjusted. Identify which procedures need re-thinking and/or re-teaching in order to maximize their effectiveness and begin to make a plan for change.

What Is Working and What Needs Work?
- Entering the classroom
- Beginning the school day
- Beginning the class period
- Taking attendance
- Returning from absences
- Dealing with tardies
- Distributing materials
- Collecting materials
- Assigning homework
- Handling missing assignments
- Dealing with broken or missing supplies
- Responding to requests for restroom visits and drinks
- Asking for and receiving help
- Making transitions
- Providing work for earlier finishers
- Leaving the classroom
- Setting up group work
- Ending the period or day
- Going to and returning from lunch and recess
- Cleaning up
- Moving in and out of groups
- Signaling for attention
- Dealing with fire and disaster drills

*Access template for identifying procedures on the CD-ROM.

Procedure Potpourri

Potential Problem Times

Careful thought and attention to detail in advance is essential for these moments. It is best to have "Plan B" ready to roll on a moment's notice because even the procedures that have been working well up until this time may fall apart here! Do not be surprised and do not take it personally!

- The day(s) before a big holiday or school break
- The day of or the day after Halloween
- The day report cards and/or progress reports are distributed
- The first few minutes after a long weekend or holiday
- Friday afternoons before a three-day weekend
- The last week of school (especially if the swimming pools are open and/or it's hot)
- Immediately before or after a pep rally or assembly
- Right after a fire drill
- The last few minutes before lunch and the first few minutes after lunch
- The first substitute of the year
- Power outages
- First snow of the year (especially in Florida)

See *Why Didn't I Learn This in College?* for extensive information on organizing a productive learning environment.

Collegial Collaboration

XI

Creating a Culture for Learning

An Array of Formats
from Professional Learning Communities to Parking Lot Chats!

The essential question for all educators must be: **What do schools look like when they are organized around the commitment of high standards by all students**? We know that part of the answer has to be collaborative efforts of all those engaged in the process of educating these learners. The current buzz word for such collaboration is professional learning communities. While we should all aspire to create real learning communities in our schools the reality is that some school personnel call any gathering of two or more educators a learning community.

Given the huge body of literature on professional learning communities, this chapter will explore the small steps we can take to move in that direction. The collaborative formats described in this chapter can certainly be used in professional communities already established or be seen as stepping stones toward their creation.

Whatever collaborative efforts are a part of your professional life, constantly seek to have those efforts
- include ongoing discussions about current reality and best practice
- have a commitment to continuous improvement
- be results oriented
- involve more and more colleagues over time

Literature on Professional Learning Communities

North Central Regional Educational Lab (NCREL)
www.ncrel.org/sdrs/areas/issues/content/currclum/cu3lk22.htm

Southwest Educational Development Lab (SEDL)
www.sedl.org/change/issues/issues61.html

National Staff Development Council (NSDC)
www.nsdc.org/standards/learningcommunities.cfm

All Things Professional Learning Communities
www.allthingsplc.info/about/aboutPLC.php

Self-Assessment
Collegial Collaboration
Practices that Promote School Success

Educators who use their knowledge, skills, and energy to engage in the following practices greatly increase the probability of higher student achievement. Given that, assess the way you and your colleagues collaborate. Mark each practice as

Often (O), Sometimes (S), Not Yet (N)

Do we...

_____ analyze standards and design instruction and assessments to match those standards

_____ design and prepare instructional materials together

_____ design and evaluate units together...especially those based on clearly articulated national, state, or local standards

_____ research materials, instructional strategies, content specific methodologies, and curriculum ideas to both experiment with and to share with colleagues

_____ design lesson plans together (both within and across grade levels and disciplines)

_____ discuss/reflect on lesson plans prior to and following the lesson

_____ examine student work together to ensure match to high standards, to refine assignments, and to analyze the results and make adaptations and adjustments for future instruction

_____ observe and be observed by other teachers

_____ analyze practices and their productivity

_____ promote the concepts of repertoire and reflection

_____ teach each other in informal settings and in focus groups

_____ develop, use, and analyze results of common assessments

_____ use meeting time for discussions about teaching and learning rather than administrivia

_____ talk openly and often about what we are learning or would like to learn

_____ concentrate efforts and dialogue on quality and quantity of student learning, rather than on how many chapters have been covered in the text

_____ share with each other what we learn at conferences, in college classes, from professional readings, and other professional development endeavors

Teacher Leaders

Once upon a time, teachers were responsible for their own students and their own instructional programs. Although many teachers have always been informal teacher leaders, the only way to officially change roles and responsibilities in K-12 education was to become an administrator. Now, the landscape has changed. There are many opportunities for teachers to become teacher leaders. We have mentors, lead mentors, instructional coaches, induction coaches, reading coaches, math coaches, second language coaches, team leaders and on and on. This is both a wonderful development and a dangerous opportunity.

It is a wonderful development because talented teachers can share their tremendous knowledge and skills with others and a dangerous opportunity because excellence as a classroom teacher does not always easily translate into success as a coach and teacher of adults; there is also the very real danger that multiple coaches can come from different perspectives and that the messages can be garbled.

Points to Ponder as a New Coach
- Clarify your role and job parameters. The greatest cause of conflict is unmet expectations and the greatest cause of unmet expectations is unclear expectations. It is not only the coach that needs to have clarity about his role; the teachers who are to be coached also need clarity about the coach's role. The reality is that coaches often end up being perceived as and/or assuming responsibilities of a quasi-administrator.
- Be assertive in asking for professional development and a support system. Establish systems for "staying in the loop." Information is power. Conversely, keep the principals with whom you are working and your coaching colleagues in the know about the work you are doing so that there are no surprises.
- Inquire about the program evaluation soon after assuming the coach role. If a program evaluation has not been written, contact neighboring districts or do research into how other districts are evaluating the impact of the program.
- Hold data-driven discussions. Always support opinions with evidence.
- Fine tune your communication skills. The top two tips are: listen more than you talk and avoid I, me, mine.
- Know that you will go through Michael Fullan's implementation dip.

Points to Ponder with Multiple Coaches
The best case scenario is one in which all coaches work together as a team with individual members recognizing and appreciating the expertise of each of the team members. Be sure that all the coaches are operating from the same construct of best practice in teaching and learning and consistently using the same vocabulary.

Through the Voice of...
Looking at Data as a Team

Marcia Baldanza, Principal on Special Assignment, Broward County Public Schools, Ft. Lauderdale, Florida, designed the process presented here for use in team analysis of student performance data. The team members systematically review work using the following questions.

- What do we know from looking at this data?

- Do we know which students are learning and which are not?

- What patterns can we observe?

- What concerns are raised by a review of the data?

- What other data sources will help to clarify and inform our teacher practice?

- How do the programs we have in place connect with the concerns we have identified?

- What additional data can we collect?

- How well, overall, are our students doing on each standard?

- Do all of the items on each standard have a high percentage of correct answers?

- If not, which items under each standard have a high percentage of incorrect answers?

- On the incorrect test items, is there an incorrect answer that was selected by a high percentage of students?

- What kind of mistake is represented by this choice?

- What items do we need to disaggregate to find out if there is a pattern of students not doing well such as boys, girls, children in poverty, or students who have an ESL or special education designation?

Marcia Baldanza, Broward County Public Schools, Ft. Lauderdale, FL

Learning Clubs

Learning Clubs are small groups of teachers who meet regularly to discuss their lives as teachers. During a learning club meeting, **each teacher takes a turn** discussing some aspect of her teaching life. In running her part of the meeting, the teacher selects one of four kinds of discussion:

Review

The teacher asks the group to focus on an instructional strategy they have studied together and explain how it is working in each of their classes. The discussion would focus on issues of how it worked, what they learned from their initial attempts to use the strategy, and its impact on student learning.

Problem Solving

The teacher presents a problem he is currently facing and asks the group for help in clarifying the problem and brainstorming possible actions to take. A structured problem solving model will yield the best results.

Now Hear This!

The teacher announces that she wants to use her time to either share a success story about a recent or current instructional encounter, or to complain about a dilemma she is facing. In a **Now Hear This** session, the group members' responsibility is to appear interested and use active listening. They do not offer solutions or suggestions.

Lesson Design

The teacher asks the group to help plan a lesson or unit, or to review a plan he has designed.

After a teacher has announced what kind of help he wants, and the group has focused on his issues for approximately 15 minutes, his turn ends and another teacher begins her turn by declaring what kind of session she wants. Once each group member has had a turn, the group spends five to ten minutes discussing the ideas shared during the meeting and the implications of each for their professional practice.

3-D Teams
Data-Driven Decision Teams

Groups of teachers meet once or twice a month to review and analyze student work in an effort to use data to make solid instructional decisions. The analysis, reflection, and collegial collaboration provides a framework for decision making about future instruction. This practice is a particularly useful tool for teachers who are striving for consistency across classrooms in a standards-based learning and assessment environment.

The group members bring samples of student work to the meeting. Hanson, Silver and Strong, in descriptions of their Authentic Achievement Teams, suggest that each teacher bring six pieces of students' work to the meeting; they further recommend that the samples represent different achievement levels or different levels of success on this particular assignment. For example, two might be from the top third of a class, two from the middle, and two from the bottom. An alternative approach would be to analyze the work of "regular" students and that of ESL, advanced, or inclusion students. It is also helpful to bring copies of any directions given to the students.

If the group members have not planned together, ten to fifteen minutes are spent looking through the student work samples and any teacher artifacts so that all participants get a good idea of what kind of work they will be discussing and analyzing.

- The participants can agree to analyze all the work of their students around the same set of criteria, or each teacher can indicate the questions, concerns, or criteria to be considered for that set of student work. In either case, the outcomes of the discussion might be directed toward:
- checking for **validation** about the appropriateness of the work for the developmental stage of the students
- checking to ensure that the task is **congruent** with the stated mastery objective and/or state or district standards
- checking for **consistency** of opinion about the assessment and evaluation of the work
- possible **adjustments** in teacher directions and **support** for all/some of the students.

Focus Groups

Focus Group Meetings

These meetings are opportunities for educators to spend dedicated time in the discussion of classroom practice. These discussions usually include the presentation or demonstration of new strategies or areas of study and the sharing of action research in the classroom.

Logistics

Meeting time varies from thirty minutes to two hours. If the group has more than eight to ten members, break into smaller groups for discussions of issues and action research. Multiple sessions on the same topic facilitate follow-up discussion after classroom implementation.

Meeting Formats

- **Presentation and Demonstration**

    The group leader, a member, or a guest presents an instructional technique and demonstrates it. Follow-up discussion is focused on implications for classroom practice.

- **Magazine/Book Club**

    Prior to the meeting, group members all read an article or a chapter in a jointly selected book. The meeting revolves around a discussion of the book and the implications for classroom practice. An alternative is to have each member of the group bring a different article related to a group identified issue or to have each member read a different book. Each participant then shares a review of that article/book over a series of meetings. Once again, discussion focus is on implications for classroom practice.

- **Brainstorming and Problem Solving**

    Group members brainstorm responses to a common problem such as students coming late to class, poor performance on homework, how to explain a concept the learners have trouble grasping, etc. Each group member picks an alternative from the list to try before the next meeting.

- **Curriculum Discussions**

    Teachers share techniques or discuss ways to teach a particular subject/concept. The standards movement makes this particular type of focus group an important one. Each member agrees to try this method of instruction and to report back on the outcomes for student learning.

Collegial Discussions

Use these questions to structure your discussions about what you did differently in your classroom as a result of your previous focus group, learning club, or workshop.

1. What You Tried

> Give a brief description of the strategy(ies) you tried. Identify the standard on which the learning was focused and explain why you chose to use this strategy.

2. How It Went

Successes Experienced

- What worked well?
- What pleased you?
- How were you able to know that the use of this process helped achieve the desired learning?

Problems Encountered

- What frustrated you?
- Was the process a good one for the content to be learned?
- Were there any logistical problems?

3. What You Learned

Possible Revisions

- What changes might you make when you use this strategy again?
- What revisions would deal specifically with the problems you encountered?

Critical or Interesting Incidents

- How did your behavior, or that of your students, match what you expected?
- What intrigued you?
- What questions were raised in your mind?

4. Next Steps

- Where do you go from here? Where might you use this strategy next?
- What do you need to do to remember to use this strategy again?
- With whom should you share your success/the usefulness of this strategy?
- With whom could you problem solve?

Adapted from Geoff Fong and Ray Szczepaniak, Department of Defense Dependent Schools (DoDDS), Europe

Let's Hear It for Peer Coaching & Peer Poaching!
Dynamic Discussions

No one questions the power of peer observation. Everyone seems to question the reality of finding the time (and training) to do it well.

The full process of conferencing prior to and following a peer observation is highly encouraged. If, however, you have yet to find the time and training to engage in peer observation, there is no reason to delay any longer. **Discussions about teaching prior to delivery of instruction, classroom observations, and discussions about teaching after delivery of instruction are valuable in their own right.** Coaching, practicing good communication skills, problem solving, reflective questioning, and observing are a part of our professional lives each and every day. The next step is asking for and providing one another the same support we provide our students.

Ideas for what you and a colleague might discuss prior to, or following, an observation are offered for use within the complete process or in isolation. Choose from this menu and add your own. Don't delay. It is the cheapest and most accessible form of staff development available to you. Go for it!

Planning Conference Questions

- What is it that you want students to know and be able to do as a result of the lesson today?
- How is this related to district or school standards or priorities?
- Where are you and your students in this particular unit of study?
- What kinds of related and important learning experiences have occurred during the past few weeks in your class?
- How do you intend to follow up on those experiences during the next week?
- What activities will you have the students engaged in during this lesson?
- Why did you select these activities for use at this time?
- What do you expect your students to learn from each of these activities?
- Do you plan to use the text? In addition to the text, what materials or resources will you use to present the concepts and have students process their learning?
- How will you determine whether or not your students have learned what you want them to learn during the lesson? At the conclusion of the unit of study?
- As you currently see the lesson, what will be the sequence of events?
- When will transitions from whole class instruction to small group work occur?
- How will student movement be built into the learning activities?

Dynamic Discussions

- As you see the lesson unfolding, what exactly will students be doing?
- What do you see yourself doing to make all this happen? Do you envision any particular problems or confusions?
- Given that the class period is an extended instructional period, how do you plan to chunk activities during the ninety minutes?
- Are there any special circumstances in the classroom that affect learning/the learning environment? What do you do to accommodate those circumstances?
- Does any particular student, or group of students, within this class present special challenges? How are you dealing with them?

Reflective Conference Questions

- As you look back on the lesson, how do you think/feel it went?
- What happened that makes you think/feel that way?
- What do you remember about your actions during the lesson?
- What do you remember about student work and behavior during the lesson? How did their actions match what you expected/hoped would happen?
- How successful were the students in moving toward competency with the standard?
- What do you think caused some of the students to not quite "get it?"
- What did you notice that caused you to...?
- What did you learn from this teaching and/or conferencing experience that will influence your future thinking and planning?

Peer Observations

At last, the practice of peer observations is becoming part of the fabric of school cultures. It is about time!

It was in the1980s that peer observations first become a topic of conversation among the staff developers with whom I worked. We quickly embraced the idea because we believed that Judith Warren Little was right on the mark with her research findings. She found that student achievement could be directly linked to collegial collaboration when it included frequent concrete talk about teaching, use of a common vocabulary and concept system, asking for and providing one another assistance, and frequent observation of one another in our practice. Embracing the idea was one thing; implementation was another story. Despite the best counsel of Sue Wells Welsh and Beverly Showers and words of wisdom from Art Costa and Bob Garmston, teachers with whom we worked in the 80s and 90s completed the rounds of peer observations required as a part of course work. They then retreated back into the privacy of their classrooms. This occurred even though almost all who completed those required peer observations wrote glowingly about how much they learned from the experience. The reason for not continuing was almost always the same. Time! That is, there was no time to do the observation, participate in planning or reflective conferences, prepare the lesson plans to leave for the substitute, or to deal with the fall-out from having a substitute in the classroom. Perhaps we managed to make the process too complex.

Over twenty years later peer observation is coming into its own. One of the primary reasons is the increase in the number of induction and mentoring programs that require, or at least recommend, peer observations as a format for mentoring interactions. Another reason for the widespread use of this professional development approach is that many colleges and universities include classroom visitations in their teacher preparation programs and require pre-service teachers to both observe and be observed with more focus and frequency. A third reason is that we are redefining peer observation to better match the realities of the work life of teachers. Finally, the Gen-Xers and Millenials, who have grown up receiving information and instant feedback through technology, want and expect instant feedback at work. Two or three observations a year culminating in a formal appraisal in the spring is not their idea of instant feedback. In fact, most young teachers are more than eager to not only be observed but to be given the opportunity to observe other teachers.

One approach to building **peer poaching** or observing to gather ideas to use in one's own classroom was used by Dianna Lindsay, at Worthington-Kilbourne High School, Worthington, Ohio. Dianna implemented a **Peer Poaching Pass** program designed to promote classroom observations by all teachers. She provided each

Peer Observations

staff member with three peer poaching passes. Upon leaving a classroom they had visited for the purpose of "poaching" teaching and learning strategies, teachers left their passes on the observed teacher's desk. The teacher who was observed signed the pass and put it in a fish bowl in the front office. Once a month Dianna drew a pass out of the fish bowl to identify winners who were applauded for their collaborative practice and public teaching with time to talk and plan or materials they could use in their instructional programs.

Videotape Analysis

If your school district does not provide release time for teachers to get into one another's classrooms, the use of technology can fill the void. Watching videotaped episodes of teaching and learning together can provide a powerful alternative to actual classroom visitations. If staff members are not quite ready to videotape themselves for self or peer analysis, there are many commercially prepared videotapes that provide exemplars of teaching and learning suitable for viewing and analysis by educators. One of the richest sources of such videotapes is the Association for Supervision and Curriculum Development's (ASCD) Lesson Collection which can be accessed on-line at www.ascd.org. These tapes run from ten to twenty minutes in length and are organized by grade level and content area.

Watching and analyzing videotaped teaching and learning episodes can lead to a strong desire by mentor and protégée to observe together in actual classrooms in their own school or at other school sites. These peer observations can be extended and focused observations of expert teachers or a series of short visits in multiple classrooms across the school. When a particular area of interest or need for growth is identified in the protégée's practice, a twenty to twenty-five minute walk through multiple classrooms observing how different teachers handle that situation provides rich data for dialogue about repertoire and decision making.

Learning Walks

Shared experiences around teaching practice are important for professional growth. Meetings and conferences where classroom practice is discussed are the usual forum; the reality is that we have been missing important learning labs all around us. When small groups of teachers identify a focus and then walk through their own buildings looking for evidence of that focus, the learning curve is steep, the dialogue is rich, and professional relationships are strengthened.

If those participating in a learning walk are participating in a learning club, book club, or focus group, they can make the focus of their learning walk the same as the focus of their study group. Other focuses might include areas identified in school, department, or grade level improvement plans.

 ©Just ASK Publications

Getting Started with
Action Research

According to St. Vrain Valley School District's (Longmont, Colorado) **Results-Based Professional Development Models**, action research is:

- A methodical evaluation of topics or issues about teaching practice and student performance
- Research-based, data-driven, and centered on student learning
- A structure for determining areas of focus for research, for gathering data, and for writing summary reports that describe observations and findings
- Generating information that is talked about, shared with students and colleagues, and acted upon

While action research may be conducted by an individual teacher, the results should be shared with colleagues and impact their practice as well. A team approach to action research could provide valuable school improvement information and probably develop on-site expertise on the selected area of study.

The Results-Based Professional Development Models cited above, as well as several **Tools for Schools** from the National Staff Development Council (NSDC) and a variety of books from the Association for Supervision and Evaluation (ASCD), provide in-depth information on the action research process.

Possible Purposes of an Action Research Project

- to develop reflective, inquiry-based skills as a teaching professional
- to enhance teacher decision-making
- to pursue, in depth, a topic or research question that is important to you or your students
- to enhance student learning opportunities
- to transfer your discoveries to classroom practices

Questions to Ask When Selecting a Research Question or Topic

- What questions do I have about instruction either in a general sense or in the context of my own teaching? (Example: How should phonics be incorporated in instruction? How should I teach spelling? When/How should I group for math instruction?)
- What issues have I been wrestling with as a teacher?
- What teaching methods would I like to investigate more fully in an action research study?
- What topics interest me most?
- Based on student data, what do I/we need to know or learn?

Getting Started with Action Research
Data Collection Possibilities

We are surrounded by data. We need to get over being defensive about it and use it to inform our practice. This list provides a starting point for thinking about the data that is, or could easily be, available to us.

- Pre/post test scores
- Attendance reports
- Grade distribution sheets
  - Across departments
  - Across teachers
  - Across schools
  - Longitudinal
- Standardized test results
- Student portfolios
  - Across students
  - Same students across time
- Student work
  - Across the same assignments
  - Across grade levels
  - Across schools
  - Across teachers
  - Using rubrics
- Field notes
- Audiotapes
- Chart patterns over time
- Videos
- Student journals
- Interviews
- Questionnaires
- Surveys
- Review of the literature
- Document analysis
  - Provides perspective
  - Provides context and background
- Case studies
- Chart patterns over time

©Just ASK Publications

Getting Started with Action Research
Important Questions to Consider

Issue
- What is the focus of your action research?
- Why is this an important challenge or issue?
- What needs to be understood or developed?
- How will learning more about this issue contribute to improved learning for students?

Guiding Questions or Hypotheses
- What do you know already?
- What does research or a review of the literature tell you?
- What question or hypothesis will guide your research?

Methods and Procedures
- What will you do to answer the question?
- How will you do the research and what resources will be used?

Data Gathering and Reporting
- What data will you gather?
- How might that data answer your question?
- How can you ensure that data gathering methods are replicable?
- How can you use multiple sources of data?
- How will you include multiple perspectives?

Data Analysis
- What does the analysis of the data reveal?
- What patterns or trends did you discover?
- What relationships did you see between data?

Action Planning Implications and Significance
- What have you learned and what will you do as a result?

Reporting Results
- What new questions emerged as a result of your study?
- What documentation will you include with your report?
- How will the results be shared with colleagues?

Looking at Assignments & Student Work

Much is being written about ways to productively look at student work in collaborative settings. When teachers engage in these processes, it makes a great deal of sense for the principal to sit in on the meetings. Several of the protocols or processes currently in use are described below.

Education Trust's Standards in Practice

Education Trust created this process to help teachers align classroom work with standards. The scoring tool is used to focus participants on the quality of classroom assignments and their direct connection with standards. Use of this approach can help teachers design rigorous assignments. Analysis of student products helps identify adjustments needed in the assignment directions and levels of teacher support needed to ensure student success. The process is:

- The teacher presenting the assignment explains how and when the assignment was given and what the students were expected to learn as a result of completing the assignment. The presenting teacher also spends a few minutes working through the problem or explaining what the response should look like.

- The collaborative group asks questions about the assignment. They in essence do a task analysis of what students would have to know and be able to do to successfully complete the assignment.

- Next the group identifies the standards, benchmarks, and level of thinking required by the task using Bloom's Taxonomy.

- The team then generates a rubric or other scoring tool to describe successful completion of the assignment.

- The teacher presents student work from the assignment and the team scores the work using the scoring tool they have generated.

- After the scoring, the group discusses possible revisions to the assignment and what to do about students who did not demonstrate competency with the standards the assignment addressed.

The last step in the Education Trust process is quite different from traditional practice around the data obtained from student work. In the past the norm was to simply record the number correct or the grade in the grade book and move on. While planning standards-based instruction is a challenge in and of itself, revision of instruction and assignments as a result of the analysis of student work requires a completely new way of thinking and working. Discussions about the significance of this shift provide learning opportunities for both teachers and administrators.

Looking at Assignments & Student Work

Project Zero

Steve Seidel and his colleagues at Harvard's Project Zero created a process that provides opportunities for teachers to examine and discuss pieces of student work in structured conversation with their peers, coaches, and supervisors.

Project Zero's Collaborative Assessment Conference

Getting Started: The presenting teacher or team shares copies of the selected student work without making comments about the work or the assignment.

Describing the work: The other participants examine the work and describe what they notice without making any judgments about the quality of the work or their personal preferences.

Raising questions: They then pose questions about the student, the assignment, the curriculum, or any other area. The teacher/team members take notes but do not respond.

Speculating about what standards are the focus of the student work: The participants "guess" what the child was working on when he/she created the piece. This could include the standards, benchmarks, and indicators on which the student was focused or the skills the child was trying to master, questions the child was trying to answer, or ideas he/she was trying to express.

Teacher response: The teacher or team responds to the comments made in the review process. She/they provide information to clarify intent and contextual background, engage in reflective discussion with the reviewers and ask their own questions.

Closing the Conference: The group reflects on their learning and the process. The presenting teacher's efforts and presentation are acknowledged.

The implications of this process for teaching, learning, and leading are tremendous. Attention and energy is appropriately focused on the work of students and of the school. It does, however, require that there be a high level of trust in the competence and benevolence of all participants and that the presenting teacher or team of teachers not be defensive about data, data analysis and questioning.

Resources for Looking at Student Work

- www.lasw.org (lasw = looking at student work.) This website features the collaborative assessment conference and provides multiple links to related web sites.
- www.annenberginstitute.org/Products/list.php

Looking at Assignments & Student Work

Writing Rubrics Using Student Work

This process is a productive way to engage staff in collegial discussions about student work and to establish consistency across teachers about what work does and does not meet the standards of performance established by the school community. As the educational leader, you can either facilitate or participate in these discussions and at the same time gather data about the thinking of teachers about what excellent work looks like. These discussions help staff meet school goals of consistently clear and high expectations, provide the opportunity for informal professional development for staff, and the teaching staff leaves the meeting with rubrics ready for classroom use.

The Process

- Sort the work in to broad categories: **excellent**, **okay**, and **needs work**.
- Identify two or three strong examples of each category.
- Start with the **excellent** examples and list the attributes that make them excellent.
- Continue the process with the **okay** and **needs work** examples.
- Write these attributes into a holistic rubric.
- Be sure that an attribute listed in any one category is also listed in the other two. If you want to turn your holistic rubric into an analytical rubric, sort by attributes and assign a rating to each of the attributes.

Getting Started

The ninth grade English team at West Springfield High School, Springfield, Virginia, developed a rubric to assess student writing. On Thursdays they have a brown bag lunch and score the work of each other's students using the rubric they designed.

Teachers in Churchville-Chili School District, Churchville, New York, examined second grade student work using a district-wide writing rubric. A collection of student writing samples from September, November, January, and March were scored and the ratings recorded in a different color for each month. This enabled them to see growth over time and to pose questions as to what the data told them and to design next steps in working with those students.

Fundamentals of Co-Teaching

Successful co-teaching relies on effective communication. Simple matters, if not clarified, can lead to misunderstandings that interfere with the co-teaching success. Before you co-teach, and throughout the process, be sure to discuss these and any other fundamental issues you identify.

Instruction and Assessment

What are students to know and be able to do, and how will they demonstrate that learning? When you are working together in a standards-based classroom there must be a clear understanding of what standard(s) is the focus of the instruction. Adaptations around assessment for special needs students may require much discussion. Will rubrics or performance task lists be used? What flexibility is built in and what might be areas of contention?

Planning

Who is going to take responsibility for which parts of the planning? When does planning get done? Does it happen one year, one month, one week, or one day in advance? Who designs the tasks, the assessment, and the criteria for demonstrating competency?

Instructional Format

How will the lesson be delivered and who will deliver it? What will be acceptable additions or clarifications? Which option for co-teaching will you use? How will a wide array of resources be assembled and organized? Who will take the lead for which tasks?

Teacher Status

How will it be clear to you and the students that you hold **equal status**? For example, think about how to do introductions to students, parents, and others, titles to be used, which names are on the report cards, who calls parents, and classroom allocation of adult space (such as desks and chairs).

Noise

How will the sound level in the classroom be monitored and adapted? Noise includes teacher voices, instructional activities, noise of machines or equipment, student voices, movement, and environmental sounds.

Fundamentals of Co-Teaching

Classroom Routines

What expectations does each teacher have for how classes should operate? This includes everything from headings on student papers to permission to use the pencil sharpener or restroom. **Equal status** means that each teacher has input into such decisions.

Discipline

What are the acceptable standards for student classroom behavior? What is absolutely intolerable for each teacher and what is okay some of the time in some situations? What are the systems for rewards and consequences for behavior?

Feedback

When will you meet to assess how the co-teaching arrangement is operating and how you will discuss both successes and problems? Identify timelines for feedback and the format of the feedback in advance.

Grading

What will be the basis for grades and who will assign them? A discussion of the effect of instructional/assessment modifications on grades is an important topic.

Data Gathering and Analysis

What data will you need to gather to make future instructional decisions? How will this data about the effectiveness of instructional decisions and about student learning be gathered and analyzed?

Teaching Chores

Who scores assignments and tests? Who duplicates materials, reserves films, contacts speakers, arranges field trips, corrects papers, records grades, and so on?

Pet Peeves

What other aspects of classroom life are critical to you? The issue for you could be the extent of organization of materials, the ways students address teachers, or the fact that it really bothers you when someone opens your desk drawer without asking. Try to identify as many as possible in advance.

Options for Co-Teaching

Many teachers think of co-teaching as one or two approaches to having two adults instructing students in a classroom setting. In fact, there are many ways to approach co-teaching. The single most important issue to consider in any co-teaching setting is that the teachers, the students, and all other interested parties must believe and act as if the two teachers are of equal status. With that given in place, any of these options can be selected to accomplish the identified objectives and tasks.

One Instructor, One Observer

One teacher has primary instructional responsibility, while the other observes and gathers data on students, their performance, their interactions, and their behavior in general; each teacher can assume either role.

One Instructor, One "Floater"

One teacher has primary instructional responsibility, while the other assists students with their work, monitors behavior, corrects assignments, etc. Each teacher can assume either role.

Station Teaching

Teachers divide instructional content into two parts (e.g., vocabulary and content, or new concepts and review). Each teacher instructs half the class in one area. Both groups of students rotate through instruction with each teacher.

Parallel Teaching

Each teacher instructs half the student group; the same content is taught simultaneously to all students though instructional methods may vary.

Remedial Teaching

One teacher instructs students who have mastered the material to be learned, while the other works with students who have not mastered the key concepts or skills.

Options for Co-Teaching

Supplemental Teaching

One teacher presents the lesson in standard format. The other works with students who have difficulty mastering the material, simplifying, and otherwise adapting instruction to meet their needs, or works with students who have already mastered the material to provide enrichment and extension. This option is often used when special education teachers and regular education teachers first work together.

Team Teaching

In this, the most sophisticated form of co-teaching, the teachers collaborate to present the lesson to all students. In fully developed team teaching situations, the teachers are so comfortable with their roles, the content, and the students that they are able to pick up on nuances and read each other's signals so well that they essentially teach as one.

Finding the right formula(s) for co-teaching is like figuring out how to get a strike in bowling. It takes lots of practice, trust in the process, thoughtful alignment with the goal, and thorough follow-through by the bowlers...and the teachers!

Mentoring Relationships

Since we cannot possibly learn all we need to know about the act of teaching during pre-service education, learning during the induction period must continue at an intensive level. Careful selection of mentors is an essential component of designing productive mentoring relationships. Whether you are identifying your own mentor, or deciding whether to become one yourself, include the following criteria in assessing the appropriateness of the choice. A teacher teaching a new grade level or a new subject area may need a mentor just as much as a beginning teacher.

Potential mentors are educators who
- demonstrate strong content knowledge
- have and use a wide repertoire of teaching strategies
- use a wide range of assessment tools
- are willing to give special attention to students who need remedial or compensatory help as well as to students who need enrichment
- demonstrate success in facilitating high student performance and achievement
- are reflective about their own practice
- are life-long learners

Mentors need knowledge of and skillfulness with
- a variety of teaching and learning styles
- strong communication skills
- adult learning theory
- generational differences
- providing growth-producing feedback
- capacity to match interactions and responses to knowledge, skills, and trust level of the novice teacher

Formats for mentor interaction
- face-to-face interactions including conversations, meetings, conferences, co-teaching, and socialization
- peer observations
- telephone/email conversations
- written communications including notes and dialogue journals
- professional development and networking opportunities
- online mentoring

Mentoring Relationships

The goal of 21st century mentoring programs is to have a fully satisfied and fully qualified teacher in every classroom. Fully qualified means that the novice teacher can demonstrate competency with the district's teacher performance criteria and fully satisfied means that the novice teacher feels supported, valued, and productive as a person and as a professional educator and, therefore, stays in the teaching profession.

Helpful Mentor Actions

- Introduce the beginning teacher to members of the administrative staff, teachers, and other school employees.
- Go over all school routines, rules, and policies, especially the unwritten ones!
- Take the new teacher on a tour of the school grounds and even of the school attendance zone.
- Escort and sit with the new colleague at faculty meetings and staff development opportunities.
- Remember to include the new staff member in informal social gatherings in the lounge and outside of school.
- Observe the new teacher and give feedback as appropriate.
- Encourage the new teacher to observe other teachers who teach the same subject/grade and/or the same students.
- Teach a demonstration lesson or co-teach in the new teacher's classroom.
- Involve the new teacher in co-curricular activities.
- Help the new staff member recognize and appreciate the knowledge and expertise he/she brings to the profession.
- Guide the new teacher through state and district standards; share time-proven lessons and assessments that are efficient and effective in moving students toward meeting the standards.
- Assist the new teacher with identifying a wide variety of materials and resources appropriate for the content and the students.
- Inform the new staff member of how to obtain audio-visiual equipment and supplies as well as how to obtain all other supplies.
- Coach the new colleague in how teachers collaborate around special needs students, whether it be in an inclusion model or a pullout model.
- Explain the teacher supervision and evaluation system and go over the criteria for teaching performance used in the district.
- Hold regularly scheduled meetings/conferences...daily, at first, and then weekly.

See **The 21st Century Mentor's Handbook** and the e-newsletter **Mentoring in the 21st Century** available at www.justaskpublications.com for in-depth information on mentoring.

Resources & References

Allen, Janet. **Words, Words, Words**. Portland, ME: Stenhouse Publishers, 1999.

Alllington, Richard. **What Really Matters for Struggling Readers: Designing Research-Based Programs**. Boston: Allyn & Bacon, 2005.

Anderson, Loren, and David Krathwohl. **A Taxonomy for Learning, Teaching, and Assessing: A Revision of Bloom's Taxonomy of Educational Objectives**. New York: Addison Wesley Longman, 2001.

Armstrong, Thomas. **Multiple Intelligences in the Classroom, 2nd Edition**. Alexandria, VA: ASCD, 2000.

Armstrong, Thomas. **The Myth of the A.D.D. Child**. New York: Penguin Books, 1997.

Aronson, Elliot and Shelley Patnoe. **The Jigsaw Classroom: Building Cooperation in the Classroom, 2nd Edition**. New York: Addison Wesley-Longman, 1997.

Ashlock, Robert. **Error Patterns in Computation, 9th Edition**. Upper Saddle River, NJ: Prentice Hall, 2006.

Avery, Patricia, Jacqueline Baker and Susan Gross. "Mapping Learning at the Secondary Level." **The Social Studies**. September/October, 1996, pp 217-223.

Beyer, Barry. **Improving Student Thinking**. Boston: Allyn & Bacon, 1997.

Black, Susan. "The Truth About Homework." **The American School Board Journal**. October, 1996, pp 48-51.

Bloom, Benjamin, Max Englehart, Edward Furst, Walter Hill, and David Krathwohl. **Taxonomy of Educational Objectives, the Classification of Educational Goals – Handbook I: Cognitive Domain**. New York: McKay, 1956.

Bonk, Curtis Jay. "P254/M201 Course Packet of Notes." Bloomington, IN: Indiana University, 1995.

Bower, Bert, Jim Lobdell, and Lee Swenson. **History Alive!** Menlo Park, CA: Addison-Wesley,1994.

Brain and Learning, The Facilitator's Guide. Alexandria, VA: ASCD,1998.

Breaking Ranks: Changing an American Institution. Reston, VA: NASSP, 1996.

Breaking Ranks II: Strategies for Leading High School Reform. Reston, VA: NASSP, 2004.

Resources & References

Brooks, Jacqueline and Martin Brooks. **In Search of Understanding: The Case for Constructivist Classrooms**. Alexandria, VA: ASCD, 1993.

Brophy, Jere. **Motivating Students to Learn, 2ⁿᵈ Edition**. Mahwah, NJ: Lawrence Earlbaum Associates, 2004.

Burke, Kay. **What To Do With The Kid Who..., 3ʳᵈ Edition**. Thousand Oaks, CA: Corwin Press, 2008.

Caine, Renate Nummela and Geoffrey Caine. **Education on the Edge of Possibility**. Alexandria, VA: ASCD, 1997.

Caine, Renate Nummela and Geoffrey Caine. **Making Connections**. Alexandria, VA: ASCD, 1994.

Calkins, Lucy. **The Art of Teaching Reading**. New York: Longman, 2001.

_____ **The Art of Teaching Writing**. Portsmouth, NH: Heinemann, 2000.

Campbell, Linda, Bruce Campbell and Dee Dickinson. **Teaching and Learning Through Multiple Intelligences, 2ⁿᵈ Edition**. Needham Heights, MA: Allyn & Bacon, 1998.

Canady, Robert Lynn and Michael Rettig. **Teaching in the Block**. Larchmont, NY: Eye on Education, 1996.

Carey, Lou. **Measuring and Evaluating School Learning, 3ʳᵈ Edition**. Boston: Allyn & Bacon/Longman Group, 2000.

Coloroso, Barbara. **Kids are Worth It!** New York: Harper Collins, 2002.

Connors, Neila. **Homework**. Columbus, OH: National Middle School Association, 1991.

Cooper, Harris. "Synthesis of Research on Homework." **Educational Leadership**. November 1991, pp 85-91.

Costa, Arthur, Editor. **Developing Minds, Revised Edition**. Alexandria, VA: ASCD, 1991.

Costa, Arthur and Robert Garmston. **Cognitive Coaching: A Foundation for Renaissance Schools, 2ⁿᵈ Edition**. Norwood, MA: Christopher-Gordon, 2002.

Costa, Arthur and Bena Kallick, Editors. **Assessment in the Learning Organization**. Alexandria, VA: ASCD, 1995.

Resources & References

Cruckshank, Donald, Deborah Bainer, and Kim Metcalf. **The Act of Teaching, 2ⁿᵈ Edition**. New York: McGraw-Hill, 1998.

Cruz, Emily. (2003). "Bloom's Revised Taxonomy." in the **Encyclopedia of Educational Technology**. Retrieved December 11, 2007, from coe.sdsu.edu/eet/Articles/bloomrev/start.htm

Curwin, Richard and Allen Mendler. **Discipline with Dignity, 2ⁿᵈ Edition**. Alexandria, VA: ASCD, 1999.

Daggett, Willard. "The New 3 Rs for a New Generation." **Instructional Leader (Texas Elementary Principals and Supervision Association Newsletter)**. vol 20, no 2, March, 2007.

Daniels, Harvey. **Literature Circles: Voice and Choice in the Student-Centered Classroom, Revised 2ⁿᵈ Edition**. York, MN: Stenhouse Publishers, 2002.

Davey, Beth. "Think Aloud Modeling." **Journal of Reading**. October, 1983.

Deschenes, Cathy, David Ebeling and Jeffery Sprague. **Adapting Curriculum and Instruction in Inclusive Classrooms: A Teacher's Desk Reference, 2ⁿᵈ Edition**. Bloomington, IN: Indiana Institute on Disability and Community at Indiana University, 2000.

Dreikurs, Rudolf, Bernice Bronia Grunwald and Floy Childers Pepper. **Maintaining Sanity in the Classroom: Classroom Management Techniques**. Boca Raton, FL: Taylor & Francis, 1998.

DuFour, Rick and Robert Eaker. **Professional Learning Communities at Work**. Bloomington, IN: Solution Tree, 1998.

Dyrli, Kurt. "Picture This." **District Administration**. November, 2007, pp 43-48.

Easton, Lois Brown, Editor. **Powerful Designs for Professional Learning**. Oxford, OH: NSDC, 2004.

Ebbinghaus, Hermann. **Memory**. Columbia University Press, 1913.

Educators in Connecticut's Pomeraug Regional School District 15. **Performance-Based Learning and Assessment**. Alexandria, VA: ASCD, 1996.

Erickson, Lynn. **Concept-Based Curriculum and Instruction: Teaching Beyond the Facts**. Thousand Oaks, CA: Corwin Press, 2002.

Resources & References

_____ **Concept-Based Curriculum and Instruction for the Thinking Classroom**. Thousand Oaks, CA: Corwin Press, 2007.

Frayer, Frederick, and Herbert Klausmieir. **A Schema for Testing the Level of Cognitive Mastery: Technical Report Paper No. 16**. Madison, WI: Wisconsin Research and Development Center, 1969.

Freidman, Thomas: **The World is Flat: A Brief History of the 21ˢᵗ Century,** New York: Farrar, Straus and Giroux, 2006.

Gardner, Howard. **Frames of Mind: The Theory of Multiple Intelligences, 10ᵗʰ Edition**. New York: Basic Books, 1993.

Gibbs, Jeanne. **Reaching All by Creating Tribes Learning Communities, 30ᵗʰ Anniversary Edition**. Santa Rosa, CA: Center Source Publications, 2006.

Gilbert, Judy, Editor, with the Northern Colorado BOCES SBE Design Team. **Facilitator's Guide and Workbook: Common Ground in the Standards-Based Education Classroom**. Alexandria, VA: Just ASK Publications, 1997.

Glasser, William. **Control Theory in the Classroom**. New York: Harper & Row, 1986.

Goleman, Daniel. **Emotional Intelligence**. New York: Bantam Books, 2005.

Good, Thomas and Jere Brophy. **Looking in Classrooms, 10ᵗʰ Edition**. New York, NY: Allyn & Bacon, 2007.

Gronlund, Norman. **Measurement and Evaluation in Teaching, 6ᵗʰ Edition**. New York: MacMillan, 1990.

Gunter, Mary Alice, Thomas Estes and Jan Schwab. **Instruction: A Models Approach, 4ᵗʰ Edition**. Boston, MA: Allyn & Bacon, 2002.

High Schools for the New Millennium. Bill and Melinda Gates Foundation. Retrieved October 20, 2007 at www.gatesfoundation.org

Hunter, Madeline. **Mastery Teaching**. El Segundo, CA: TIP Publications, 1982.

Jacobsen, David, Paul Eggen and Donald Kauchak. **Methods for Teaching: Promoting Student Learning in K-12 Classrooms, 7ᵗʰ Edition**. Upper Saddle River, NJ: Prentice Hall, 2005.

James, Jennifer. **Thinking in the Future Tense**. New York: Simon & Schuster, 1997.

Resources & References

Jensen, Eric. **Teaching with the Brain in Mind, 2ⁿᵈ Edition**. Alexandria, VA: ASCD, 2005.

Johnson, David. **Every Minute Counts: Making Your Math Class Work**. Palo Alto, CA: Dale Seymour Publications, 1982.

_____**Making Minutes Count Even More: A Sequel for Every Minute Counts**. Palo Alto, CA: Dale Seymour Publications, 1986.

Johnson, David and Roger Johnson. **Leading the Cooperative School, 2ⁿᵈ Edition**. Edina, MN: Interaction Book Company, 1993.

Johnson, David, Roger Johnson, and Edythe Johnson Holubec. **Cooperation in the Classroom**. Edina, MN: Interaction Book Company, 1998.

Jones, Beau Fly, Annemarie Sullivan Palinesar, Donna Sederburg Ogle, and Eileen Gylnn Carr. **Strategic Teaching and Learning: Cognitive Instruction in the Content Areas**. Alexandria, VA: ASCD, 1987.

Joyce, Bruce, Beverly Showers and Michael Fullan. **Student Achievement Through Staff Development (3ʳᵈ Edition)**. Boston: Allyn & Bacon, 2002.

Joyce, Bruce and Marsha Weil. **Models of Teaching, 7ᵗʰ Edition**. Boston: Allyn & Bacon, 2003.

Kagan, Spencer. **Cooperative Learning Resources for Teachers**. San Juan Capistrano, CA: Kagan Cooperative Learning, 1997.

Keene, Ellin and Susan Zimmermann. **Mosaic of Thought**. Portsmouth, NH: Heinemann. 1997.

Kounin, Jacob. **Discipline and Group Management in the Classroom**. New York: Holt, Rinehart and Winston, 1970.

Kulla, Bridget. "10 Majors That Didn't Exist 10 Years Ago." Retrieved October 20, 2009 at fastweb.com/resources/articles/index/110381

Lambert, Linda. **Building Leadership Capacity in Schools**. Alexandria, VA: ASCD, 1998.

Lapp, Diane, James Flood and Nancy Farnan. **Content Area Reading and Learning: Instructional Strategies**. Mahwah, NJ: Lawrence Erlbaum Associates, 2007.

Larkin, Martha. "Using Scaffolded Instruction to Optimize Learning." December 2002. Retrieved December 30, 2007 from cec.sped.org

Resources & References

Lee, Jackson and Wayne Pruitt. "Homework Assignments: Classroom Games or Teaching Tools." **Clearing House.** vol 53, 1979, pp 31-35.

Little, Judith Warren."Norms of Collegiality and Experimentation: Workplace Conditions of School Success." **American Educational Research Journal**. vol 19, no 3, Fall 1982, pp 325-340.

Looking at Student and Teacher Work to Improve Students' Learning. National Middle School Association, 2005.

Marzano, Robert and Debra Pickering. **Building Academic Vocabulary: Teacher's Manual**. Alexandria, VA: ASCD, 2005.

Marzano, Robert, Debra Pickering, and Jane Pollock. **Classroom Instruction That Works: Research-Based Strategies for Increasing Student Achievement**. Alexandria, VA: ASCD, 2001.

McCarthy, Bernice and Dennis McCarthy. **Teaching Around the 4Mat Cycle**. Thousand Oaks, CA: Corwin Press, 2005.

McKenzie, Gary R. "Data Charts: A Crutch for Helping Pupils Organize Reports." **Language Arts**. vol 56, no 7, October, 1979, pp 784-788.

Morison, Kay and Suzanne Brady. **Homework: Bridging the Gap**. Redmond, WA: Goodfellow Press, 1994.

Murnane, Richard, and Frank Levy. **Teaching the New Basic Skills**. New York: Martin Kessler Books, 1996.

Novak, Joseph. "Clarify with Concept Maps." **The Science Teacher**. October, 1991, pp 45-49.

Oliver, Bruce. " Rethinking Assessment Practices." **Just for the ASKing!** April 2006. Access at www.justaskpublications.com

_____ "Growth Producing Feedback." **Just for the ASKing!** April 2005. Access at www.justaskpublications.com

Palinesar, Annemarie and Anne Brown. "Reciprocal Teaching of Comprehension-Fostering and Comprehension-Monitoring Activities." **Cognition and Instruction**. no 2, 1984, pp 117-175.

Pink, Daniel. **A Whole New Mind: Why Right-Brainers Will Rule the Future**. New York: Riverhead, 2006.

Resources & References

Prensky, Marc. "Listen to the Natives." **Educational Leadership**. December 2005/January 2006, pp 8-13.

_____ "Digital Natives, Digital Immigrants." **New Horizons**. University Press, October 2001.

Raphael, Taffy, Kathy Highfield and Kathryn Au. **QAR Now: A Powerful and Practical Framework That Develops Comprehension and Higher-Level Thinking in All Students**. New York: Scholastic, 2006.

Readence, John, Thomas Bean, and Scott Baldwin. **Content Area Reading: An Integrated Approach, 8th Edition**. Dubuque, IA: Kendall/Hunt, 2004.

Results that Matter. Partnership for 21st Century Skills. Retrieved October 20, 2007 at www.21stcenturyskills.org

Rief, Sandra. **How to Reach and Teach ADD/ADHD Children: Practical Strategies and Interventions, 2nd Edition**. San Francisco, CA: Jossey-Bass, 2005.

Rief, Sandra and Julie Heimburge. **How to Reach and Teach All Students in the Inclusive Classroom: Practical Strategies, Lessons, and Activities, 2nd Edition**. San Francisco, CA: Jossey-Bass, 2005.

Rodriquiz, Rely, Editor. **Instructional Strategies for All Students: A Compendium of Instructional Strategies for High School Teachers**. Fairfax, VA: Fairfax County Public Schools, 1995.

Rosenholtz, Susan. **Teacher's Workplace: The Social Organization of Schools**. New York: Longman, 1989.

Rosenshine, Barak and Robert Stevens. "Teaching Functions." **Handbook of Research on Teaching, 3rd Edition**. New York: Macmillan, 1986, pp 376-391.

Roy, Patricia and Shirley Hord, Project Directors. **Innovation Configurations, Volume I**. Oxford, OH: NSDC, 2003.

Rutherford, Paula. **The 21st Century Mentor's Handbook**. Alexandria, VA: Just ASK Publications, 2005.

_____ **Why Didn't I Learn This in College?** Alexandria, VA: Just ASK Publications, 2002.

Resources & References

Saphier, Jon and John D'Auria. **How to Bring Vision to School Improvement**. Carlisle, MA: Research for Better Teaching, 1993.

Saphier, Jon, Mary Ann Haley-Speca and Bob Gower. **The Skillful Teacher**. Carlisle, MA: Research for Better Teaching, 2008.

Saphier, Jon and Mary Ann Haley. **Activators**. Carlisle, MA: Research for Better Teaching, 1993.

_____ **Summarizers**. Carlisle, MA: Research for Better Teaching, 1993.

Saphier, Jon and Matthew King. "Good Seeds Grow in Strong Cultures." **Educational Leadership**. March, 1985.

Slavin, Robert. **Using Student Team Learning, 4ᵗʰ Edition**. Baltimore, MD: The John Hopkins University Press, 1994.

Smaller Learning Communities Program. Retrieved on October 20, 2007 at .ed.gov/programs/slcp/index.html

Schmoker, Mike. **Results Now**. Alexandria, VA: ASCD, 2006.

Spitzer, H. F. "Studies in Retention." **Journal of Educational Psychology**. 1939, pp.641-656.

Standards-Based Classroom Operator's Manual. Developed by Centennial BOCES SBE Design Team. Alexandria, VA: Just ASK Publications, 2002.

Stevenson, Harold and James Stigler. **The Learning Gap**. New York: The Free Press, Simon & Schuster, 1999.

Strategic Teaching and Reading Project Guidebook. NCREL, 1995.

Sylwester, Robert. **A Celebration of Neurons**. Alexandria, VA: ASCD Publications, 1995.

Taba, Hilda. **Teacher's Handbook to Elementary Social Studies: An Inductive Approach**. Reading, MA: Addison Wesley Publishing Company, 1971.

Tierney, Robert, and James Cunningham. "Research on Teaching Reading Comprehension." **Handbook of Reading Research**. 1984, pp 609-641.

Tierney, Robert, John Readence and Ernest Dishner. **Reading Strategies and Practices**. Boston: Allyn & Bacon, 1995.

Resources & References

Tomlinson, Carol Ann. **How to Differentiate Instruction in Mixed-Ability Classrooms, 2ⁿᵈ Edition**. Alexandria, VA: ASCD, 2001.

Tovani, Cris. **I Read It, But I Don't Get It**. Portland, ME: Stenhouse, 2000.

Tyler, Ralph. **Basic Principles of Curriculum and Instruction**. Chicago, IL: The University of Chicago Press, 1949.

VanDrimmelen, Jeff. "Eight Ways to Use Camera Phones in Education." Retrieved November 17, 2007 at edutechie.com

_____ "Five Ways You Can Use Video in Education." January 23ʳᵈ, 2007. Retrieved on November 17, 2007 at edutechie.com

_____ "Four Things Good Teachers Do To Get Students Really Involved in Projects." Retrieved on November 17, 2007 at edutechie.com

Vacca. Richard and Jo Anne Vacca. **Content Area Reading: Literacy and Learning Across the Curriculum**. New York: Allyn and Bacon, 2004.

Villa, Richard, and Jacqueline Thousand. **Creating an Inclusive School, 2ⁿᵈ Edition**. Alexandria, VA: ASCD Publications, 2005.

Vygotsky, Lev. **Mind and Society: The Development of Higher Mental Processes**. Cambridge, MA: Harvard University Press, 1978.

Response to Intervention: An Implementation and Technical Assistance Guide for Districts and Schools. West Virginia Department of Education. October 2006. Retrieved at wvde.state.wv.us/ose/RtiImpGuide91906.DOC on December 19, 2007.

Wiggins, Grant. **Educative Assessment**. San Francisco: Jossey-Bass, 1998.

Wiggins, Grant and Jay McTighe. **Understanding by Design**. Alexandria, VA: ASCD, 2005.

Winebrenner, Susan. **Teaching Gifted Kids in the Regular Classroom**. Minneapolis, MN: Free Spirit, 2001.

Wood, Judy. **Adapting Instruction for Mainstreamed and At-Risk Students, 3ʳᵈ Edition**. Columbus, OH: Merrill, 1998.

Index

A

B

About the Author

Paula Rutherford is the author of four books, *Instruction for All Students*, *Leading the Learning: A Field Guide for Supervision and Evaluation*, *The 21ˢᵗ Century Mentor's Handbook*, and *Why Didn't I Learn This in College?* She writes an e-newsletter titled: *Mentoring in the 21ˢᵗ Century*.

Paula is president of Just ASK Publications and Professional Development, established in 1989 and based in Alexandria, Virginia. She works extensively with districts as they engage in long-term multifaceted work to align all the system processes in the interest of student learning. She also leads *Mentoring in the 21ˢᵗ Century Institutes* across the country and has developed a comprehensive *Mentoring in the 21ˢᵗ Century Resource Kit* so that districts can replicate the Just ASK institutes and provide extensive follow-up support for mentors. Paula is committed to building in-house capacity and has developed Certified Local Trainer (CLT) programs based on *Instruction for All Students* and *Why Didn't I Learn This in College?*

In addition to her extensive work as a consultant and trainer, Paula's professional experience includes work in regular education K-12 as a teacher of high school history and social sciences, physical education, Spanish, and kindergarten, as well as a special education teacher, coordinator of special education programs, school administrator at the middle school and high school levels, and as a central office staff development specialist.

She can be reached at paula@justaskpublications.com.

Ordering Information

Books	Order #	Price
Instruction for All Students Second Edition	11027	$ 34.95
Leading the Learning (3-ring binder)	11004	$ 59.95
Leading the Learning (bound)	11005	$ 34.95
Meeting the Needs of Diverse Learners	11033	$ 34.95
Results-Based Professional Development Models	11011	$ 70.00
Standards-Based Classroom Operator's Manual	11012	$ 45.00
The 21st Century Mentor's Handbook	11003	$ 34.95
Why Didn't I Learn This in College?	11002	$ 29.95
Why Didn't I Learn This in College? and *The 21st Century Mentor's Handbook* Save 20%	11029	$ 50.00

Videos and DVDs	Order #	Price
Collegial Conversations DVD	11031	$ 295.00
Common Ground Video and Facilitator's Guide CD-ROM	11020	$ 30.00
Helping New Teachers Succeed DVD	11021	$ 60.00
How to Co-Teach to Meet Diverse Student Needs (ASCD) VHS	11024	$ 95.00
How to Use Interactive Notebooks (ASCD) VHS	11023	$ 95.00
How to Scaffold Instruction for Student Success (ASCD) VHS	11022	$ 95.00
Lesson Collection: Biology Visual Learning Tools (ASCD) VHS	11026	$ 95.00
Lesson Collection: HS Geometry Surface Area and Volume (ASCD) DVD	11034	$ 95.00
Lesson Collection: HS Reciprocal Teaching (ASCD) DVD	11035	$ 95.00
Lesson Collection: Primary Math (ASCD) DVD	11025	$ 95.00
Points to Ponder DVD	11016	$ 29.95
Principles in Action DVD	11019	$ 19.95
Success Factors in a Standards-Based Classroom DVD	11017	$ 75.00

Other Products	Order #	Price
ASK Poster Pack	11006	$ 16.95
Just for the ASKing! CD-ROM	11042	$ 19.95
Mentoring in the 21st Century™ Resource Kit	11028	$ 985.00
Visual Tools: The Complete Collecton CD-ROM	11041	$ 375.00
Visual Tools: Instruction for All Students CD-ROM	11036	$ 100.00
Visual Tools: Leading the Learning CD-ROM	11039	$ 100.00
Visual Tools: Meeting the Needs of Diverse Learners CD-ROM	11040	$ 100.00
Visual Tools: The 21st Century Mentor's Handbook CD-ROM	11038	$ 100.00
Visual Tools: Why Didn't I Learn This in College? CD-ROM	11037	$ 100.00
What Do You Do When... Cards	11032	$ 49.95

Prices subject to change without notice

To Order

Call
800-940-5434

Fax
703-535-8502

Online
www.justaskpublications.com

Mail
2214 King Street, Alexandria, VA 22301

Order Form

Just ASK Publications & Professional Development

<table>
<tr><th colspan="2">Ship To</th><th colspan="2">Bill To (If different)</th></tr>
<tr><td>Name</td><td>_____</td><td>Name</td><td>_____</td></tr>
<tr><td>Title</td><td>_____</td><td>Title</td><td>_____</td></tr>
<tr><td>School/District</td><td>_____</td><td>School/District</td><td>_____</td></tr>
<tr><td></td><td>_____</td><td></td><td>_____</td></tr>
<tr><td>Address</td><td>_____</td><td>Address</td><td>_____</td></tr>
<tr><td>City_____ State___ ZIP_____</td><td></td><td>City_____ State___ ZIP_____</td><td></td></tr>
<tr><td>Email</td><td>_____</td><td>Email</td><td>_____</td></tr>
<tr><td>Telephone</td><td>_____</td><td>Telephone</td><td>_____</td></tr>
<tr><td>Fax</td><td>_____</td><td>Fax</td><td>_____</td></tr>
</table>

Order #	Title	Quantity	Unit Price	Total Price

Please attach a sheet of paper for additional products ordered

Sub Total

Shipping and Handling
$6 S&H minimum per order
15% on orders under 10 units, 10% on orders 10 units and more
$49 S&H Mentoring in the 21st Century™ Resource Kit

TOTAL

Contact us for quantity discounts and special offers
Call 800-940-5434

Payment Method (Select One)

☐ Check (Please make checks or Purchase Orders payable to Just ASK Publications)

☐ Purchase Order   Purchase Order Number_____

☐ Credit Card   ☐Visa   ☐MasterCard   ☐AMEX

Name as it appears on the card _____

Credit Card # _____

Expiration Date ☐☐ / ☐☐
Month   Year

Mail or Fax to:
Just ASK Publications
2214 King Street
Alexandria, VA 22301
Fax: 703-535-8502

☐ Check here to receive information about Just ASK workshops, institutes, and train-the-trainer opportunities.